Visi
SOUTH

SOUTHERN
ITALY

SOUTHERN ITALY

ROME
l'Aquila
Sulmona
Alatari
Alfedena
Lesina
Saepinum
Benevento
NAPLES
Castellamare di Stabia
Salerno
Bay of Naples
CAPRI
Morano Calabro
Barletta
Matera
Massafra
Martina Franca
Lecce
Porto Badisco
Rossano
Catanzaro
Gerace
Reggio Calabria
Messina
PALERMO
Solunto
Tindari
Selinunte
Enna
Palazzolo Acreide
Siracusa
SICILY

TREMITI ISLANDS

ADRIATIC SEA

TYRRHENIAN SEA

AEOLIAN ISLANDS

IONIAN SEA

MEDITERRANEAN SEA

0   180km
0   100 miles

VISITOR'S GUIDE
SOUTHERN ITALY

Amanda Hinton

MPC

HUNTER

Published by:
Moorland Publishing Co Ltd,
Moor Farm Road West, Ashbourne,
Derbyshire DE6 1HD England

ISBN 0 86190 296 3

Published in the USA by:
Hunter Publishing Inc,
300 Raritan Center Parkway, CN 94, Edison, NJ 08818

ISBN 1 55650 578 7 (USA)

British Library Cataloguing in Publication Data:
A catalogue record for this book is available from the British Library.

Colour origination by: P. & W. Graphics Pte Ltd, Singapore

Printed in Hong Kong by: Wing King Tong Co Ltd

Cover photograph: *Gondolas, Venice* (International Photobank)
Rear Cover: *Mask Shop in Sorrento* (W. Astill)

The illustrations have been supplied by Italian National Tourist Office:
pages 19,23; all the remainder by Amanda Hinton

MPC Production Team:
Editorial: Tonya Monk
Design: Daniel Clarke & Ashley Emery
Cartography: Alastair Morrison
Typesetting: Christine Haines

CONTENTS

	Introduction	7
1	Rome	11
2	Lazio and Upper Campania	41
3	Lower Central Appennines	76
4	Upper Central Appennines	90
5	Tyrrhenian Coast	114
6	Northern Sicily	138
7	Southern Sicily	167
8	Ionian Coast	190
9	Salentine Peninsula	214
10	Murge and Adriatic Coast	242

Fact File	**270**
Accommodation	270
Additional Information	271
Climate	272, 274
Credit Cards	272
Currency Regulations	273
Customs Regulations	273
Electricity	273
Embassies & Consulates	273
Emergency Services	275
Health Care	275
Holidays & Festivals	276
Language	276
Maps	280
Police Registration	280
Post & Telephone Services	280
Photography	281
Travel	281
Index	**285**

Key to Symbols Used in Text Margin and on Maps

🏃	Recommended walks	⛪	Church/Monastery
❀	Garden	⊞	Building of interest
🏰	Castle/Fortification	Π	Archaeological site
✳	Other place of interest	🏛	Museum/Art Gallery
⋏	Winter sports	🔭	Beautiful view/Scenery, Natural phenomenon
🦙	Nature reserve/Animal interest	♣	Parkland

Key to Maps

▬▬▬	Motorway		City
▬▬▬	Main Road	●	Town /Village
═══	Minor Road		River/Lake
·‚_‗‗‗‗	Department Boundary	◼ ═══════ ◼	Tunnels

How To Use This Guide

This MPC Visitor's Guide has been designed to be as easy to use as possible. Each chapter covers a region or itinerary in a natural progression which gives all the background information to help you enjoy your visit. MPC's distinctive margin symbols, the important places printed in bold, and a comprehensive index enable the reader to find the most interesting places to visit with ease. At the end of each chapter an Additional Information section gives specific details such as addresses and opening times, making this guide a complete sightseeing companion. At the back of the guide the Fact File, arranged in alphabetical order, gives practical information and useful tips to help you plan your holiday — before you go and while you are there. The maps of each region show the main towns, villages, roads and places of interest, but are not designed as route maps and motorists should always use a good recommended road atlas.

INTRODUCTION

The *Visitor's Guide to Southern Italy* covers most of the major sights, as well as many remoter spots, in the lower part of the Italian peninsula, from Rome to Sicily. By contrast to the northern part of Italy, Southern Italy has less in the way of fine art and architecture, its public services are less efficient, and the standard of living enjoyed by the population is lower. However, part of the attraction of Southern Italy is its very muddle and confusion, its happy-go-lucky attitude, and the slower pace of life. The southern part of the Italian peninsula is drier and hotter than the north and has a landscape which ranges from the rugged and rocky crags of the Apennines to the gentle coastal lands around the Ionian and Mediterranean Seas. It is littered with traces of the region's long history; rock-hewn Byzantine monasteries are tucked away in secluded valleys, and numerous castles and towers stand sentinel over the now unthreatened coasts. The coastal lands were settled by the Greeks and Romans, and the ruins of their cities, including the marvellously preserved cities of Pompei and *Paestum*, offer visitors an opportunity to catch a glimpse of a past age. The modern towns often contain splendid Norman and Romanesque cathedrals, as well as a wealth of exuberant Baroque architecture.

Southern Italy also offers good and simple food. Fresh fish, mussels, lobsters and other seafoods are available along the coasts, while tasty cheeses, cured hams and salamis are produced in the mountains. In Puglia, olives grow to the size of small plums; in Calabria the tomatoes and peppers are the sweetest and juiciest in Italy; and in Campania the *mozzarella*, which is made from buffalo's milk, is rich and succulent.

The ten chapters in this book are organised into thirty-six, carefully planned itineraries, each of which can be tailored to meet the individual needs of the visitor as alternative routes are suggested in many places. The itineraries generally suggest the most picturesque route from one place to the next, and only where there is little of interest, or where the roads are congested, are visitors recommended to take motorways. Each itinerary is well-packed with sights and excursions, and can be generally regarded as about two days worth of travelling.

The Regions

The eight regions covered in this book are: Abruzzo, Molise, Lazio, Campania, Basilicata, Calabria, Puglia and Sicily. Each region has a distinct character and landscape. The central Apennines run through Abruzzo and Molise, both of which have high, mountainous interiors, but relatively flat coasts. Lazio and Campania contain the great metropolises of Rome and Naples respectively, and are low lying, well-cultivated and densely populated regions. Basilicata and Calabria, remote and cut off from the rest of the peninsula by their geographic position at the bottom of the boot, have rugged, wild landscapes, while Puglia, with its long coastline, is flatter and more gentle. Sicily has an identity, quite separate from the mainland, and is far more lush and verdant than the southern peninsula.

With the exception of the Abruzzo, Molise and Lazio, cities in the southern regions of Italy, tend to suffer more from crime and can in parts be rather rough and sleazy. Providing visitors take sensible precautions, however, such as removing all personal effects from their vehicles and leaving them in a secure place, and avoid carrying valuables around when sightseeing, they should have little cause to be alarmed.

The Seasons

The coasts of Southern Italy, and in particular Sicily, are the main holiday destination for Italians during the long August break. The coastal resorts suddenly burst into activity with festivals and entertainments and accommodation is often hard to come by. Most people spend the day on the beach, with a long *siesta* from midday until five or six in the evening when the sun is often unbearably hot. To avoid the crowds, and also the high season prices, it is far preferable to travel around Southern Italy in the spring or early autumn, when it is warm enough to swim, but not uncomfortably hot. During the winter, the weather is generally damp and mild along the coasts, while inland it is colder with mountain roads and remote villages often being cut off by snow.

History

Southern Italy with its long and exposed coastline has been subjected to attack and invasion ever since the Stone Age when the first infiltrations of people from the Eastern Mediterranean occurred. This was a trend that was to continue throughout Southern Italy's history. From the eleventh century BC onwards, the Ancient Greeks founded colonies along the coasts of Southern Italy and Sicily which later became known as the territories of *Magna Graecia*. Greek expansion in Southern Italy was curtailed by the expanding and increasingly powerful Roman Empire to the north, and eventually the whole peninsula came under their control. At the fall of the Roman Empire, the Eastern Mediterranean once again exerted its influence over Southern Italy, this time, however, it was the Byzantines from *Constantinople* who were the rulers. During this period, the sixth century, Lombards were forcing there way down through Italy from the north, taking all but Campania, Puglia, Calabria and Sicily, which remained under Byzantine control. The gradual decline of the Byzantine Empire's power in the region, allowed the southern cities an increasing amount of independence, and Naples and Amalfi became autonomous maritime states in the eighth century. It also heralded the beginning of the Saracenic invasions that were to threaten Southern Italy for the next few centuries, for by AD902 the Saracens had already conquered Sicily, which served them as a convenient base from which to attack mainland Italy.

The next great period in the history of Southern Italy is that of the Norman Conquest which took place between 1030 and 1130. When the Saracens were finally dislodged in 1127, Roger II made Palermo the capital of his Norman kingdom, setting the scene for one of the most outstanding periods in Southern Italy's history, which culminated in the reign of Frederick II in 1208. Frederick II, however, died heirless, and although both his illegitimate son, Manfred, and his sixteen-year-old grandson, Conradin, attempted to continue the line, neither escaped death in battle. The dominant foreign powers at the time, namely the French and Spanish, assumed control and in 1288 the Spanish claimed Sicily, and the House of Anjou the mainland. The Angevins eventually fell to the Spanish who exploited Southern Italy for the next few hundred years in order to finance the endless Franco-Spanish wars. Peasants were taken from their homes as cannon fodder and taxes levied which crippled the local economy. There were revolts against this Spanish austerity, the most significant being that in Naples in 1647, but the Spaniards managed to suppress them and keep the upperhand.

Even after the Peace of Utrecht in 1713, which saw the end of Spanish domination in Southern Italy, the situation remained dire, and famine was far from uncommon. By the nineteenth century when Garibaldi started out on his campain of liberation in Sicily, a large proportion of the population was disaffected, and he was able to rely on considerable local support in the south. After Italy was liberated and unified, an achievement brought about largely by Garibaldi, the picture in Southern Italy remained bleak, with large areas of the region being depopulated as workers migrated to the north and to the USA in search of better lives. The problem of the backward economy in the south began to be tackled in the 1950s as projects to stimulate development were established. Many of these, such as the Cassa per il Mezzogiorno, have, unfortunately, had only limited success, even though they have injected vast amounts of money into Southern Italy, as funds have been poorly managed and mis-directed. So the problem persists to this day, giving rise, and to a certain extent due, to the activities of mafia-type operations.

1

ROME

This chapter, the most northerly in the book, is devoted entirely to Italy's capital, **Rome**. The first impression one gets of the city is one of noise and incessant movement, but gradually one becomes aware that beneath the bustle and the traffic there is a clear sense of order and of permanence. Ancient structures poke through Rome's modern exterior in great profusion, like the bones of a skeleton, and in parts the city resembles an architectural dig where all the layers and strata are exposed to view. The site was settled as early as the tenth century BC, although according to the ancient historian Varro, Rome itself was founded in 753BC. The true origins of its early rulers are unclear; myth has Romulus and Remus as the founders and a series of legendary kings as their successors, but what is known for sure is that the city was ruled by three Etruscan kings from 616BC to 509BC. The deposition of the last Etruscan king, Tarquinius Superbus, in 509BC marked the beginning of the Roman Republic and was quickly followed by the introduction of the Senate as the city's ruling body. Over the following centuries the city expanded rapidly as Rome conquered great tracts of land in and around the Mediterranean basin. After the murder of Julius Caesar in 44BC, the appointment seventeen years later of his nephew Octavian (later to be named Augustus) as the first Emperor of Rome, heralded the Golden Age of the city. By the end of the first century Rome had already conquered half the known world and was unequalled in its wealth and power. Its pre-eminence, however, was not to last forever, a point made very forceably by Constantine I, who chose Constantinople as his capital in AD330 and divided the Empire in two, east and west. In AD410 the city was humiliated at the hands of the Visigoths, under Alaric, and again in AD455 by the Vandals, under Genseric. It never really made much of a recovery during the following centuries, and it was only in AD800, when Charlemagne was crowned here and the Holy Roman Empire established, that things began to look a bit brighter. The next 600 years saw the city periodically afflicted by both plague and civil strife, but the presence of the papacy ensured the city's place at the centre of western Christianity. During the exile of the papal court to Avignon between 1305 and 1376 Rome degenerated, and it was not until 1420, with the return of papal authority under Martin V, that the city recovered some of its former glory. By the time Julius II came to the papacy in 1503, Rome had resumed its place as one of the world's foremost cities, and became a major centre of the Renaissance. Italy's general decline in the seventeenth century also took its toll on Rome, and the city was under foreign domination for almost two centuries before being made the capital of united Italy in 1871. The city has grown rapidly ever since.

Today, Rome possesses an astounding wealth of art and architecture, with 7km (4 miles) of galleries in the Vatican alone, many ancient monuments and grand churches, numerous well-endowed museums, as well as major works by names such as Michelangelo and Raphael. So much in fact that the visitor can expect to see but a fraction of what is on offer before their appetite is sated. Added to this, the city has a great many attractive squares, over a thousand fountains as well as obelisks and statues left, right and centre.

Visitors should be cautioned that traffic is a real problem in Rome. It roars through the city from daybreak to the early hours of the morning, creating a considerable amount of noise and fumes. August, when the Romans are on holiday, is the city's quietest month, but it is also when the museums are busiest with tourists. The large number of tourists has unfortunately attracted a growing number of thieves. It is very rare to leave Rome without either having been robbed yourself or having witnessed someone else being robbed. The culprits are usually seemingly-innocent children, who hang around the major tourist sights, namely the Colosseum, the Forums, the Pantheon, the Vatican and usually around the railway station too. They approach tourists in groups and proceed to search through pockets and bags for likely valuables at lightening speed. If you are attacked in this way, grab the children, who are often only 'pint-sized', and search their clothing, by which time the police will have probably arrived on the scene. Moped riders can be another danger, their tactic is to whisk past removing a handbag as they go. It is obviously safest to leave all your valuables in the hotel safe, carrying sufficient money for the day in a zipped bag or pocket. Remember to take extra caution around tourist sights, and avert confrontation by clutching your pocket or bag whenever anyone suspicious approaches, letting them know that you are aware of their game.

The chapter is divided into four itineraries, each of which covers a different district of Rome. The first three itineraries start from Piazza Venezia, the city centre, while the fourth, itinerary 1D, is devoted to the Vatican. Itinerary 1A takes in the sights of ancient Rome and the east of the city, itinerary 1B concentrates on the historic centre which is contained within a bend of the River Tiber, and itinerary 1C explores the north of the city and the beautiful Villa Borghese park. Each route could easily take 2 or 3 days, so those in a hurry are recommended to pick and choose rather than try to visit everything on the itinerary. It should be noted that to cover all four of the itineraries on foot, involves a walk of some 50km (31 miles), and that therefore using public transport is advisable. The bus service is good, the main terminus is next to the Termini rail station and tickets are available from *tabacchi*, kiosks and at main bus-stops. There is a metro too, which although the stops are quite widely spaced, is useful for getting about the city. Visitors in cars are advised to leave them outside the city and take public transport in, as parking is either difficult or expensive, and thieving, particularly of car stereos is commonplace.

Route 1A

Piazza Venezia, the centre of Rome, is towered over by the colossal, white marble monument, the Vittoriano, which was built to commemorate the founder of modern Italy, King Vittorio Emanuele II. It was constructed between 1885 and 1911 as an attempt to recreate the pomp and grandeur of ancient Rome. It fails perhaps, not because it is not immensely impressive and truly monumental, but because its sheer size completely dwarfs everything around it, unlike Greek and Roman architecture which was essentially articulated on a more human scale. The top of the monument is crowned with a pair of bronze chariots, which can be seen from most parts of the city, however, the focal point is the 16m (52ft) equestrian statue of the king.

The opposite side of the piazza is filled by the early-Renaissance **Palazzo Venezia**. Built in 1455, it was the residence of various popes, as well as Napoleon, before becoming Mussolini's headquarters. The balcony from where Mussolini made many of his speeches looks over the piazza, while the interior of the building, complete with its original Renaissance decoration, is used as an exhibition space and has a collection of the applied arts, dating from medieval to Renaissance times.

Leave Piazza Venezia, passing to the right of the Vittoriano, and

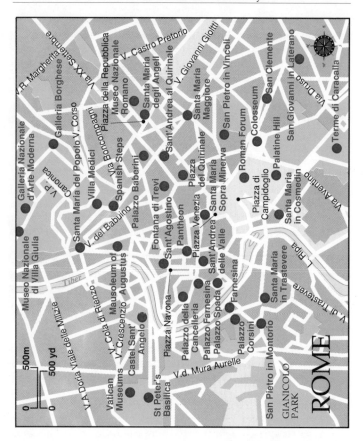

climb up the first flight of steps on the left to **Santa Maria in Aracoeli**. The church was built in 1250 and lies at the summit of the ancient Capitoline hill on the site of a former Roman shrine to Juno. Its interior is covered by a magnificent, coffered ceiling which was added in 1575 to commemorate the victory at Lepanto over the Turks. The wide central aisle, which has remnants of its original, thirteenth-century Cosmati paving, is lined along either side with chapels. The first chapel on the right contains a beautiful fresco cycle, depicting the *Life of San Bernardino* by Pinturicchio (around 1485), while in the third chapel on the left there is a fine fresco of *Sant'Antonio da Padova* by B. Gozzoli (around 1449). The door at the back of the church on the right leads out to Michelangelo's Piazza di

*Palazzo dei
Conservatori*

*Roman Forum and
San Luca Church*

Campidoglio and saves the effort of descending the church steps only to climb the next flight, the Cordonata, back up again. The Cordonata is a monumental stairway that starts at the foot of the church steps, a little way to the south.

Piazza di Campidoglio is the site of the ancient Capitol, and **Palazzo Senatorio**, along its eastern side, stands on the foundations of the Roman Senator's Palace. Ancient remains from the site are housed in the **Musei Capitolini** which fill the twin palaces lining either side of the piazza. Palazzo Nuovo, along the left side, has a colossal antique statue decorating a fountain by G. della Porta in its courtyard. To the right of the fountain is a second-century, bronze, equestrian statue of Marcus Aurelius which once stood at the centre of Piazza di Campidoglio and was the prototype for many of the equestrian statues made during the Renaissance. Stairs lead up from the right side of the courtyard to the main part of the collection, which is on the first floor. Unfortunately, none of the statues are labelled, but it is fairly easy to identify the most famous, including the *Dying Gaul* in the first room, the *Old and Young Centaurs* sculpted from grey marble in the third room, the *Capitoline Venus* in the small octagonal room off the main corridor, and the statue of *Elena*, Constantine's mother, in the fifth room, along with some sixty-four busts of Roman emperors.

Palazzo dei Conservatori on the right side of the piazza also contains a fine collection of ancient sculpture. Its courtyard holds some impressive fragments of a colossal statue of Constantine, but pass through the door on the right into the museum shop and upstairs to the museum itself. On the first floor, numerous statues, including important bronzes such as the Etruscan *Capitoline She-Wolf* in Room 4 and the *Boy Removing Thorn* in Room 3, are displayed in a grand suite of rooms, complete with their sixteenth-century frescoes and friezes depicting the *History of Rome*. Other antiquities are housed in the series of rooms at the back of the palace, including the Galleria degli Orti Lamiani which has sculptures found on the Esquiline hill, the Sala dei Bronzi which contains an impressive, first-century, bronze bed, and the Museo Nuovo which holds a good collection of pottery, funerary urns and sculptures, dating from both Hellenistic and Roman eras. Continue up to the Pinacoteca on the second floor, where there is a fine collection of paintings dating from the fourteenth to seventeenth centuries, including the *Rape of the Sabine Women* by P. da Cortona, the *Gypsy* by Caravaggio and other well-known works by Bellini, Veronese, Lotto and Tintoretto.

Before leaving Piazza di Campidoglio it is worth walking along the right side of Palazzo Senatorio, down Via del Campidoglio, from

where there is a panoramic view of the **Roman Forum** with the
wooded hill of the Palatine to the right, and the Colosseum in the
distance to the left. Return to Piazza di Campidoglio and head along
the left side of Palazzo Senatorio, passing a short column surmounted by a replica of the *Capitoline She-Wolf*, and take the steps
down, passing alongside the church of San Pietro in Carcere, which
was built on the site of the Roman prison where St Peter is believed
to have converted the guards. Next to it is the Baroque church of San
Luca, which was designed by P. da Cortona. On the right, opposite
the church, is the beautifully-carved Arch of Septimus Severus
which marks the westernmost end of the Foro Romano, the Roman
Forum. The entrance to the Forum is a little further on the right, along
Largo Romolo e Remo.

A ramp leads down from the ticket office onto Via Sacra, the main
ancient road through the Forum. Turn right and follow the road to
the **Arch of Septimus Severus**. It was built in AD205 to celebrate the
tenth anniversary of Severus' reign and is richly-carved with reliefs
depicting the Emperor's campaigns. The large brick building to the
right, the **Curia**, was constructed in AD303 as the seat of the Senate,
but was converted to a church in the seventh century. The interior is
comprised of a large hall, 27m (88ft) long and 18m (59ft) wide, and
has fragments of its original marble paving as well as good reliefs
depicting the life of Trajan (AD117-138).

To the left of the Arch of Septimus Severus, is **Colonna di Foca**, a
solitary column, 14m (46ft) high, which was reconstructed with the
original Roman stones in AD608. Heading past the column, the
Temple of Saturn with its eight Ionic columns is on the right, and
there is a good view of the ancient Tabularium upon which Palazzo
Senatorio stands. The remains of **Basilica Giulia**, which was
founded in 54BC by Julius Caesar, lie just south of the Temple of
Saturn. Follow along the steps of the Basilica, past the circular
Temple of Vesta, before turning right into the **Casa di Vestali**, the
house of the Vestal Virgins, where statues on pedestals surround a
large courtyard which has two pools at its centre.

Return to Via Sacra, heading north of the Casa di Vestali towards
the impressive, second-century portico of the **Temple of Anthony
and Faustina** which is incorporated into the façade of a Baroque
church. Turn right, following Via Sacra past the Temple of Romulus
on the left, to the massive brick-built walls of the **Basilica di
Massenzio**. The entrance to the Basilica, which is 80m (262ft) long
and 60m (197ft) wide, is just before the seventeenth-century façade
of San Francesco Romano. The Basilica was started by Maxentius in
AD306, but completed by Constantine in AD330. The north aisle

with its three vast, coffered vaults is the best-preserved part of the structure.

The **Arch of Titus**, to the right of the church, San Francesco Romano, marks the easternmost end of the Forum. It was erected after the death of Titus by the Emperor Domitian in AD81, and is decorated on the inside with reliefs depicting the capture of Jerusalem. Head towards the Palatine Hill, past the arch, and climb the steps to the ruined, sixteenth-century Palazzo Farnese, which is surrounded by a formal Italian garden. During the Republican Era (509-31BC), the Palatine was a wealthy residential area, but by medieval times the once-fine buildings had either tumbled down or had been exploited for their stone. The Renaissance interest in classicism, once more made the Palatine a popular residential area, although little was done to preserve the ruins, and Palazzo Farnese with its extensive gardens was laid out by the cardinal, Alessandro Farnese, on top of the ruins of Tiberius' palace.

The best ruins are on the southern side of the hill and are reached by heading through the Farnese gardens and descending the steps at the end to the scant remains of Casa di Livia. From here the Cripto Portico, a 122m (400ft) long tunnel, leads to the former imperial palace. Follow the tunnel, taking the first passage on the right, which emerges amongst the scattered foundations of the Palazzo dei Flavi, built by Domitian between AD81 and AD96. Head east of these ruins, past the Antiquarium, the excavation headquarters, to the stadium of Domitian. This sunken arena, littered with column fragments, is an impressive 160m (525ft) long and 80m (262ft) wide. The ruined brick walls of the Baths of Septimus Severus lie on the other side of the stadium, where steps lead down to the exit on Via di San Gregorio.

From Via di San Gregorio there are three options: the first is to end the tour by heading north to the Colosseum and returning to Piazza Venezia along Via dei Fori Imperiali; the second, best attempted by bus or car as the roads are busy and unpleasant, is south to the Roman Circo Massimo, continuing along Via dei Terme di Caracalla to the massive, crumbling, brick walls of the thermal baths, built by Caracalla in AD217; the third is to spend some time exploring the less-frequented spots in the eastern part of the city. To do the latter, cross over Via di San Gregorio and take the first steps up from the main road, passing the Baroque church of San Gregorio Magno, before continuing up the Celio hill along Clivo di Scauro. After 100m (110yd) the walls of **Santissimi Giovanni e Paolo**, a twelfth-century church built on top of a Roman house, are passed to the left. The façade, with its attractive portico made up of eight ancient columns,

Chiesa di San Carlo a Catinari, one of Rome's many churches

looks onto a small piazza at the right side of which, is the prettily-decorated, Romanesque, *campanile*, built on the site of the Roman Temple of Claudius. From the interior of the church, stairs lead down to the remains of the Roman house where St Paul and St John are believed to have been executed. The house dates from the second century and a number of its original frescoes remain intact.

An entrance to the park of **Villa Celimontana** lies opposite the church, at the top of the piazza on the right. Follow the path through this charming public gardens, which contains a children's playground as well as the graceful, sixteenth-century Villa Celimontana, to the east gate. Cross over Via Claudia and head east along Via di San Stefano Rotondo. After 90m (96yd) turn off right to visit the church of **San Stefano Rotondo**. This small, circular building dates back to the fifth century and contains good seventh-century mosaics as well as later seventeenth-century frescoes. After continuing along Via di San Stefano Rotondo for some 500m (547yd) the road opens out into the busy **Piazza San Giovanni in Laterano**, at the centre of which is the tallest of Rome's Egyptian obelisks (31m/102ft). Along the south and east sides of the *piazza* is **San Giovanni in Laterano**, the cathedral church of Rome and the papal residence up until their exile to Avignon in 1309. The baptistery, on the south side of the piazza, dates back to the founding of the church by Constantine in the fourth century, and contains fine mosaics. Both the baptistery and the church were, however, remodelled between 1646 and 1649 at the request of Pope Innocenzo X by one of the greatest architects of the Baroque era, Borromini. The portal to the left of the baptistery, which is flanked by two small towers, leads into the right transept of the church. The vast interior, divided into five aisles, is covered by a highly decorative, coffered ceiling, studded with rosettes and coats of arms, while the domed ceiling in the apse holds a mosaic in the style of the thirteenth century on a gold ground. The ornate Gothic tabernacle in front of the apse dates from 1367 and holds relics of St Paul and St Peter. A door in the left aisle leads through to a charming, thirteenth-century cloister which is surrounded by double columns and stone-carved remnants of the earlier church. A room in the left corner contains a tapestry of 1599 which depicts the *Life of St John the Evangelist*, as well as a collection of chalices and papal garments. It is worth going out of the church through the main entrance to see the grand façade, which is adorned with massive Corinthian columns and monumental statues. It faces onto a large, busy piazza, on the left side of which is the Scala Santa, a flight of twenty-eight marble steps transported by Elena, Constantine's mother, to Rome from Pilate's house in Jerusalem.

Return to Piazza San Giovanni in Laterano and leave from its north-west corner along Via San Giovanni in Laterano, continuing along it to the small church of **San Clemente** on the right. Although this church is not very remarkable from the outside, the interior is of considerable interest. It has three aisles divided by ancient columns with an attractive choir made from sixth-century stone originating from the former basilica. The dome of the apse holds a splendid, thirteenth-century mosaic depicting the *Triumph of the Cross* with fourteenth-century frescoes on the lower walls of *Jesus, Mary and the Apostles*. In the left aisle, the Cappella di San Caterina d'Alessandria, holds some fine Renaissance frescoes of scenes depicting the *Life of Saint Catherine*, the *Crucifixion*, and an *Annunciation*. Other frescoes, dating from the sixth to twelfth centuries can be seen in the Chiesa Inferiore, the remains of the former basilica, which is reached by descending the stairs from the sacristy. It is also possible to visit the Roman remains of a Temple of Mithras behind the apse of the church.

The **Colosseum** is a further 300m (328yd) west of San Clemente along Via San Giovanni in Laterano. This magnificent building dates from AD72 when Vespasian, the first of the Flavian emperors, commissioned its construction on the former site of Nero's pleasure palace. It was used for public spectacles, mostly bloody in nature, although dramatic and athletic performances were also staged here, and could hold up to 50,000 spectators. It remained in use up until the sixth century, after which it was transformed into a fortress, later to be plundered for stone. In 1740, Pope Benedict XIV consecrated the Colosseum in memory of the Christians who were martyred here during gladiatorial spectacles and the monument was given the respect it deserved. A large section of the outer walls, clad in the original travertine marble, remain standing to a height of 57m (187ft) and are made up of three arcaded tiers, the first in the Doric order, the second in the Ionic and the third in the Corinthian. The wall making up a fourth tier was added by Titus in AD80. The entrance is on the west side and although visitors are admitted free of charge into the eliptical arena, which is 76m (250ft) long and 46m (151ft) wide, a ticket must be bought in order to climb to the upper levels.

Constantine's Arch, just to the left of the Colosseum entrance, is one of the best-preserved, ancient buildings in Rome. It was erected between AD313 and AD315 to celebrate Constantine's conquest over his rival Maxentius. It has three monumental arches and is richly decorated with carved reliefs. The panels on the column bases depict Constantine's good deeds, while in the circular medallions above the arches, the Emperor is shown hunting. The frieze along the top was removed from an earlier building, dating from the second century, and is carved with scenes from the *Life of Marcus Aurelius*.

Those who wish to return to the city centre can follow Via dei Fori Imperiali from the west side of the Colosseum to Piazza Venezia. The itinerary, however, continues by heading north from the Colosseum, up a flight of steps to Via Nicola Salvi. Take the first left, Via delle Terme di Tito, where, after 150m (164yd) visitors can choose either to continue right along Viale dei Monti Opio to visit the Terme Traiano, the scant remains of Trajan's Baths, or turn left, passing through Largo delle Polveriera, to Via Eudossiana which, shortly after passing the Engineering University, opens out into **Piazza di San Pietro in Vincoli**. The main attraction of the church in the north-east corner of this piazza, is Michelangelo's *Memorial to Julius II*, which stands inside, at the back of the right aisle. It is a far cry from the original project which was designed to stand in splendour at the centre of the Pantheon, but it is nonetheless impressive. The central figure, Moses, was just one of the numerous large statues designed for the original monument and gives some idea of the scale upon which it was envisaged. In the niches either side of Moses (1514-16) are statues of Leah and Rachel (1542), the rest of the monument is the work of Michelangelo's pupils. The church also contains the chains which are believed to have held St Peter prisoner in Palestine. They are on display in a glass casket beneath the fine bronze tabernacle (1477) in the main apse. The apse itself is decorated with frescoes and the central aisle, which is lined with antique Doric columns along either side, is covered by a fine ceiling painted by F. Fontana. Also of interest is the small, Byzantine mosaic of St Sebastian, dating from the seventh century, in the second chapel along the left aisle.

Leave the piazza following Via delle Sette Salle along the left side of the church and descend the first steps on the left to Largo Viscevelosta. Turn right and follow Via Cavour for 450m (492yd) to Piazza dell'Esquilino where a monumental flight of steps skirts the apse of **Santa Maria Maggiore**. Enter the church from the top of the steps and head for the dome of the apse, which contains a beautiful thirteenth-century mosaic depicting the *Coronation of the Virgin*, while the triumphal arch in front is covered by a cycle of mosaic scenes of the *Childhood of Christ*, dating from the church's foundation in the early fifth century. The main part of the church is comprised of a very wide central nave with aisles at either side divided by antique columns. The high walls supported above the columns are also decorated with fifth-century mosaics, arranged in panels depicting scenes in the lives of Abraham, Moses and Joseph. The grand, coffered ceiling covering the nave was designed by G. da Sangallo (1493-8), while the Cosmati paving on the floor dates from the twelfth century. The ornate, eighteenth-century baldachin in front of the altar is built over relics from the crib at Bethlehem. To its right, a large domed chapel contains the decorative tombs of Popes Sixtus V and Pius V, while to its left another chapel holds a small, thirteenth-century painting of the *Madonna*.

From Piazza dell'Esquilino, which has an ancient obelisk from the Mausoleum of Augustus at its centre, it is possible to continue for a further 250m (273yd) to Piazza dei Cinquecento where the Termini rail station is on the right, and the **Museo Nazionale Romano** on the left. The museum stands on the site of the Terme di Dioleziano which was built by Diocletian in AD298. Its collection of ancient art is contained in one of the vast rooms of the baths and in the cloister of a convent that was built amongst the ruins in the sixteenth century. It is one of the most important collections of ancient art in the world and includes numerous mosaics, statues and frescoes dating from Roman times. On the west side of the baths complex, looking onto Piazza della Repubblica, is the church of **Santa Maria degli Angeli**, designed by Michelangelo in 1566 on the site of the ancient tepidarium. A large domed hall leads into a very wide but short nave with seventeenth- and eighteenth-century paintings decorating the walls.

The curved porticoes (1896-1902) surrounding Piazza della Repubblica stand over the former exedra, a semi-circular recess, of

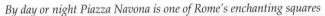

By day or night Piazza Navona is one of Rome's enchanting squares

the Diocletian baths. There are no antique remains visible, but the piazza has an attractive fountain at its centre, decorated with bronze statues dating from 1901. Take a bus if possible along Via Nazionale which heads south from the piazza towards the city centre. Those who wish to visit the **Mercati Traianei** (Trajan's Market), should stop at Largo Magnanapoli. Designed by the architect Apollodoro di Damasco (AD107-112), the market, was originally five-storeys high, and has a fine curved façade looking over Trajan's forum (closed to the public). Next to it stands the **Torre Milizia**, a stout, thirteenth-century tower which can be ascended and offers good views of the city. From Torre Milizia head down the first steps on the left to **Trajan's Column**, which is 38m (125ft) high and is covered by a spiral of carved scenes depicting Trajan's victory over the Dacians. Piazza Venezia, the starting point for Route 1B, is a short distance to the west of the column.

Route 1B

Itinerary 1B leaves Piazza Venezia from its north side, and follows Via del Corso for 150m (164yd) before turning left to Piazza del Collegio Romano. **Galleria Doria-Pamphili** is housed in the grand, eighteenth-century palazzo in the north-east corner of the piazza, and contains an important collection of paintings dating from the fifteenth to eighteenth centuries. Amongst the most famous works in the collection are: *Portrait of Two People* by Raphael; *Flight into Egypt* by Caravaggio; and *Innocent X* by Velazquez.

Head west from the piazza for 200m (218yd) to **Piazza della Minerva**, at the centre of which is Bernini's rather whimsical elephant (1667), supporting a small Egyptian obelisk on its back. The simple, Renaissance façade of **Santa Maria Sopra Minerva**, along the east side of the piazza, belies its finely decorated interior, which has three vast aisles lined with chapels along either side. There are also chapels in the transepts, the one in the right transept is decorated with frescoes by F. Lippi (1489-93), that in the left contains the tomb of the great Florentine painter, Fra Angelico. Also of importance is the small statue by Michelangelo of *Christ Bearing the Cross* (1519-21) which is to the left of the main altar.

One of Rome's most outstanding monuments, the **Pantheon**, is within easy striking distance as it lies just a short distance to the north-west of Piazza della Minerva. This circular building is crowned by a large dome and fronted by a massive portico, eight columns wide, which is surmounted by a high pediment. The inscription on the portico states that the Pantheon was built by Marcus Agrippa in 27BC, although the present structure was erected between AD120 and AD125, by Hadrian. It was an extraordinary feat of engineering, for the dome, the largest in the history of architecture, was supported, without the aid of buttresses, by the immense walls, which were up to 6m (20ft) thick. Its period of glory, however, was relatively short-lived, for being a pagan temple, it was closed in AD399 in accordance with Christian law. The building was plundered and generally neglected up until AD608, when Pope Boniface IV consecrated it as a church. It is, nonetheless, remarkably well-preserved. The interior is still complete with its splendid, coffered dome, the diameter of which is equal to the overall height of the building. The pilasters and columns lining the lower walls are made of the original *giallo antico*, a very rare, yellow, Numidian marble, while the alternately curved and oblong recesses which once held statues, now contain tombs and altars. The first recess on the right has a fresco of an *Annunciation* by M. da Forli, while the second, next to it, contains the revered tomb of King Vittorio Emanuele II (died 1878). Another famous tomb, that of Raphael, is on the left, between the second and third recesses.

Head across the piazza in front of the Pantheon, past its fountain, and follow the street from the left corner to the impressive façade of **San Luigi dei Francesi**. This church was built for the French community in 1518, although the richly decorated interior with its variegated marbles, stucco and gilt work, dates from the eighteenth century. It contains a fine fresco depicting the *Life of St Cecilia* in the second chapel on the right, and three important paintings by Caravaggio of the *Story of Matthew* (1598-1601) in the fifth chapel on the left.

Follow Via della Scrofa north of San Luigi dei Francesi and take the second turning on the left to the church of **Sant'Agostino**. Constructed between 1479 and 1483, this was one of the first Renaissance churches to be built in Rome. Its interior is divided into three aisles by square pillars which are decorated with statues and frescoes of saints and prophets. The third pillar on the left has a painting of Isiah by Raphael (1512). The most important statue in the church, the *Madonna del Parto*, is set in a niche to the right of the main door and is by J. Sansovino (1521).

Take Via Sant'Agostino south of the church, passing under an arch into Piazza delle Cinque Lune from where a passage, Passetto delle Cinque Lune, leads through to **Piazza Navona**. This elongated piazza stands on the site of Domitian's stadium which was built in AD86. There are no ancient remains, but the absence of traffic, and the richly coloured façades of the fine surrounding buildings, make this one of the most charming spots in Rome. At the centre of the piazza are four elaborate Baroque fountains designed by Bernini, the largest of which, the Fountains of the Four Rivers, is surmounted by an obelisk and dates from 1651.

Leave the piazza from its east side and follow Corsia Agonale to the high walls of the sixteenth-century Palazzo Madama. Turn right and continue along Corso del Rinascimento, passing **Palazzo Sapienza** (number 33) which contains Borromini's quaint Chapel of St Ivo (1660) inside its courtyard. Continue to the end of Corso del Rinascimento and cross over the busy street, Corso Vittorio Emanuele, to the grand Baroque façade of **Sant'Andrea delle Valle**. The church was started in 1591 by G. della Porta, but it was not finished until 1625 when Maderno designed its distinctive dome, the second highest in Rome. The interior, with its richly decorated ceiling, is lit by the number of windows that pierce the high drum of the dome. The ceiling of the dome holds a fine fresco of the *Glory of Paradise* by Lanfranco (1625) while the pendentives below the drum are decorated with the *Evangelists* by Domenichini (1628).

On the opposite side of Corso Vittorio Emanuele at number 141 is the sadly neglected **Palazzo Massimo**. The building was commissioned by the descendant of an ancient Roman family, Prince Pietro Massimo, who wanted a house in the style of his patrician forefathers. The project was undertaken by B. Peruzzi (1532-36), one of the most important architects of the High Renaissance. Given the awkward shape and size of the site, Peruzzi did well to create a townhouse that in many ways resembles one of Augustan Rome. The columned portico has a finely moulded ceiling and niches at either end. A long passage leads to the first courtyard, modelled on the ancient atrium, and continues to a second courtyard, the peristylium, private quarters.

Continue for a short distance along Corso Vittorio Emanuele to the **Museo di Roma**, a museum of the life and history of Rome, which is on the right, and the **Museo Barraco**, which occupies a fine, Renaissance palazzo designed by A. da Sangallo and contains a collection of ancient statues, on the left. Take the next left turn to **Palazzo della Cancelleria**, another fine Renaissance building. It was constructed between 1483 and 1517 and is the seat of the apostolic chancellery. It is possible to peek into the courtyard, which was designed in the style of the great architect, Bramante, and is surrounded by elegant arches on two storeys.

Head south through the colourful market on Piazza Campo di Fiore to **Palazzo Farnese**. This grand palazzo, set on a quiet piazza, was started by A. da Sangallo in 1514 and completed by Michelangelo in 1546. It was built for Alessandro Farnese, later Pope

Paul III, and is now the seat of the French Embassy. The two fountains in the piazza contain ancient granite basins removed from the Caracalla baths. **Palazzo Spada**, a short distance east of Palazzo Farnese, along Via Capo di Ferro, is also very impressive. Built in 1540, it surrounds a charming courtyard decorated with ancient statues. On the left side of the courtyard there is a short corridor which Borromini, through the use of *trompe-l'oeil* made appear quite long.

From here the itinerary crosses the River Tiber to the west bank and the district of **Trastevere**. It is a delightful part of Rome, the narrow streets are filled with small restaurants and the absence of traffic in them is a welcome change from the busy main roads in the centre of Rome. Head south of Palazzo Spada, along Via Polverini and cross over Ponte Sisto, a pedestrianised bridge, to Piazza Trilussa. Follow Via di Ponte Sisto to the crenellated gate, Porta Settimana, and turn right, through the gate, following Via della Lungara to **Palazzo Corsini** on the left. This large Baroque palazzo, built in 1736, houses the **Galleria Nazionale d'Arte Antica** which contains a notable collection of paintings dating from the sixteenth to eighteenth centuries. The **Farnesina**, on the opposite side of the road, houses a collection of fifteenth- to nineteenth-century prints, but the building itself is perhaps of more interest. Set in fine gardens on the bank of the Tiber, the villa was designed by B. Peruzzi between 1508 and 1511 and is a good example of Roman High Renaissance architecture. Raphael frescoed the *Galatea* on the ground floor, and the *Marriage of Alessandro and Roxana* by Sodoma is on the first floor.

Return to Porta Settimana and head south along Via della Scala to the lovely twelfth-century church of **Santa Maria in Trastevere**. Its façade, which looks onto a peaceful piazza, is decorated with bands of mosaics, dating from the twelfth and thirteenth centuries. The interior also contains fine mosaics, both in the dome of its apse and on the lower walls. Those in the dome depict the *Redeemer, Virgin and Saints* and date from 1140, while the six mosaic panels on the lower walls showing the *Life of Mary* date from the end of the thirteenth century. The church also has fine Cosmati paving on its floor and a rich, gilt, coffered ceiling which was added in 1617 by Domenichino.

Visitors may wish to head uphill from here, visiting the small Renaissance church of **San Pietro in Montorio**, which is famous for the circular Tempietto del Bramante in its courtyard. Just beyond it is the **Gianicolo**, a park which covers the top of the ancient Janiculum hill. Shaded by lofty umbrella pine trees, it offers fine views over the city and contains an equestrian statue of Garibaldi, commemorating his valiant defense here in 1849 against the French. Those who do not wish to climb up to these sights should head east from Santa Maria in Trastevere along Via della Lungaretta, to the Tiber. Continue in an easterly direction following the river bank, past the small island, Isola Tiberina, which was the site of the ancient Aesclepion, a medical centre, and is now a hospital. The bridge crossing the Tiber to the island, **Ponte Fabricio**, is one of the oldest in Rome and dates back to 62BC. Take the next bridge, Ponte Palatino, across the river to **Piazza Bocca della Verita** which holds the remains of two small temples. The rectangular temple on the left, Tempio di Portuno, is well-preserved and stands complete with its Ionic columns. It dates from 100BC. The Augustan circular temple to the right, Tempio d'Ercole, is also in good condition and is surrounded by attractive columns of the Corinthian order. At the southern end of the piazza, looking onto a fine Baroque fountain (1715), is the façade of the Greek basilica, **Santa Maria in Cosmedin**, with its pretty, Lombardic *campanile*. The basilica dates from the eighth century, although it was largely reconstructed in 1123 and is typical of Romanesque architecture. Inside its portico, against the wall on the left, is the Bocca della Verita, a marble stone, carved into a face, which was used in Roman times as a drain cover. During the medieval period the superstition began that anyone who put their hand into the gaping hole of the mouth and told a lie would have it bitten off. The interior of the church is well-restored and has a traditional, flat ceiling which is painted with stars in the section over the central nave. The excellent Cosmati paved floor dates from 1123, while the choir, which is complete with its original marble walls, pulpits and seats, as well as the iconastasis, a screen that divides the nave and choir from the sanctuary, dates from the medieval period.

Return to the city centre by heading north of Santa Maria in Cosmedin along Via Teatro di Marcello. The church of **San Nicola in Carcere**, passed on the left, has numerous ancient columns built into its walls, while the remains of an Augustan gate lie nearby. **Teatro di Marcello**, with its impressive ancient curved walls, is passed a short distance further on. The theatre was built by Julius Caesar between 13BC and 11BC, and was later dedicated by Augustus to his nephew Marcellus. The three columns just to the right of the theatre are all that remain of the Tempio di Apollo Sosiano, an Augustan temple. Piazza Venezia, the starting point for itinerary 1C, is 400m (437yd) further north.

Route 1C

Itinerary 1C starts at the north-east corner of Piazza Venezia and heads up Via IV Novembre. At the top of the hill turn left and follow Via Pilotta, a small street beneath a series of four arches, to **Galleria**

Colonna, which is at number 17 on the left. The gallery is housed in part of the vast Palazzo Colonna and contains a good collection of paintings dating from the fifteenth to eighteenth centuries, with works by well-known artists such as Tintoretto, Poussin, Van Dyck and Rubens. Continue along Via Pilotta and keep straight on along Via Lucchese to **Fontana di Trevi**. This splendid Rococo fountain, created in 1762, is the most impressive of all Rome's many fountains. It was designed by Bernini in the seventeenth century, but the project was abandoned and only came to fruition over a hundred years later, when Pope Clement XII commissioned the little-known architect, N. Salvi, to build it. A colossal statue of Neptune stands at the centre of a Roman triumphal arch, being drawn on a cockle-shell by winged sea-horses, which are led by tritons, across a foaming sea. Water cascades from the sea, over sculpted rocks, before spilling into the vast basin below.

Return back along Via Lucchese and turn left up Via della Dataria just before the small church of Santa Croce. At the top of the hill, which is the highest of Rome's Seven Hills, is **Piazza del Quirinale**. Palazzo Quirinale, along the left side of the piazza, was the residence of numerous popes and kings from the sixteenth century up until 1946 when it became the presidential palace. The grand, white marble building along the east side of the piazza is **Palazzo della Consulta** (1734), while set in the gardens at the centre of the square is an Egyptian obelisk, flanked on either side by the antique statues of Castor, Pollux and their horses. These statues originally stood in the Roman Baths of Constantine. There is a good view from the piazza across the city's roof tops to the dome of St Peter's.

Follow Via del Quirinale out of the east corner of the piazza, between the two palaces, to the little church of **Sant'Andrea al Quirinale** which is on the right. Designed by the papal architect, Bernini, in 1658, it has a large, curved portico with Corinthian pilasters at either side, surmounted by a classical pediment. The oval-shaped interior, sumptuously decorated with rare marbles, porphyry and gilded stucco, is covered by a shallow dome with a high lantern.

Continue down Via del Quirinale to another small, Baroque church, **San Carlo alle Quattro Fontane**, designed by Bernini's contemporary, Borromini. It was built exactly twenty years before Bernini's Sant'Andrea, in 1638, and has all the sinuous curves and elaborate decoration typical of the Baroque style. The interior, which is long and narrow, has an eliptical ground plan and is decorated with ornate stucco work. The church stands at a really remarkable crossroads, there being a Rococo fountain on each corner and long views down each of the four roads. Looking back down Via del Quirinale it is possible to see the obelisk on Piazza Quirinale. Obelisks are also visible at either end of Via del Quattro Fontane, while at the end of Via XX Settembre is Michelangelo's gate, Porta Pia. Those interested in the work of Bernini should make the excursion along Via XX Setembre to the church of **Santa Maria della Vittoria** which contains one of his greatest sculptural works, the *Ecstasy of St Teresa*. It stands in the fourth chapel on the left. The church, also notable for its rich marble decoration, was designed by Maderno, the papal architect before Bernini, in 1605.

The itinerary, however, heads down Via del Quattro Fontane, in a north-westerly direction, to **Palazzo Barberini**, on the right. This grand Baroque *palazzo*, surrounded by pleasant gardens, was started by Maderno in 1625 with the help of Borromini, and finished by Bernini in 1633. It houses the Galleria Nazionale d'Arte Antica, the other part of which is visited on itinerary 1B (Palazzo Corsini). The paintings the gallery contains, date from the thirteenth to eighteenth centuries and include notable works such as: the *Madonna and Child* and *Annunciation* by F. Lippi in Room 2; *La Fornarina* by Raphael in Room 6; *Judith and Holofernes* by Caravaggio in Room 13; and *Henry VIII* by Holbein in Room 19. It is also possible to visit the Rococo apartments on the second floor which contain seventeenth-century paintings, as well as furniture, porcelain and costumes of the period.

Piazza Barberini is a short distance further down the hill beyond the *palazzo*. It contains a fountain designed by Bernini which is decorated with the three bees of the Barberini coat of arms. From the piazza continue in a north-westerly direction along Via Sistina, to the massive obelisk which stands in front of the Baroque, **Santa Trinita dei Monti**. The church was built for the French king, Louis XII, in 1502, but the façade, which has bell-towers at either side, dates from 1585 and was designed by Maderno. From the top of the steps which lead up to the portal there is a fine view across the city and of Villa Medici to the right. The interior, made up of a single aisle, has deeply recessed chapels along either side. The frescoes in the second chapel on the left of the *Descent from the Cross*, and also in the third chapel on the right of the *Ascension of Mary*, are by the sixteenth-century painter, D. da Volterra.

Just below the church are the famous Spanish Steps, the **Scalinata della Trinita dei Monti**, designed in 1723 by F. de Sanctis. They take their name from the Spanish Embassy which was established here in the same year. The piazza at the foot of the steps, which contains a fountain by Bernini (1629), has been the popular abode of numerous foreign writers and musicians over the years including George Eliot,

James Joyce, Stendahl, Balzac, Wagner, Henry James and Byron. The house where Keats died in 1821 is on the right of the steps and is now a museum, the **Keats and Shelley Memorial House**, and contains an assortment of memorabilia. The Babington Tea Rooms, which is as popular today as it was when it was established in 1896, are on the left side of the steps.

Climb back up the steps to Trinita dei Monti and turn left, following Via Trinita dei Monti past Villa Medici, designed by A. Lippi in 1544. The first ramp on the right after the Villa leads up to the **Pincio**, a formal garden dotted with the busts of Roman patriots. At the end of the garden there is a vast terrace, above Piazza Popolo, with a magnificent panorama. Rome's largest park, **Villa Borghese**, stretches over an area of 6sq km (2sq miles) behind the Pincio. Take the Magnolia-lined, Via dei Magnoli, one of the principal roadways through the park, to Piazzale Canestre, and continue up Viale Pietro Canonica, passing Piazza Siena, a horse-riding centre, to **Museo Canonica**. The museum, a low crenellated building, resembling a fortress, is built round a courtyard and contains the work of the sculptor Pietro Canonica (1869-1959) as well as a number of antique statues.

Continue up to the four columns at the top of Viale Pietro Canonica and follow Viale Antonino e Faustina to Viale delle Due Piramide. Turn left up Viale delle Due Piramide and at the top of the hill turn right, following Viale dell'Uccelliera for 200m (218yd) to **Galleria Borghese**. The gallery is arranged in the seventeenth-century villa of Cardinal Scipione Borghese, who founded the park between 1613 and 1616, and contains a good collection of paintings and sculpture. The sculpture collection ranges from antique to Baroque, and includes Canova's famous statue of *Pauline Borghese* (1805), who was Napoleon's sister. There are also numerous famous paintings by well-known masters such as Raphael, Caravaggio, Correggio and Titian.

Return back along Viale dell'Uccelliera and continue past the **Zoo**, which is the best in Italy and covers some 12 hectares (30 acres), to Viale delle Belle Arti. The **Galleria Nazionale d'Arte Moderna** is a short distance along this road on the right. It was built in 1911 as an exhibition centre and houses Italy's largest collection of modern art, which dates from the nineteenth and twentieth centuries. Continue along Viale delle Belle Arti for a further 400m (437yd) to **Museo Nazionale di Villa Giulia**. This is a museum not to be missed: it contains the best collection of Etruscan finds in the world, and is arranged in a magnificent, Late Renaissance villa, which was built for Pope Julius III in 1551. The collection, which is displayed according to the geographical locations of the sites, fills the thirty-two rooms around the large central courtyard. The courtyard contains formal gardens and has a large nymphaeum, or fountain, at its centre. To the left of the nymphaeum there is an impressive reconstruction of an Etruscan temple from *Alatri*, which is just to the south of Rome.

Return to Galleria Nazionale d'Arte Moderna and head south to Viale Washington. The gate at the bottom of Viale Washington leads into Piazzale Flaminio, at the left side of which another gate, the large sixteenth-century Porta de Popolo, leads through to **Piazza del Popolo**. This large oval piazza took on its symmetrical appearance in 1816 when it was re-arranged by G. Valadier. Just inside the gate on the left is the church of **Santa Maria del Popolo**, with its mirror-image on the right, which was commissioned by the Renaissance pope, Sixtus IV in 1477. Its interior, divided by attractively carved pillars into three aisles, is lined with chapels along either side. The first chapel on the right contains a fine fresco by Pinturicchio dating from 1485, the second chapel on the left was designed by Raphael for the Chigi family. Also of interest is the thirteenth-century, Byzantine *Madonna* on the main altar.

Cross to the far side of Piazza del Popolo, passing the Egyptian obelisk at its centre, and follow Via di Ripetta to the **Ara Pacis** monument, which is enclosed within a glass show room on the right. The monument was built between 13 and 9BC in celebration of the peace that ensued during the Augustan era. It is very finely carved and has beautiful reliefs depicting the imperial procession of Augustus and his family, as well as scenes of sacrifice and of fertility rites. The large, grassy tumulus on the opposite side of the road is the Mausoleum of Augustus, which was built in the Etruscan style in 28BC. Converted to a fortress in medieval times, it now stands in a state of neglect, and is best viewed from a distance.

To join the start of itinerary 1D, head south along the banks of the Tiber to Ponte Sant'Angelo. Otherwise return to the city centre along Via del Corso, from where a great many pleasant pedestrian shopping streets lead off from either side. On the way it passes through **Piazza Colonna**, where there is the beautifully-carved column of Marcus Aurelius.

Route 1D

Itinerary 1D begins at Ponte Sant'Angelo, one of the many fine bridges spanning the River Tiber. Cross over the bridge, which is lined with statues by Bernini (1669-71), to **Castel Sant'Angelo**. This circular edifice was built first as a mausoleum for Hadrian in AD135, but was later surrounded by a wall and converted to a fortress to defend the Vatican. Today it contains a collection of arms and armour, as well as the papal apartments complete with their Renaissance decor and furnishings.

From Castel Sant'Angelo head west along the monumental road, Via della Conciliazione, which was built in 1937 to celebrate the reconciliation of Mussolini and Pope Pius XI, to **St Peter's Basilica**. The basilica, the largest and most important in the Catholic world, stands majestically above Bernini's circular, colonnaded piazza which can hold a crowd of 400,000 and has an Egyptian obelisk at its centre. The original Basilica was built by Constantine in AD324 on the site of Nero's Circus where St Peter was martyred. Plans for the present building were, however, drawn up in 1452, although it was not until more than fifty years later that building actually commenced. Over ten of Rome's leading architects, including Michelangelo, Bramante, Bernini and Maderno, were involved in its construction and it was not completed until 1667. The façade, which was designed by Maderno (1606), has eight gigantic Corinthian columns and four pilasters. It is surmounted by a balustrade which is adorned with statues of Christ and the Apostles. Of the five massive bronze doors which lead into the building, that in the centre is the oldest. It was cast between 1433 and 1445.

The interior, overwhelming both in size and decoration, was designed by Bernini who embellished every facet with polished marble, gilded stucco or rich fresco. The vast pillars that divide the interior into three immense aisles are clad with umpteen statues. However, the most important statue in the basilica is that in the first chapel on the right, the *Pieta* by Michelangelo, which was carved in 1499, when the sculptor was still in his early twenties. A magnificent gold coffered ceiling leads up to the famous dome which was started by Bramante in 1506, then taken over by Michelangelo, and finally completed in 1593 by G. della Porta. The bronze baldachin, under the dome, was designed by Bernini (1633), and stands above the tomb of St Peter. Other works in bronze can be seen in the treasury, the entrance of which is in the left aisle. The collection is well-displayed and includes the bronze sepulchre designed by Pollaiolo (1489-93) for Sixtus IV. To visit the crypt, descend the steps from the right transept. A circular passage, beautifully-decorated with frescoes, leads to St Peter's tomb, while a wide corridor, lined along either side with the tombs of many Popes, leads out of the basilica, emerging near the entrance to the dome, which can be ascended by lift.

The **Vatican** is a tiny state, covering little more than 40 hectares (100 acres), but it has its own army of Swiss Guards, its own stamps

and coins, a duty-free supermarket and one of the richest collections
of art in the world. The Vatican museums can either be reached by
taking the service bus through the Vatican gardens from St Peter's
Square, or by walking around the Vatican walls to the entrance at its
north side. To do the latter, turn left out of St Peter's Square, passing
the barracks of the Swiss Guards and follow Via di Porta Angelica to
Piazza del Risorgimento, from where Via Leone IV heads uphill to

St Peter's Basilica, the largest and most important in the Catholic world

Shopping in Rome

The main shopping area is the historic centre of Rome in the network of streets around Piazza di Spagna. High fashion shops are in Via Sistina and Via Gregoriana, other boutiques fill the area around Via Condotti, Via Frattina and Via del Corso. For antiques and art objects, Via del Babuino has the best reputation, but lower prices are found on Via dei Coronari, between Piazza Navona and Tor di Nona and on Via Gulia and Via Giubbonari.

La Rinascente is Rome's most prestigious department store, and has branches on Piazza Colonna and Piazza Fiume. Otherwise, the only chain department stores are Upim and Standa, both with branches throughout the city.

A lively flea market is held in Trastevere, every Sunday, in the streets around Porta Portese. In Via Sannio, near Porta San Giovanni there is a daily market of new and second-hand clothes. Every morning, except Sunday, prints and reproductions are sold in a street market on Piazza Fontanella Borghese. For general food markets, the most interesting are on Piazza Vittorio, Via Andrea Doria and Campo dei Fiori. There is also a colourful flower market held on Tuesday morning in Via Trionfale.

the museum's entrance. Either take the lift or walk up the massive circular staircase to the ticket office on the upper floor.

There are four colour-coded itineraries around the museum, each of varying length. The fourth, the yellow itinerary, is the longest and most comprehensive. With some 7km (4 miles) of galleries it is impossible to visit all of the Vatican's collection and hope to appreciate it, so it is best to select a few of the most important things and concentrate on them. The museums are arranged around two mas sive courtyards. In the left corner of the first courtyard, Cortile della Pigna, is the **Museo Gregoriano Egizio**, which houses a well-displayed collection of ancient Egyptian statues, mummies, carved reliefs and artefacts. Along the west side of the courtyard is **Museo Pio Clementino** which contains an outstanding collection of Greek and Roman statues, including the Hellenistic *Laocoon Group*, and the first-century BC *Belvedere Torso* which was greatly admired by Michelangelo. The Braccio Nuovo, New Wing, along the south side of the courtyard also houses classical statues.

The **Sistine Chapel**, probably the most famous feature of the Vatican, is at the southernmost end of the second courtyard, joined, in actual fact, to the right aisle of St Peter's Basilica. The chapel was built between 1475 and 1481 by Pope Sixtus IV. In 1508 Pope Julius II commissioned Michelangelo to paint the ceiling, which having recently been restored, can now be seen in all its former splendour. Michelangelo worked single-handed for four years to complete the massive project. The scenes depicting the *Creation* and the *Flood*, amongst others, and the sculpturally painted figures are composed on an architectural grid and demonstrate Michelangelo's astounding ability to use light and dark, and vivid colour to maximum effect. The fresco of the *Last Judgement* filling the apse is also by Michelangelo, although it is a later work and dates from 1534. The walls of the chapel are frescoed by other artists, including Botticelli, Perugino and Pinturicchio.

Pinturicchio also decorated the **Borgia Apartments** which are next to the Sistine Chapel, while the **Cappella di Niccolo V**, also nearby, contains beautiful frescoes by Fra Angelico, depicting scenes from the lives of San Stefano and San Lorenzo (1448-50). On the upper floor, directly above the Borgia Apartments are the **Stanze di Raffaello**. These four rooms were frescoed by Raphael at the same time as Michelangelo was working in the Sistine Chapel. From here, one of the most impressive of the Vatican's galleries extends along the entire length of both courtyards, back to the entrance. The first section of the gallery, the **Galleria delle Carte Geographiche**, has maps of the Roman provinces frescoed on the walls along either side. It continues into the **Galleria degli Arazzi** which contains an extraordinary collection of vast tapestries, and includes numerous sixteenth-century Brussels tapestries designed by Raphael. The last section of the gallery, the Galleria dei Candelabri, is divided into six parts and is filled with antique statues.

The **Pinacoteca**, which looks out onto the Vatican gardens, in the small courtyard at the entrance, is well worth visiting. It contains many fine altarpieces dating from the thirteenth to fifteenth centuries, and religious paintings by well-known artists such as Giotto, Fra Angelico, F. Lippi, Pinturicchio and Perugino. The largest room, Room 8, is devoted to the work of Raphael and includes ten tapestries made to his designs, as well as a *Transfiguration* and the small panels of a predella depicting the *Coronation of the Virgin*.

Additional Information

Places to Visit in Rome

Route 1A

Museo di Palazzo Venezia
Via del Plebiscito 118
☎ (06) 6798865
Open: Monday to Saturday 9am-1.30pm, Sunday 9am-12.30pm.

Musei Capitolini
Piazza del Campidoglio
☎ (06) 6782862/67102771
Open: winter, Tuesday, Saturday 9am-1.30pm, 5-8pm. Wednesday, Thursday, Friday 9am-1.30pm. Sunday 9am-1pm. Summer, Tuesday 9am-1.30pm, 5-8pm. Wednesday, Thursday, Friday 9am-1.30pm. Saturday 9am-1.30pm, 8-11pm. Sunday 9am-1pm.

Foro Romano e Palatino
Via dei Fori Imperiali
☎ (06) 6790333
Open: winter, Tuesday to Sunday 9am-3pm; summer, Monday, Wednesday, Thursday, Friday, Saturday 9am-6pm. Tuesday, Sunday 9am-1pm.

Terme di Caracalla
☎ (06) 5758626
Open: winter, daily 9am-3pm. Summer, Tuesday-Saturday 9am-6pm., Sunday, Monday 9am-1pm.

San Clemente Scavi
Via San Giovanni in Laterano
Open: daily 9am-12noon, 3.30-6.30pm.

Colosseo (Colosseum)
☎ (06) 735227
Open: winter, daily 9am-3pm. Summer, Mon, Tues, Thurs, Fri, Sat 9am-7pm Wed, Sun 9am-1pm.

San Pietro in Vincoli
Piazza di San Pietro in Vincoli.
Open: daily 7am-12.30pm, 3.30-6pm.

Museo Nazionale Romano
Viale E. De Nicola 79
☎ (06) 460530
Open: Tuesday- Saturday 9am-2pm, Sunday 9am-1pm.

Mercati Traianei
Via IV Novembre 94
☎ (06) 67102070
Open: winter, Tuesday to Saturday 9am-1.30pm, Sunday 9am-1pm; summer, Wednesday, Friday, Sunday 9am-1.30pm. Tuesday, Thursday, Saturday 9-1.30pm, 4-7pm. Sunday 9am-1pm.

ROUTE 1B

Galleria Doria Pamphili
Piazza del Collegio Romano 1a
☎ (06) 6794365
Open: Tuesday, Friday, Saturday and Sunday 10am-1pm.

Pantheon
Piazza della Rotonda
☎ (06) 369831
Open: Monday to Saturday 9am-2pm, Sunday 9am-1pm.

Museo Barraco
Corso Vittorio Emanuele 168
☎ (06) 6540848
Open: Tuesday to Saturday 9am-2pm, Sunday 9am-1pm.

Museo di Roma
Palazzo Braschi
Piazza San Pantaleo
☎ (06) 6875880

Galleria Spada
Piazza Capodiferro 3
☎ (06) 6861158
Open: Monday to Saturday 9am-2pm, Sunday 9am-1pm.

Galleria Nazionale di Palazzo Corsini
Via della Lungara 10
☎ (06) 6542323
Open: Monday to Saturday 9am-2pm, Sunday 9am-1pm.

ROUTE 1C

Galleria Colonna
Via della Pilotta 17
☎ (06) 6794362
Open: Saturday 9am-1pm, closed in August.

Galleria Nazionale d'Arte Antica a Palazzo Barberini
Via Quattro Fontane 13
☎ (06) 4814591
Open: Monday to Saturday 9am-2pm, Sunday 9am-1pm.

Keats and Shelley Memorial House
Piazza di Spagna 26
☎ (06) 6784235

Open: winter, Monday to Friday 9am-1pm, 2.30-5.30pm; summer, Monday to Friday 9am-1pm, 3-6pm.

Museo Canonica
Viale Pietro Canonica
Villa Borghese
☎ (06) 8842279
Open: Wednesday, Friday, Saturday, Sunday 9am-2pm, Tuesday, Thursday 9am-2pm, 4-7.30pm.

Galleria Borghese
Villa Borghese
☎ (06) 8548577
Open: Tuesday to Saturday 9am-7pm, Sunday 9am-1pm.

Giardino Zoologico
Villa Borghese
Open: daily 8am-5pm.

Galleria Nazionale d'Arte Moderna
Viale delle Belle Arti 131
☎ (06) 8082751
Open: Tuesday to Saturday 9am-2pm, Sunday 9am-1pm.

Museo Nazionale di Villa Giulia
Piazzale di Villa Giulia 9
☎ (06) 3201951
Open: Tuesday to Saturday 9am-7pm, Sunday 9am-1pm.

Ara Pacis Augustae
Via Ripetta
Open: winter, Tuesday to Saturday 9am-1.30pm, Sunday 9am-1pm; summer, Wednesday, Friday 9am-1.30pm. Tuesday, Thursday, Saturday 9am-1.30pm, 4-7pm. Sunday 9am-1pm.

ROUTE 1D

*Museo Nazionale di Castel
   Sant'Angelo*
Lungotevere Castello
☎ (06) 6544572
Open: Monday 2-6pm, Tuesday-
Saturday 9am-2pm, Sunday 9am-
1pm.

Musei Vaticani
Viale Vaticano
☎ (06) 6983333
Open: Monday to Saturday 9am-
2pm. Last Sunday of every month
9am-2pm (free).

Useful Information

Events and Festivals

6 January, Feast of the Epiphany
(Toy fair on Piazza Navona).

18-19 March, Festa di San Giuseppe
(Festival of St Joseph, celebrated in
the Trionfale district with *bigne*,
doughnuts, and fritters).

April, Festa di Primavera
(Spring festival, flowers on steps of
Trinita dei Monti).

24 June, Festa di San Giovanni
(Festival of St John, celebrated in
the San Giovanni district, with
snails and suckling pig to eat).

July-August, Summer Festival
(Concerts, dance, folklore and opera).

1 August, Festa delle Catene
(The chains of St Peter are dis-
played during a service at San
Pietro in Vincoli).

Tourist Information Centres
Ente Provinciale per il Turismo
Via Parigi 5
☎ (06) 4881851

ENIT (Italian National Tourist
   Board)
Via Marghera 2
☎ (06) 49711

Transport
Termini Railway Station
☎ (06) 4775/464466

ATAC (City Transport)
☎ (06) 46951/46954444

ACOTRAL (Underground and
   Provincial Transport)
☎ (06) 5915551

Emergencies
Polizia di Stato (Police)
Via San Vitale 15
☎ (06) 4686

Police — Foreigners' Bureau
☎ (06) 46862987

Polizia Stradale (Traffic Police)
☎ (06) 5577905

Pronto Soccorso (First Aid Service)
☎ (06) 5100

Guardia Medica (Medical Officer)
☎ (06) 4756741

Automobile Club d'Italia
Via Marsala 8
☎ (06) 49981

Telephone 1921 to find out which
pharmacies are open. Daily
newspapers also publish lists of
pharmacies on rotation duty, as
well as the 24 hour pharmacies.

Leisure and Entertainment
Listings for coming events in Rome
can be found in the local Saturday
supplement, *Trovaroma,* of the daily
newspaper *La Repubblica.* Local
editions of other daily national
newspapers, such as *Il Messaggero,*

also have listings. Otherwise, Ente Provinciale per il Turisimo, the local tourist board, produce a monthly listings called *Carnet di Roma*.

Concert and opera venues are as follows:

Teatro dell' Opera
Piazza Beniamino Gigli
☎ (06) 461 755
Open: December to June.

Terme di Caracalla
Via delle Terme di Caracalla
☎ (06) 5758302
Open: July and August.

Saint Cecilia Conservatory of Music
Via dei Greci 18
☎ (06) 6784552
Open: October to May.

Postal Services
Main Post Office
Piazza San Silvestro
☎ (06) 6771
Open: Monday to Friday 8.30am 9pm,
Saturday 8.30am-12noon.
Services: current accounts, telegraphic money orders, postal, poste restante, telegrams. 24 hour telegram service ☎ 6795530

Central Post Office
Via della Mercede 96
☎ (06) 6795167
Open: Monday to Saturday 8.30am-12noon.
Services: information, current accounts, money orders, emergency services.

Parcel Post Office
Piazza dei Caprettari
☎ (06) 6545901
Open: Monday to Friday 8.30am-3.30pm. Saturday 8.30am-12noon
Services: parcels, packages.

Disabled
Organisations which can provide information for disabled travellers are as follows:
A.I.A.S. (Italian Association to Spastics)
Via Cipro 4/H
☎ (06) 316312

Associazione per la Terapia e la Riabilitazione degli Handicappati Psicofisici (Association for the therapy and Rehabilitation of the Pyscho-Physically Handicapped)
Opera Sante de Sanctis
Via Conte Verde 47
☎ (06) 7008311

Car Hire
Hertz (Car Hire)
Via Sallustiana 28
☎ (06) 463334

Avis (Car Hire)
Piazza Esquilino 1
☎ (06) 47011

Maggiore (Car Hire)
Via Po 8
☎ (06) 858698

Budget (Car Hire)
Via Sistina 37
☎ (06) 4755726

Automobile Club d'Italia
Via Marsala 8
☎ (06) 49981

2

LAZIO AND UPPER CAMPANIA

The routes covered in this chapter head south from Rome to Naples, passing through the province of Lazio with its many fine Roman hill-towns, to Upper Campania, which is more urbanised, particularly around the region of Naples. Just before entering Campania the route takes in two impressive abbeys, Casamari and Montecassino. Visitors should note, however, that due to their opening times, it is difficult to visit both abbeys in the same afternoon. From Montecassino, those who prefer not to continue south, can head inland along the SS6 to Isernia, and proceed northwards along the routes in chapter 3.

Chapter 2 continues south to Naples and then along its sweeping bay, visiting the famous archaeological sites of *Herculaneum* and Pompei, as well as the crater of Mount Vesuvius. From Naples, visitors have the choice, either of continuing south down the coast in chapter 5, or returning to Caserta and crossing inland to Benevento, from where chapter 3 can be followed northwards.

Route 2A • Rome to Ferentino

Route 2A heads south of Rome on the A1 Autostrada del Sole, for 20km (12 miles), along the foothills of the Colli Albani, to the San Cesareo junction. From here, follow the SS155 for a further 10km (6 miles) to the ancient Roman, hill-town of **Palestrina**. As the road approaches the town's south walls, turn right, passing by the public gardens, before turning left, along Viale della Vittoria, to the parking area on Piazzale Santa Maria degli Angeli. Continue on foot along the narrow shopping street, Via Antica, to the town centre, Piazza Regina Margherita, in which stands the attractive, medieval belfry of the duomo *(cathedral)*. In ancient times, the piazza was the site of a forum, and remnants of Roman *Praeneste* are incorporated into the

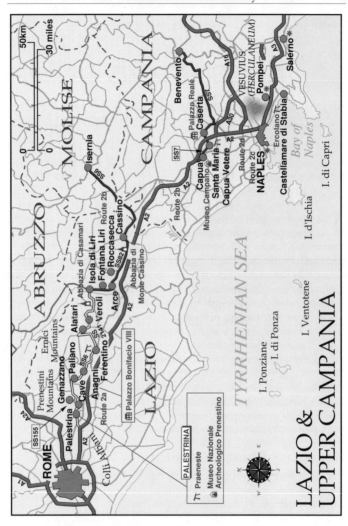

surrounding buildings. In the north-west corner of the piazza, below the entrance to the Seminario Vescovile, is a flight of ancient steps, while at the back of the Seminario, behind the apse of the *duomo*, a lower temple precinct is under excavation.

π   The most impressive remains of ancient *Praeneste* are, however, the upper temple precinct, the Tempio della Fortuna Primigenia, which was amongst the most extensive religious complexes in

Roman times. The temple oracle, who was highly regarded, continued to operate at the site until as late as the fourth century. The temple is built on the steep slopes of Monte Ginestro, above the town, along with the vast, seventeenth-century Palazzo Barberini which houses the Museo Nazionale Archeologico Prenestino. Visitors who wish to visit the site by car, should follow the main road up. Those on foot should be prepared for a stiff, ten-minute climb, starting from the north-east corner of Piazza Regina Margherita along Via Thomas Mann, and continuing up through Piazzetta del Borgo.

The temple's massive vaults, ramps and stairways, and colonnaded terraces, drop steeply down, in front of the Barberini palace, and can be visited on the same ticket as the museum when there are staff available. The main body of the temple lies beneath the palace itself, the façade of which has the same ground plan. Evidence of this can be seen in each of the palace's ground floor rooms where the bases of ancient columns, originally forming a curved colonnade, can be seen through glass panes set in the floor. On the first floor of the museum there is a scale model of the temple which gives a good idea of its former grandeur. Other rooms contain finds from the temple precinct, including some fine bronze urns. The show-piece of the museum is, however, the excellently-preserved, Roman mosaic on the top floor, *The Nile in Flood*, which dates from the first century BC. It is comprised of a series of intricate and delicately-coloured scenarios set along the banks of the Nile, with troops of Roman soldiers, maidens in grottoes and a host of jungle animals.

By continuing up the road above the museum, after several hairpin bends, the visitor will arrive at the site of the ancient acropolis, Castel San Pietro Romano, which is at a height of 752m (2,466ft). There are remains of an ancient polygonal wall and on the hill summit the ruins of a fifteenth-century castle. However, perhaps the most impressive aspect is the fine panorama, which offers views that extend as far as Rome.

The route continues along the SS155 di Fiuggi, winding between the steep rocks that reach down from the Prenestini mountains. After passing through **Cave**, 6km (4 miles) east of Palestrina, where there is a tenth-century church, San Lorenzo, and the scant remains of a castle, the visitor may wish to make a short excursion off the route to **Genazzano**. This small, medieval town has many attractive, narrow streets and a fifteenth-century castle.

The SS155 di Fiuggi continues through an undulating and well-cultivated landscape, until the squat fortress of Paliano, now a prison, comes into sight, atop a small hill. Turn off right and follow the road up through **Paliano**, a small but busy town with an attractive centre. Heading down from Paliano, fork right to **Anagni**, which lies a further 12km (7 miles) along a narrow and winding road.

This charming, medieval hill-town is surrounded by impressive walls, parts of which date from Roman times. It is best to park outside the walls, preferably near the east gate, Porta Santa Maria, from where it is a short walk along Via Vittorio Emanuele to the town's main monument, the *cattedrale*. Built in 1077 on the site of the former Roman acropolis, the cathedral is remarkably well-preserved, complete with its free-standing, Romanesque *campanile* and its original interior. The floor inside the church is covered by a fine Cosmati pavement dating from 1227, while the main apse holds the original Romanesque ciborium. There is also a fine candle holder and an episcopal throne, which was designed by P. Vassalleto in 1260. The large, vaulted crypt below the church, the Cripta di San Magno, holds further Romanesque delights, including another beautiful Cosmati paved floor, dating from 1231, and a wealth of frescoes of the same era. The frescoes were painted by Benedictine masters, and depict saints, men of science (including Galen and Hippocrates), as well as scenes from the Old Testament, and show the influence of both Byzantine and Romanesque art.

Heading west of the cathedral, along Via Vittorio Emanuele, Palazzo Bonifacio VIII (1295) is passed to the left. It takes its name from the Pope (one of several to be born in Anagni), who was held captive in this building by French troops when he threatened to excommunicate their King. It now contains a small archaeological collection of locally-excavated finds in its attractively-frescoed rooms. Via Vittorio Emanuele, lined with attractive, fourteenth-century buildings along either side, continues to Piazza Cavour, at the corner of which is the twelfth-century Palazzo Comunale. Those with time may wish to continue along Via Vittorio Emanuele to Casa Barnekow, one of the finest fourteenth-century houses in the town. It is named after the Swedish painter, Baron Albert von Barnekow, who lived here in the late nineteenth century.

Route 2A heads east from Anagni, following the SS6 Caselina for 11½km (7 miles) before turning off left to **Ferentino**, another of Lazio's attractive, medieval hill-towns built on top of Roman remains. Park outside the town's ancient, cyclopean walls, which date from the fifth century BC, and head up to the site of the ancient acropolis at the top of the hill. It was here that the Hernici, an indigenous, pre-Roman tribe, built their sturdy fortress in the fourth century BC. Its foundations and the remnants of later Roman additions still remain, but the major building on the site of the acropolis now, is the eleventh-century *duomo*. Its simple Romanesque façade belies an attractive interior, which is complete with a fine Cosmati, paved floor and, in the main apse, a Romanesque ciborium, pashcal candelabra and bishop's throne, which are also decorated with inlaid Cosmati mosaic.

Most of Roman *Ferentinum* has been dismantled and incorporated into the medieval buildings in the town, but the Mercato Romano, a vaulted, covered market, on Via Don Morosini, which dates from the first century BC is well-preserved. The original town gates, in particular Porta Maggiore and Porta Sanguiniaria, are also in good condition. Near the latter, is Santa Maria Maggiore, a thirteenth-century, Gothic-Cistercian church with a fine rose window and an attractive portal carved from Roman marble.

The route continues north of Ferentino on a minor road, signposted to Alatri, from the top end of the town. The road winds up and down, along the foothills of the Ernici mountains, which in ancient times were the territory of the Hernici people. After 5 ½km (3 miles) take the second fork right and head downhill, through Dodici Marie, to the modern outskirts of **Alatri**. A sharp left turn leads into the town, through a gate, from where signs indicate the way up to the acropolis. Alatri was founded by the Hernici in the sixth century BC as *Aletrium*, but had become a Roman colony by the fourth century when the magnificent, polygonal wall that rings the acropolis was constructed. Built of finely-cut, white stone, the wall, 2km (1 mile) long and standing to a height of 3m (10ft), has two well-defended gates, making it the best-preserved, fortified acropolis in Italy. The large, flat area inside the walls contains the seventeenth-century *duomo*, and a pleasant park with a children's playground. Footpaths lead around the tops of the walls from where there are fine views across the bleached roofs of the town and of the surrounding countryside. The walls themselves are best seen from the small road that runs around their base.

Other than the acropolis, Alatri also has a lovely medieval quarter, surrounding a large central piazza which contains the Romanesque-Gothic church of Santa Maria Maggiore. The church was built on the foundations of the ancient Temple of Jove in the thirteenth century and has a fine rose window set into its plain façade. Inside, the first chapel on the left holds a wooden sculpture of the *Madonna of Constantinople*, which dates from the twelfth century. The Franciscan church, San Francesco, which is a short walk to the east, has a similar façade to that of Santa Maria Maggiore and dates from the late thirteenth century.

Route 2B • Alatri to Naples

Route 2B heads due east from Alatri for 6km (4 miles), along a narrow country road, which gradually climbs up to **Veroli**. Situated on a foothill of the Ernici mountains, this small town has a well-preserved and pedestrianised, historical centre, which has numerous small Romanesque and Baroque churches. High on the hill above the town are the remains of a dilapidated castle.

Leave the town by following signs to **Abbazia di Casamari**. The road winds steeply downhill before turning left onto the SS214. The abbey appears on the left after a further 7km (4 miles) opposite a large carpark. The abbey was originally founded in 1035 by Benedictine monks, but was taken over in 1140 by the Cistercian Order. As in the rest of Europe, the Cistercians, who originated from France, brought with them the French Gothic architecture of the era. By 1203, the abbey had been endowed with many of the characteristics of French architecture, and today, it remains a unique example of the Burgundian-Gothic style. The abbey, still very much alive, attracts a

*A picturesque view of the bleached roof tops and
surrounding countryside at Alatri*

great many visitors. The monks wear the traditional white habits of the Cistercian Order, and continue to follow their strict monastic codes of conduct. Physical discipline and strenuous manual labour are distinguishing features of the Order, and the vow of absolute silence is enforced.

The abbey complex is entered through a gatehouse which has two deep arches and a fine loggia above. The arches lead through to the abbey's outer courtyard which has the monks' living quarters on the right and the church on the left. The church façade has a simple rose window with six alabaster petals, above an elegant portico which is made up of three arches. The main portal is surrounded by multiple bands of carvings and has a richly carved lunette. The church interior is simple but spacious, and glows in the gentle light that filters in through the alabaster windows.

Those that wish to tour the interior of the abbey should head to the right corner of the courtyard. The original medieval pharmacy, on the right, is still in use, while the abbey entrance is just to its left. Wait just inside the doors until a monk, who is exluded from the vow of silence, appears to act as a guide for visitors. The tour starts from a pretty inner courtyard which looks out over the countryside. Steps lead up from the left side of the courtyard to a charming cloister which is edged by twin-columns and has colourful flower gardens and a well at its centre. Along the right side of the cloister is the *aula capitolare*, the chapterhouse, which has an impressive rib-vaulted ceiling, typical of the French Gothic style. Along the left side of the cloister is the *reffetorio* (refectory), which also has a fine, rib-vaulted ceiling, supported on six central columns, and simple tables and benches lining the walls. The church flanks the remaining side of the cloister, and can be entered through an attractively-carved, side portal.

The route follows the SS214 for 9km (6 miles) east of Abbazia di Casamari, to the pleasant town of **Isola di Liri** which is situated on a fork of the River Liri. The road crosses over both arms of the river, the second of which has an impressive waterfall to the left of the bridge, known as the Cascate Valcatoio e Grande. After the waterfall, turn right onto the SS82, which is signposted to Arce. The road follows the Liri river past **Anitrella**, where there is another waterfall, and then gradually winds down to **Fontana Liri**, the upper town of which is picturesquely clustered on a hilltop.

Continuing south through Arce, the SS214 heads through the hilly, wine-growing region of Colfelice, passing by the ruined castle of Roccasecca, high on a crag, to the left of the road. After Roccasecca, the road continues along the foot of the mountains, traversing a wide plain to **Cassino**, above which, looms the massive, white bulk of the Abbazia di Monte Cassino.

The abbey was founded in AD529 by St Benedict and has been the headquarters of the Benedictine order ever since, despite its destruction, in 1349 by an earthquake, and most notably in 1944, when it was razed to the ground by bombing. It was the last key Nazi stronghold on the Gustav line and after a prolonged ground battle, which cost some 30,000 lives, the Allies resorted to a devastating air attack which reduced the abbey to a pile of rubble. It was gradually rebuilt, stone by stone, after the war had ended, but most of the medieval frescoes and paintings were irretrievably lost.

Today, the abbey attracts thousands of tourists every year, but visitors are obliged to respect the peace and also the dress code imposed by the Benedictines. Visitors wearing shorts or skimpy clothing are not allowed to enter. It is also forbidden to take photographs inside the abbey. The steep, winding road up to the abbey is clearly signposted from the modern town of Cassino which lies at the foot of the hill. On the way up, the road passes by the Museo Archeologico Nazionale, which houses finds from the adjacent site of ancient *Casinum* where there are the Roman remains of a theatre, an amphitheatre, tombs, and a paved road dating from the first century. Continuing up the hill, after no less than six hairpin bends, the road ends at a carpark (payment by donation) below the walls of the abbey. A rampway leads up from the carpark to the abbey entrance, where there is a postcard shop. The colonnaded Hall of Honour leads off right from here, along the south edge of the complex which is 122m (400ft) long. Straight ahead from the entrance are two large cloistered courtyards with a panoramic loggia along the west side. Along the east side a flight of steps leads up to a third cloister, the Chiostro Benefattori, which was rebuilt to A. da Sangallo's design of 1510. It is named after the statues of the abbey's benefactors which are set in niches around the cloisters' walls. The entrance to a small museum, documenting the history of the abbey and containing a collection of art works, is on the north side of the cloister, while the façade of the church lies along the east side. The church has massive bronze doors which were cast in 1951 by P. Canonica, with the exception of the central ones which were brought from Constantinople in the eleventh century. The luxuriant Baroque interior which is encrusted with gilded stucco and bedecked with inlaid polished marbles, was reconstructed following C. Fanzago's eighteenth-century design. The entrance wall is covered by a fresco depicting *The Glory of St Benedict*, which was painted in 1978 by P. Annigoni, who was also responsible for the decoration of the dome and vault above the choir. The high altar is built over the mortal remains of St Benedict, and his sister, St Scolastica. The crypt of St Benedict, which is accessible from the museum, is the only part of the fifteenth-century abbey structure to have survived the World War II bombardment. Its attractive decoration was completed in 1900 by German monks from the Benedictine monastery of Beuron.

The route continues by heading south of Cassino, onto the A2 *autostrada* which should be followed in the direction of Napoli. After 10km (6 miles) the road crosses over the Lazio border and enters into Upper Campania. From here on the roads become increasingly busy with traffic, and the towns lose some of the polish and prosperity of those in Lazio. A visit to **Capua**, which is just over 30km (19 miles) north of Naples, will confirm this. Those who wish to visit this town should leave the motorway at the Capua junction and follow the SS7. At the outskirts of the town fork left, and cross over the Volturno river, to the *centro storico*. After passing through the sixteenth-century town wall follow Corso Appio straight ahead to the attractive main square, Piazza dei Giudicci, where visitors can park. Along the south side of the piazza, set into the lower walls of the *municipio*, which dates from 1561, are seven marble busts taken from the Roman amphitheatre at Santa Maria Capua Vetere. From the north side of the piazza, follow Via Duomo for 100m (110yd) to the *duomo's* massive, square bell-tower, which dates from AD861 and is Lombardic in style. The *duomo* itself was flattened in 1942 and the building that has reared up in its place is unprepossessing, although the atrium, or small courtyard, in front of the entrance contains some fine columns topped by Corinthian capitals dating from the third century. The Museo Campano is a further 225m (740yd) along Via Duomo in Palazzo Anignano. This fine building, with its elegant Catalan-Gothic portal, dates from the fifteenth century. Contained within its forty attractive rooms is a large collection of archaeological relics of ancient Capua, *Casilinum*, including some two hundred votive statues, dating from the seventh to the first centuries BC, on the ground floor, and an interesting medieval section on the first floor.

The site of ancient Capua is at present day **Santa Maria Capua Vetere**, which is just 5km (3 miles) east along the SS7. It is hard to imagine that this sprawling, agricultural town was in Roman times one of the most prosperous in southern Italy. However, a magnificent amphitheatre, the second largest in Italy after the Colosseum, stands as testimony. It is positioned in the north-west corner of the town and is reached by taking the left turn, after passing through Hadrian's Arch, at the gardens on Piazza Adriano. The amphitheatre originally stood four storeys high and was encircled by eighty arches, only two of which remain. Indeed, the constant plundering for stone over the centuries has left little above ground level, there being only three covered galleries beneath the arena, one around its circumference, and six vaulted entrance ways. It is still possible nonetheless to get an impression of its original scale, and it is no small affair, measuring as it does some 170m (558ft) by 140m (459ft).

The busy and rather uninspiring town of **Caserta**, 6km (4 miles) east of Santa Maria Capua Vetere, also holds a sight of considerable interest, the Palazzo Reale. Often referred to as the 'Versailles of Naples', this grandiose palace was begun in 1752 under Charles III and finished in 1774 by Ferdinand I, to a design by L. Vanvitelli. The main road from Capua Santa Maria Vetere leads straight to its façade, which looks out over a circular piazza, similar to Bernini's St Peter's in Rome. The lavishly decorated apartments inside, which surround four internal courtyards, were lived in by the Bourbon kings of Naples and Sicily, before becoming the Allied headquarters in World War II. The *appartamenti reali* are complete with their neo-Classical furnishings and rich stucco and painted decor. The *appartamento nuovo* contains the throne room which dates from 1845, while the *appartamento del Re*, added in 1816, has Francesco II's luxurious bedroom. Also of interest is the chapel, *cappella Palatina*, and the eighteenth-century theatre, *teatrino di corte*. In the *pinacoteca* a collection of portraits of the Bourbons can be seen as well as numerous nineteenth-century, still-life paintings. A large formal gardens extends behind the palace and contains umpteen fountains and waterworks, the most impressive of which is the *cascata grande*, which falls from a height of 75m (246ft) at the end of a 3km (2 mile) avenue.

Visitors should head south of Caserta on the A2 *autostrada* and so avoid the extensive slum-like suburbs that extend from here to Naples.

Route 2C • Naples

Naples is a vast, sprawling city with a population of street-sellers unmatched by any other city in Italy. It is permeated by a general air of neglect and the perpetual roar of the traffic which charges through its narrow, fume-choked streets. In some ways it is almost like a third-world city, indeed this is one of its attractions. Visitors to Naples are well-advised to take a train and not bring their cars, on account of the hectic traffic, the parking difficulties and the risk of theft. Those that do visit Naples by car, however, are recommended to stay at a hotel with a secure carpark and to never leave anything

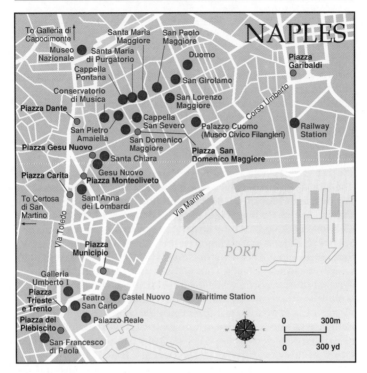

visible inside the vehicle. The main public carparks are on Piazza Garibaldi (near the railway station), Piazza del Plebiscito (near the castle), and around the port area on Via Marina, though these are often crowded and offer little in the way of security. To get about the city use public transport. Tickets for the trams and buses must be purchased in advance, and are available from booths at the major stops, or from *tabacchi* (tobacconists).

Naples was founded by Greek colonists from *Cumae* in the sixth century BC, and developed into a major port under the Romans, who captured and renamed the city *Neapolis* in 326BC. They were succeeded by the Byzantines who ruled up until the twelfth century, and then by the Normans and a series of six royal dynasties, the last of which was the House of Savoy. Many of the major historical buildings in Naples date from the Angevin period (1309-1442), although few have emerged unscathed from the rash of Baroque embellishments which were later added to the city's monuments by architects of the Neapolitan School.

The city's main sights have been organised into four itineraries. Itinerary I concentrates on the imperial quarters of the city. Itinerary II leads the visitor through the heart of old Naples, taking in numerous churches, the opening hours of which should be checked in the Additional Information section of this book before setting out, as the best features of many of them are the interiors and the works of art held there. Itinerary III visits the archaeological museum and the city cathedral. Itinerary IV covers outlying sights, namely the two major museums of Certosa San Martino and Capodimonte.

ITINERARY 1

Itinerary I starts at the castle, **Castel Nuovo**, which lies near the port. Those setting out from Piazza Garibaldi can take a number 106 or 150 bus to Piazza Municipio, the busy roundabout on which the castle stands. The castle was originally built between 1279 and 1282 for Charles I of Anjou, but the structure seen today was designed by Spanish architects to accommodate the court of Alfonso V of Aragon. Its most prominent feature is the series of round towers, built in 1446, which surround the walls. Four of the towers are built of grey stone, shipped from Majorca, while the fifth, known as the Golden Tower, is made from a local tufa, and contained Alfonso's treasury. The two western towers flank an impressive Renaissance portal, which is richly-carved from brilliant-white stone. It dates from 1454, but the design harks back to triumphal arches of the Classical era, with the victor, in this case Alfonso V, depicted in a bas-relief between the lower arch, which has Corinthian columns at either side, and the upper arch, which has Doric columns. The four classical conches, above the upper arch, each contains a statue of the four Renaissance Virtues: *Justice, Temperance, Strength* and *Prudence*.

The portal, which is reached by a drawbridge across the castle's wide moat, leads through to a central courtyard. Opposite is the Cappella Palatina, a small church with a Catalan rose window piercing its upper façade. The portal, part of the original Angevin structure, has a small carved relief, depicting *Scenes from the Life of the Virgin Mary*, with a lunette above containing *Madonna and Angels*. Unfortunately the church interior, which was once decorated with frescoes by Giotto, is now quite bare.

In the corner of the courtyard, to the left of the church façade, an open staircase leads up to the Sala dei Baroni. This grand hall is named after the Barons who met here, in 1485, to plot against Ferrante I, the illegitimate son of Alfonso V. Their conspiracy was, however, uncovered and the rebellious Barons were executed in this very hall. Today, meetings still take place here, usually between local political parties and councils, but when it is not in use it is possible to see inside. The hall measures 26m (85ft) by 28m (92ft), and is covered by a vast umbrella dome, which is divided into segments by slender ribs of grey stone. At the centre of the dome there is an oculus, a round window, while at its base there are elegant galleries, a feature of Catalan architecture.

Return across the castle drawbridge and turn left onto Via San Carlo. This busy thoroughfare passes by the gardens of Palazzo Reale, which are enclosed by high railings, before reaching the entrance to **Teatro San Carlo**, on the left. This sumptuous opera house, the largest in Italy, was built for Charles of Bourbon in 1737, but it had to be re-built in 1816 after it was destroyed in a fire. The deep, horseshoe-shaped auditorium has a total seating capacity of 3,000, and has 185 ornately-decorated boxes, steeply stacked up on six tiers.

Continue beyond Teatro San Carlo, passing through Piazza Trieste e Trento, to **Piazza del Plebiscito**. On the south-west side of this piazza, are the curved arcades and massive dome of San Francesco di Paola, which was built in the nineteenth century to a design modelled on Rome's Pantheon. On the north-east side of the piazza is the equally imposing façade of the **Palazzo Reale**. The Palazzo Reale, the imperial palace, was built in 1600 to a design by Domenico Fontana, who had already completed the Lateran Palace in Rome and been involved in planning St Peter's dome. Further construction took place in 1734, when the Bourbon King Charles III, had the palace enlarged and aggrandised, in keeping with the imperial dignity of neo-Classicism.

In 1753, the former Baroque arches along the palace façade were converted into neo-Classical niches, in which statues of the eight leading monarchs of Naples were placed. The entrance, which pierces the centre of the façade, leads through to a large inner courtyard, surrounded by the gloomy-pink and dour-grey walls of the palace apartments. On the left side of the courtyard, there is a vast vestibule with a high coffered ceiling of white and pale grey stucco, which contains a monumental marble staircase, dating from 1651. The ticket office for the palace apartments is on the right at the foot of the staircase, which leads up to the imperial apartments on the first floor.

The apartments surround the inner courtyard, on the left side of which is the palace chapel. Re-designed in the nineteenth-century, neo-Classical style, the chapel ceiling is frescoed by the Neapolitan painter, Domenico Morelli, while other paintings by the nineteenth-century Neapolitan school are hung in the small domed chapels at either side of the nave. The nave, which is headed by an ornate, inlaid altar, contains a permanent exhibition of holy vestments and treasury.

From the chapel, continue around the courtyard to the west side, and take the last door on the left, which leads into the court theatre. The theatre was built in 1768 to a design by Ferdinando Fuga, an architect whose late-Baroque style was by then well-known in Rome. As with his other commissions in Naples, however, Fuga's design for the theatre was neo-Classical in style. The upper walls are decorated with classical statues of deities, placed within niches, and the auditorium is surrounded by fluted pilasters, which are highlighted in gilt. To the right of the stage, a door leads through to the palace apartments. There are thirty rooms in total, each of which is decorated in the style of the nineteenth century, with silk wall coverings, frescoed ceilings, gilt furniture, elaborate chandeliers and elegant mirrors. The first room is notable for its beautiful Gobelin tapestries by Georges De La Tour, which date from the early seventeenth century. In the fourth room, which has a strikingly paved floor of red, green and white marble hexagons, the king's gilded throne sits beneath a heavily-embroidered, velvet canopy. On the walls, which are covered by dark red satin, there are a series of court portraits, dating from the eighteenth century. A further collection of paintings

Charles Angevin, one of the kings who once ruled Naples, on the façade of the Palazzo Reale, Naples

are hung in the fine suite of ten apartments that look out over the hanging gardens to the harbour. The paintings date from the nineteenth century and are by artists of the Neapolitan school. From the ninth room of this grand suite, turn left into the ball-room, where enormous, Neapolitan tapestries, made for the palace in the eighteenth century, cover the walls. A further series of three apartments bring the visitor to the main entrance hall, from where the monumental staircase down, is on the left.

From Palazzo Reale, return to Teatro San Carlo, and cross over the road to **Galleria Umberto I**. This glass-covered shopping arcade was built between 1887 and 1890, to a design very similar to the one in Milan, and has a central dome which is 56m (184ft) high. Turn left, along the longest of the four arms which radiate from the central dome, to Via Toledo. From here, it is a dull walk of 700m (765yd) to Piazza Carita, which is the starting point for Itinerary II. Visitors may wish to take a bus or taxi along Via Toledo.

ITINERARY II

From Piazza Carita, head north-east down Via Marconi and turn right at the crossroads to the grey, stone façade of **Sant'Anna dei Lombardi**, also known as Monteoliveto. The church was first built in 1411, and despite seventeenth-century modifications, still has a number of its original Renaissance sculptures and frescoes inside. The entrance hall, which holds the tomb of D. Fontana, the architect of Palazzo Reale, precedes a single nave with deep chapels along either side. In the first chapel on the right, there is an *Annunciation* (1489) by the Tuscan painter, Benedetto da Maiano. Also from the same period, is a terracotta group of eight figures, the *Pieta*, which can be seen in the sacristy on the right. Giuliano da Maiano, Benedetto's elder brother, was one of the leaders of the Tuscan Renaissance in Naples, and the architectural decoration of the sixth chapel on the left is typical of his work. The first chapel on the left, which contains a fine *Ascension* painted on wood, leads through to the Cappella Piccolomini. This chapel contains a funerary monument to Mary of Aragon, which was designed by B. da Maiano and his Tuscan contemporary, A. Rosselino. There is also a fine *Annunciation* in the chapel, painted in the style of Piero della Francesca.

From Sant'Anna dei Lombardi, continue downhill to **Piazza Monteoliveto**, where there is an attractive fountain decorated with lions. Cross over the piazza and head up Cala Trinita Maggiore to **Piazza Gesu Nuovo**. The piazza is dominated by a large, Baroque column which rises in front of the diamond-pointed façade of **Gesu Nuovo**. This Renaissance church was completed in 1660, but a century later had started to show structural faults and was to be left abandoned. It has since been repaired, and although the façade is truncated and the dome has been demolished, the interior is lavishly decorated in coloured marbles, stucco, frescoes and gilt work. Of particular interest is the painting by Francesco Solimena, the leading artist of the Neapolitan school in the eighteenth century, which is above the door. It depicts *Heliodorus Being Driven Out of the Temple* and is considered one of the artist's greatest works.

Opposite Gesu Nuovo, a fourteenth-century arch leads through to the walled courtyard which contains the Angevin Church of **Santa Chiara**. The church was commissioned by Robert of Anjou's wife, Queen Sancha, for the Order of Poor Clares, in 1310, and to provide a burial place for the Angevin dynasty. The simple façade, constructed from yellow tufa and grey stone, has an unusually tall central section with a small rose window, which is positioned high in the gable. The massive interior, with its single nave, is typical of the French, hall-type churches which were fashionable in contemporary Anjou, and has an open-beamed roof which stands some 45m (148ft) above the floor. The sense of height is further enhanced by long, narrow lancet windows in the high clerestory and a large Gothic tracery window in the flat apse.

Set against the wall of the apse is the elaborately carved sarcophagus of Robert of Anjou, who died in 1343 and was known to his admiring contemporaries as 'Robert the Wise'. Designed by Tuscan sculptors, the tomb stands on four columns with the king, attended by his mourners. Other carved tombs, also dating from the fourteenth century, fill the side chapels, but amongst the most prestigious funerary monuments are those mounted on the wall, either side of the king. That on the right commemorates King Charles III of Durazzo, while the one of the left is to his daughter, Maria. Both monuments are the work of Tino da Camaiano, who was one of the greatest Gothic sculptors and architects in Naples.

The two doors, piercing the apse wall, lead through to a splendid choir, which, although unusual to Italy, is a typical feature of French Gothic churches. Its high ceiling is criss-crossed by elegant rib vaults, and the end wall has lacy Gothic windows. No longer used as a choir, the room contains odd sculptural fragments and detached frescoes, salvaged after the war damage. On the right side of the choir a door gives access to Santa Chiara's charming cloisters. They are known as the Chiostro Maiolicato after the decorative majolica tiles that date from 1743. Both the walkways and walls, as well as the sixty-four columns enclosing an octagonal garden, are clad in these beautiful tiles which are decorated with landscapes and foliate motifs.

Leave Santa Chiara and turn right along Via B. Croce, passing a large, brick and stone *campanile* to the right, which was originally part of the Roman city wall. After less than 200m (218yd) the narrow street opens out on the left into **Piazza San Domenico Maggiore**, at the centre of which is a spired monument, erected in 1656, after the plague. Along the north side of the square lies the polygonal, yellow-plastered apse of **San Domenico Maggiore**. The church was first erected for the Domenican order during the Angevin era. Since then it has been rebuilt on several occasions with Baroque alterations being made in the eighteenth century, and neo-Gothic in the nine-teenth century. The portal, set into the apse wall, leads into an octagonal crypt, from where steps climb up either side of a Baroque high altar. Most of the decoration of the interior dates from 1850, although in the chapels along the side aisles there are some notable pieces of Renaissance art. The second chapel on the right, which contains the tomb of Brancaccio, is decorated with a cycle of frescoes dating from the original construction of the church. They were painted in 1309 by Pietro Cavallini who was commissioned by the Angevins from Rome. The seventh chapel on the right is of note for the *Christ on the Cross*, which is on the altar. It is associated with the legend of Christ speaking to St Thomas Aquinas who was a mendi-cant friar in the adjoining monastery during the mid-thirteenth century. A painting of *St Thomas Aquinas*, by Luca Giordano, can be seen in the small chapel to the right of the altar. Also on the right, is the sacristy, which holds the tombs of Angevin princes and other notables, and has a fine ceiling decorated with frescoes by F. Solimena. The most prestigious work of art in the church, the *Flagellation* (1607), by Caravaggio, is now in the Capodimonte mu-seum. However, a seventeenth-century copy of Andrea Vaccaro hangs in its place, in the chapel to the left of the altar.

Return to Piazza San Domenico Maggiore and head along the right side of the church, taking the first turning on the right to the **Cappella San Severo**. This unassuming, eighteenth-century chapel, painted yellow and grey, stands on a narrow street corner. It was the creation of Prince Raimondo di Sangro (1710-1771), who commissioned the numerous fine sculptural works that adorn the interior. The most important work is that of the *Veiled Christ*, which can be seen in the central nave. It was sculpted by the Neapolitan, Giuseppe Sanmartino, in 1753, and is made of polished alabaster. It was originally intended to be placed in an underground cave, illumi-nated from above, in order to show the beautiful folds of the veiled figure to full advantage. To the left of the sculpture, standing against a pillar in front of the presbytery, is a statue of *Chastity*, also draped in a flowing veil. It is one of the last works of Antonio Corradini (1751) who died a year after its completion. The figure is intended to resemble the prince's mother, Cecilia Gaetani. Against the pillar on the right of the presbytery is another notable sculpture, *Disenchantment*, by Francesco Queirolo. It depicts a male figure climbing out of a heavy rope net, the allegorical net of vice. The large and dramatic sculptural work in the main apse is of the *Deposition*, and is by another eighteenth-century, Neapolitan sculptor, Francesco Celebrano.

Continue alongside San Domenico Maggiore and turn left at the end of the street onto Via Tribunale. The church of **San Pietro a Maiella**, passed on the left, is of interest for its collection of paintings by the Calabrian artist, Mattia Pretti, which date from 1656 to 1661. Those in the nave depict the *Life of Celestin V*, while the transept holds the *Legend of Catherine of Alexandria*. Back outside the church, the former adjoining convent, has been the seat of the Conservatorio di Musica since 1826. The conservatory is one of the oldest of its kind, and was founded in 1537. Turn right, at the conservatory's entrance, and follow Vico San Pietro a Maiella to **Piazza Bellini**. This elegant piazza has a small gardens with palm trees at its centre and is surrounded by fine buildings. From the northern end of the piazza, follow Via Santa Maria di Constantino for 350m (383yd), to the **Museo Nazionale**.

The museum was built in 1790 to house the archaeological finds from the excavations of Pompei and *Herculaneum*. Today, its collection of antiquities rank amongst the most extensive and important in the world. The collection is arranged on two floors in a series of rooms surrounding two inner courtyards. The ticket office is on the left of a large entrance hall which contains a fine sarcophagus with a carved relief depicting Prometheus creating man from clay. Straight ahead, the central gallery, Atrio dei Magestri, contains a collection of Imperial Roman statues. Room 1, the Galleria dei Tirannicidi, is entered from the right side of the Atrio dei Magestri. Amongst the many fine statues displayed here, that of *Harmodius and Aristogiton*, the murderers of Hipparchus in 514BC, is one of the most important. It is copied from a Greek original made for Athens in 477BC. The Galleria dei Grande Maestri, which includes Rooms 2-6, also contains classic copies of Greek statues. Room 3 holds one of the most famous copies to be made in Roman times, *Doryphorus*, the spear-carrier. In Room 7 there is a copy, made in Imperial Roman times, of the *Palestrita*, and in Room 10 a copy of the Hellenistic *Venus Callipyge*. Room 12 contains an original Greek statue of the *Aphrodite of Sinuessa*, while the *Farnese Heracles* in the same room originates from the Roman baths of Caracalla. In Room 14 there are two fine statues from the ancient site of Capua: *Psyche* and *Venus*. Room 16 has the famous *Farnese Bull*, which, standing to a height of 4m (13ft), is the largest known statue of antiquity, and was restored by Michelangelo. On the Mezzanine Floor there is a good collection of mosaics and murals preserved from Pompei. Room 59 has two exceptional mosaics complete with the signatures of their maker. Other outstanding pieces are the *Nile Scenes* in Room 60, and the *Battle of Issus*, which shows Alexander the Great defeating the Persian Emperor Darius, in Room 61. The rooms on the first floor are mostly closed to the public, but it is usually possible to visit the Sale della Villa dei Papiri in the right wing, which contains finds from *Herculaneum*, and the collection of murals from Greek and Roman sites in Campania in the left wing. The left wing also has a collection of bronze figurines and other artefacts from Pompei and *Herculaneum*.

ITINERARY III

From the Museo Nazionale return through Piazza Bellini, to the church of San Pietro a Maiella, and continue eastwards along **Via Tribunale**. This narrow, flag-stoned street leads through an impoverished quarter of the city, where small neglected squares are used as football pitches or dumping grounds for rusted cars, and the gloomy neo-Classical churches are covered with graffiti. It is not, however, the architecture one comes to see here, but the street life. Shops and stalls display their wares out on the street, and the noise of people talking is only challenged by the many scooters.

Wandering along Via Tribunale, the Renaissance Cappella Pontana, and Santa Maria Maggiore, which has lain abandoned since it was damaged in the war, are passed to the left. The street continues, past the severe façade of Santa Maria del Purgatorio on the left, and a row of stone arcades on the right. In the shade of the arcaded vaults are dozens of small food shops with colourful displays of fresh fish, fruits and vegetables. At the end of the arcade, on the left, is the large, plastered façade of **San Paolo Maggiore**. This church was built in 1603 on the site of a Roman temple that was dedicated to the Dioscuri. A pair of antique columns have been placed at the top of the monumental staircase which precedes the façade. The staircase was designed by the master of Neapolitan Baroque, F. Grimaldi. The interior of the church is also Baroque and is typically decorated with inlaid marbles, frescoes and stucco.

A short distance further along Via Tribunale, on the right is **San Lorenzo Maggiore**. Its yellow-painted façade, decorated with pilasters and statues dates from 1742. The church, however, is much older, and the interior has been restored to its original Gothic style. Commissioned by Charles I of Anjou in 1270, it was erected on the site of a sixth-century basilica. Inside, the spacious and well-lit nave has an elegant transept arch and a rib-vaulted apse, which is surrounded by an ambulatory. The ambulatory is typical of the French Gothic style and connects a series of chapels, each of which is frescoed and has the original carved funerary monuments dating from the fourteenth century. The tomb in the first chapel is sculpted with statues of the *Virtues* by the Gothic master, Tino di Camaiano. It belongs to Catherine of Austria, who died around 1323. The chapel also has fine frescoes of *Scenes from the Life of Mary Magdalen* which are painted in the style of Giotto, as are those in the sixth chapel which depict *Scenes from the Life of the Virgin Mary*. The ninth chapel has the tomb of Maria Durazzo, while the tomb of her father, Charles Durazzo, is in the left transept along with that of Robert of Artois. Also dating from the Gothic era, is the painted crucifix, to the right of the main door.

The itinerary continues from San Lorenzo Maggiore along Via Tribunale, passing the pale, grey and white façade of San Girolamo on the left, before reaching a crossroads. Turn left at the crossroads and follow **Via del Duomo** to the city's **cathedral**, which is on the right. Undoubtedly one of Naples' most interesting historic monument, this grand cathedral was started under Charles II of Anjou in 1294, and completed by Robert of Anjou in 1323. The façade, which is built of a startling-white stone, was reconstructed in the neo-Gothic style in 1877, although the three portals are original. The central portal has a bas-relief of the *Madonna and Child* by Tino da Camaiano, and has short porphyry columns at either side, which rest on the backs of weather-worn lions, sculpted by the Pisano School.

The vast and sombre interior of the cathedral is composed of a central nave with aisles along either side. The great pillars, dividing the central aisle, have slender, ancient columns set into each side, and support high, pointed arches. Against the first pillar on the left stands a Baroque font which is made with an ancient Egyptian basin of smooth, black basalt. Cross over to the right aisle where a gilt bronze gate encloses the **Cappella San Gennaro**. This famous chapel was built in 1609, after a design by Francesco Grimaldi, to house the holy relics of San Gennaro (St Januarius), which include phials of the saint's congealed blood. According to a tradition that has taken place over the last five hundred years, the phials are brought out three times a year for the miraculous liquidification of the blood. Recently scientists have postulated that the liquifying blood is actually a medieval fake relic, devised by some expert who discovered a thixotropic substance which becomes fluid when shaken. The interior of the chapel is adorned with Neapolitan Baroque statues and has a fresco in its large central dome by Lanfranco, who was commissioned from Rome.

Some of the cathedral's finest art works are in the right transept, where the second chapel holds a large painting of the *Assumption*, by the Renaissance Umbrian artist, Perugino, and the side apse chapel has its original cycle of frescoes by Pietro Cavallini which date from 1312. The main apse itself is decorated with a theatrical marble group depicting the *Ascension*, dating from the eighteenth century. Below the main apse, steps lead down to the Cripta di San Gennaro. The crypt has an outstanding, coffered ceiling, entirely sculpted from white marble, and decorated with portraits of saints and angels. The walls are also marble clad and have statues standing in recessed niches, while the floor is intricately inlaid with coloured stone. Praying to the altar, where there is a bronze urn containing the bones of San Gennaro, is an almost life size statue of Cardinal Carafa. The Cardinal was responsible for commissioning the building of the chapel which was undertaken in the sixteenth century, by a northern Italian sculptor from Como, Tommaso Malvito.

The cathedral was built on the site of a former tenth-century basilica, the remains of which have been incorporated into the Cappella Santa Restituta, which is entered from the left aisle. At the back of the chapel, a door on the right leads through to a baptistery, which dates from an even earlier Christian basilica of the fifth century. Back in the chapel, along the left side, thirteenth-century bas-reliefs can be seen in the fifth and seventh recesses, and a mosaic, dating from 1322, of the *Virgin Enthroned*, between them.

From the *duomo*, return back down Via del Duomo and continue straight ahead for 350m (383yd) to **Palazzo Cuomo**, which is on the right. This fine Renaissance *palazzo* with its rusticated façade of dark stone, was built in 1464, and today houses the **Museo Civico** **Filangieri**. Prince Gaetano Filangieri, who lived in the *palazzo* during the nineteenth century, was an avid collector of arms. In 1943, his collection was destroyed, but an arms museum was founded in its place. The arms collection, which dates from the sixteenth century up to the eighteenth century, is displayed on two floors of the *palazzo*. The first floor also contains a collection of Neapolitan School paintings in the Grand Salon, and on the second floor there are European ceramics and porcelains dating from the sixteenth century onwards.

ITINERARY IV

The two most important museums in Naples, the Certosa di San Martino and the Galleria Nazionale di Capodimonte, lie outside the city centre.

Visitors have probably already spotted the large, white vaulted buildings of the Certosa di San Martino, which loom above the city on the Vomero hill. To get there by public transport, take the number 49 bus from Piazza Garibaldi (in front of the central railway station) to the Monte Santo Funicolare. The funicular climbs up from Stazione Cumano, to the walls of **Castel Sant'Elmo** which lies to the west of Certosa di San Martino. The castle was first built for Robert of Anjou in 1329 and is strategically placed on the summit of the Vomero, overlooking the city and the Bay of Naples. During the reign of Charles V, the original castle was demolished to make way for that seen today. Designed in the shape of a six-pointed star, the new castle was completed in 1546 and became the seat of the city's governors. The fortified walls and surrounding moat are restored, and the coat of arms of Charles V, carved from white marble, can still be seen above the entrance.

 Certosa di San Martino, situated next to the castle, was also founded during the Angevin era, as a Carthusian monastery. Much of the present building, however, dates from the sixteenth and seventeenth centuries and the monastery has been converted to a museum, with ninety rooms, containing artefacts which document the history, art and life of Naples. A tour of the Certosa di San Martino, starts with a visit to the former monastery church, which is on the left side of the first courtyard, and is preserved complete with its seventeenth-century Neapolitan art works. The church was designed in 1580 by G.A. Dosio, using the already existing skeleton of the Angevin structure, of which only the Gothic ribs remain. The ceiling is decorated with frescoes by the Roman artist, Giovanni Lanfranco. Other parts of the interior are frescoed by leading exponents of the Baroque Neapolitan School, including G.B. Caracciolo, who decorated the third chapel on the left, and who also painted the *Washing of the Disciples' Feet* which hangs in the main apse and is considered the artist's masterpiece. The apse also contains *Institution of the Eucharist* by the Veronese School, and *Communion of the Apostles*, by the Spaniard, Ribera. The portraits of the twelve prophets, above each of the chapels, were also painted by Ribera, in 1643. Ribera's best-considered work, however, *The Descent from the Cross*, is housed in the Cappella del Tesoro, the third chapel on the left, where there is a ceiling fresco of *Judith*, by the Neapolitan painter, Luca Giordano.

Return to the entrance courtyard and pass into the Chiostrino Procuratori, a small, seventeenth-century cloister at the museum's entrance. The series of rooms surrounding the cloister contain a wide ranging collection that includes naval models, portraits of Bourbon rulers and documents concerning the 1799 revolution. In Room 25, a door leads through to the Belvedere, from where there is an excellent view over the Bay of Naples. In Rooms 27-30, there is a collection of Neapolitan prints, and in Rooms 34-37 there are nativity crib scenarios, for which Neapolitans are well-known. In the western part of the monastery, surrounding the Chiostro Grande, the large cloister, is the *pinacoteca.* This contains a fine collection of Neapolitan art, starting with primitive works in Rooms 42 and 43, and progressing through the centuries, from the 1600s to the 1800s, up to Room 61. In rooms 62-70 there is a collection of Neapolitan sculpture, amongst the most important of which are the works by Tino da Camaiano, and the great Baroque sculptor, Pietro Bernini, who moved to Naples in 1584. The remaining rooms in the museum contain glass and porcelains.

Galleria Nazionale di Capodimonte lies at the northern edge of the city, some 2km (1 mile) from the centre. By public transport, take the number 24 bus, either from Piazza del Plebiscito (opposite Palazzo Reale), or from Piazza Dante. Get off the bus at the roundabout, Tondo di Capodimonte, from where a series of steps lead up to the gallery. The gallery is seated in a sumptuous hunting lodge, surrounded by its former game preserves. It was built for Charles of Bourbon, and was still in use up until 1947 by Victor Emanuele II. In 1957 the lodge was opened as a museum, housing the art collection of the Farnese family. Amongst the most important paintings in this collection are: *St Louis of Toulouse* by Simone Martini (1317) in Room 4; *Crucifixion* by Masaccio (1426) in Room 6; *Transfiguration* by G. Bellini in Room 8; *Gypsy Madonna* by Correggio in Room 17, *Portrait of Pope Paul III with his Nephews* by Titian in Room 19; and *Flagellation* by Caravaggio in Room 29. It is also very pleasant to spend time wandering around the grounds of Capodimonte, which are now open as a public park, and offer fine views across the city, to the bay of Naples.

Route 2D • Bay of Naples

The Bay of Naples is enclosed by the Phlegrean Fields to the west, and the Sorrento peninsula to the east. It is dominated by the cone of Vesuvius, which towers over the suburbs of Naples, that have gradually spread along most of the coastal land. Naples is a convenient base from which to make excursions along the bay, most places of interest being easily accessible by public transport. Those intending to continue touring the southern coast may wish to visit the sights east of Naples on the way to Castellamare di Stabia, which is the starting point of chapter 5.

The places of interest to the west of Naples are centred around the Phlegrean Fields (Campi Flegrei), an area of volcanic activity, which extends between Naples and the ancient site of *Cumae*. The landscape is made up thirteen low craters, some of which are water-filled, and dozens of crevices from where fumaroles emit puffs of sulphurous vapour. The largest town on the Phlegrean Fields is **Pozzuoli**, it stands on the ancient Roman city of *Puteoli*. Volcanic activity has altered the level of the land here and the Roman harbour has long since disappeared beneath the sea. However, near the waterfront are the remains of a Roman market and temple, dedicated to Serapis, known as the Serapeo. The three remaining columns of this first-century edifice have encrustations, up to a height of 5m (16ft), left from a period when the site had temporarily dropped below sea level. Another fine relic of the Roman settlement is the amphitheatre, the entrance to which is on Corso Terracciano, 350m (383yd) west of the Serapeo. Built in the first century, the impressive arena is the third largest in Italy and could hold 40,000 spectators. The substructures, below the arena, which were used for animals, are also well-preserved.

The Solfatara, one of the most impressive of the fumaroles on the Phlegrean Fields, lies 2km (1 mile) north-west of Pozzuoli. It issues from the basin of a now extinct crater where the mud has a temperature of 160°C (320°F) and the ground is hollow-sounding underfoot.

Those with their own transport can continue west of the Solfatara for 5km (3 miles) to the Arco Felice, a triumphal arch, built in Roman times on the ancient Domitian Way. From here it is a short distance further west to the ancient ruins of *Cumae*. First settled by early Greek colonists in the eighth century BC, the city was Romanised in 334BC. There is a carpark at the entrance to the site, from where a tunnel leads right, to Cripto Romano, a Roman crypt, used during the Augustan period. Via Sacra, the principal artery through the city, leads up hill to the acropolis. On the way, the Temple of Apollo, which was converted to a basilica in the sixth century, is passed to the right. At the summit of the acropolis stands a temple dedicated to Jove. It was first erected by the ancient Greeks in the fifth century BC, but it was rebuilt during the reign of Augustus, and was later used as a Christian basilica. There are excellent views of the coast from here.

Those who wish to explore the coast to the west of Pozzuoli will pass through **Baia**, where there is an archaeological park containing the remains of the spa resort that stood here in Roman times, and **Bacoli**, a resort town, once a popular site for Romans to build their summer villas. Hikers may wish to continue along the headland to **Miseno** from where the summit of Cape Miseno can be ascended. The ascent takes about one hour and is rewarded by outstanding views across the Bay of Naples, and also of the headland which is strewn with the scant remains of Roman villas.

The places of interest along the bay to the east of Naples can either be reached by the Circumvesuviano train, a private line that operates from a series of platforms beneath the central railway station in Naples, or by the A3 *autostrada*. **Ercolano**, the first place of interest to be reached east of Naples, stands on the site of ancient *Herculaneum*. Like Pompei, the city was destroyed in the eruption of Vesuvius in AD79, being submerged beneath a massive flow of volcanic mud. *Herculaneum*, originally founded by Greek colonists who named it *Herakleia*, had been under Roman control for less than two hundred years when the natural disaster occured. At this time it was a modest, residential town, overshadowed by the much larger and more important commercial city of Pompei. Today, Pompei is still the more important site of the two, although the ruins of *Herculaneum* are better-preserved and less crowded.

From the main carpark, which is at the north-eastern corner of the site, follow the avenue through the *palestra*, the former public games hall, to the southern end of the city, from where the itinerary begins. The city is laid out on a grid plan, and has three principal streets running north-south, and one which runs through the centre, west-east. The central one of the three north-south roads, Cardine IV, passes by the Casa dell'Atrio a Mosaico, on the right. This well-preserved house, as its name suggests, has fine geometric-patterned mosaics in its atrium. The house has a peristyle, which overlooks a garden, with sleeping quarters on the left side and a triclinum, or dining area, on the right.

Continue north along Cardine IV to Casa dei Tramezzo di Legno, which is just before the central crossroads, on the left. The façade of this house remains remarkably intact, two-storeys high, and with its original guttering which has water spouts carved into the shape of dog's heads. The house takes its name from the wooden partition which remains complete with its hinges and brackets for lamps. The interior also contains the remains of a wooden charred bed.

Casa Sannitica, on the right, at the crossroads, has a good portal and an impressive interior where the remains of a fresco depicting

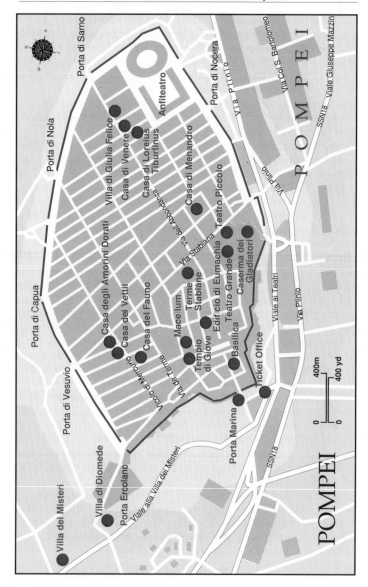

the *Rape of Europa* can be seen. Continuing northwards along Cardine IV, a large baths complex is passed to the left. It was built in 10BC, during the Augustan era, and has separate sections for men and women, with a games area at the centre. A short distance further along Cardine IV, Casa di Nettuno e Anfitrite, is on the right. As can be seen by the fittings of the interior, the front of this house was used as a shop.

Continue to the end of Cardine IV and turn right along Decumano Massimo which runs along the northern edge of the town. Casa del Bicentenario, on the right, is a large and wealthy residence with a fine entrance hall and remains of mosaics decorating the dining area. At the end of Decumano Massimo, turn right, and head south along Cardine V to the south-eastern quarter of the city, where a number

A well-preserved tiled floor at Pompei

of well-preserved houses are grouped. The first of these is the Casa dei Cervi, on the right, which is the most luxurious house yet discovered on the site. It is richly decorated with frescoes and is named after sculptures of deer that were found here. Opposite, on the left, are the Casa del Rilievo di Telefo, the largest house yet to be excavated, and next door, Casa della Gemma, which is so-named for the carved gem stone that was found in the excavations.

At the extreme southern end of Cardine V are the remains of another baths complex, the Terme Suburbane, which are well-preserved, but often flooded with water. Return back along Cardine V and turn right into the *palestra* from where it is a short distance back to the carpark.

Ercolano is also a good point from which to make an excursion to the crater of **Vesuvius** (1,281m/4202ft). Those using public transport should take a number 4 bus from outside the Circumvesuviana railway station. By road, simply follow signposts from Ercolano to Vesuvio. The road winds up through abundant vineyards, which are used in the production of the local wine, Lacrima Cristi, for 8km (5 miles) to the Osservatorio Vesuviano (609m/1,997ft). Built in 1845, the observatory contains a library and documentation of the volcano's daily activity since the mid-nineteenth century. The road continues up to a carpark, at a height to 1,017m (3,336ft), from where it is a 20-minute hike to the crater edge. A fee is charged at the crater for a compulsory guide.

The volcano is amongst the smallest in the world, but is one of the most active, having remained so ever since the major eruption of AD79. In 1631 it was recorded that 3,000 people were killed in a lava flow, and in the last major eruption of 1906, the top of the cone fell into the crater.

Pompei lies to the south-east of Vesuvius, 14km (9 miles) from *Herculaneum*. By public transport take the Circumvesuviana train to **Pompei Scavi**. The entrance to the site is 50m (55yd) from the railway station, while the ticket office is on nearby Piazza Marina. The piazza, which is directly next to the motorway exit, also holds the main carpark, for which high fees are charged. From the ticket office, follow the footpath to the entrance, and pass through a tunnel to the south-westernmost corner of the city which once looked out across its large port. It was through sea-trading that Pompei grew rich, and a commercial port was well established here by the sixth century BC. In 80BC the city was romanised, and continued to prosper up until AD79 when Vesuvius erupted. The city was completely destroyed and there were few survivors.

Take Via Marina, past the rambling brick ruins of a large basilica on the right, to the forum, the ancient market place, which is surrounded by the remains of fine buildings. Along the north end are the remains of a temple dedicated to Jove, which dates from the second century BC. Fifteen steps, cut from dark Vesuvian stone, remain intact, along with sections of fluted columns. To the left of the temple is the Granaio, a granary, now used as a store-house for umpteen amphorae. To the right of the temple, along the east side of the forum, is the **Macellum**, a former market building, originally covered by a dome. Another market building, the Mercato della Lana, which was used for the trading of wool, is also on the east side, to the right of the Macellum.

Leave the forum by following Via dell'Abbondanza, along the right side of the Mercato della Lana. This fine street is typically Pompeian, being paved with polygonal blocks of dark volcanic stone. The surface is deeply rutted by cart wheels, and at regular intervals there are raised stepping stones for pedestrians. Ruined houses line either side of the street, some of which have remnants of mosaics and frescoes. Casa Cinghiale, at number 8, has a black and white mosaic in its entrance hall of a wild boar.

After 300m (328yd) Via dell'Abbondanza passes the large baths complex, **Terme Stabiane**, on the left. The baths have separate sections for male and female with a *palestra*, or games area, at the centre. On the left of the *palestra*, which is surrounded by arcades, there is a large circular pool. The men's baths, which are the best-preserved section, are along the right side of the *palestra*. The changing rooms have stucco decorated walls, and fossilised figures, found here during the excavation, can be seen in show cases. Also of interest are the private cubicles, each of which contains a bath tub and has a high ceiling with a sky-light.

Return to Via dell'Abbondanza and turn right down Via Stabiana. After 200m (218yd), turn right again to the Teatro Piccolo, behind which is the large arcaded courtyard of the gladiators' barracks. Archways lead onto the stage of the **Teatro Piccolo** from either side. The cavea, which once held 1,000 spectators and was roofed over, has been reconstructed of small, roughly cut stone. The ends of the cavea are preserved with the attractive carvings of figures and griffons. Pass through the theatre to the **Teatro Grande**. Dating from the second century BC, this large theatre seated 5,000 spectators.

Return back up Via Stabiana and turn right along Via dell'Abbondanza. Some of the houses lining either side of the street have traces of frescoes and latin names are written on the walls in red ochre. The Casa di Larario, on the right, has a series of rooms with architectural motifs frescoed on the walls. The rooms are along the left side of an inner courtyard which has its original impluvium, used to collect rain, at its centre. Casa del Menandro, one block behind, was a large, patrician villa, named after the frescoed portrait of the poet Menander found on one of its walls. The villa also yielded great hoards of silver and precious mosaics.

Continue along Via dell'Abbondanza, past Casa Paquius Proculus, on the right, which has a fine black and white mosaic, decorated with birds within medallions, and a snarling dog on the hearth. Casa di Loreus Tiburtinus, which is also on the right has a grand portal with the original bronze doors. The doors are encrusted with lava, but the studs along the top are still intact. The atrium of this grand house has a simple marble fountain at its centre which has been restored to working order.

Take the paved road along the right side of Casa di Loreus Tibutinus, to the eastern end of the city which, shaded by lofty pine trees, contains a *palestra* and amphitheatre. The large *palestra* is surrounded by arcades on three of its sides, with the walls of the amphitheatre along the fourth side, and a large square pool at its centre. The amphitheatre, which is entered by climbing up the steps along its outer wall, is one of the first amphitheatres known to have been built in the Roman era, and dates from 80BC. It is eliptical in shape, measuring 135m (443ft) by 104m (341ft), and could hold an audience of 12,000 spectators. The entire structure is remarkably well-preserved, although sadly overgrown with weeds, and there are good views to be had from the topmost walkway, of the *palestra*, the modern town of Pompei with its Baroque church, and the hills of the Sorrento peninsula beyond.

From the north-west corner of the amphitheatre follow Regina II Insulae IV, an abandoned street of the city, past walled gardens, back up to Via dell'Abbondanza. Turn left, and follow Via dell'Abbondanze back towards the city centre. **Villa di Giulia Felice**, which is passed on the left, has a charming atrium with some of its fluted columns partially covered by red stucco, and a pretty gardens with an arbour. **Casa di Venere**, next door, also has a lovely, colonnaded garden and in one of its rooms can be seen a fossilised figure. On the corner, there is a stand with deep basins cut into the surface said to have been used for hot drinks. From here, return back along Via dell'Abbondanza to the forum.

From the forum it is possible to explore the northern part of the city and also the two outlying villas: Villa di Diomede and Villa dei Misteri. Those with their own transport, however, may wish to visit the latter by road, following Viale alla Villa dei Misteri, north of the railway station. Much of the northern city stands neglected and overgrown, but the streets are well-paved and the atmosphere of a deserted city is evocative. **Casa del Fauno**, 100m (110yd) north of the forum, on Via della Fortuna, is one of the largest houses in the city. It has an attractive atrium with an impluvium at its centre, in front of which stand copies of the small bronze statues of fauns that were found here. The floor of the atrium has a striking, geometric-patterned floor, while many of the surrounding rooms are paved with black and white mosaics. At the back of the house there is a grand peristyle with its large columns still standing. To the north of Casa del Fauno there is another impressive house, **Casa dei Vetti**, which belonged to a family of wealthy agricultural merchants. The atrium has been restored with its original roof and impluvium, and leads through to a peristyle. The surrounding rooms are decorated with simple frescoes, mainly of architectural designs, except for those in the triclinum which depict agricultural and mythological scenes.

Villa di Diomede, lies 300m (328yd) beyond the western city gate, Porta Ercolano. In the cellar of this grand villa, which has a large garden, eighteen skeletons were found, including the proprietor with the key still in his hand, and a servant behind who was carrying the household valuables.

Villa dei Misteri is a further 300m (328yd) north of Villa di Diomede. This large and complex villa dates from the third century BC and is famous for the frescoes which decorate the hall, along the south side of the atrium. The frescoes date from the first century BC and depict twenty-four, life-size figures enacting an initiation ceremony to Dionysius, known as the Mysteries.

Additional Information

Places to Visit

Anagni
Cattedrale
Piazza Innocenzo II
Open: winter daily 9.30am-12noon, 3.30-5pm. Summer daily 9.30am-12noon, 4-7pm.

Palazzo Bonifacio VIII
Via Vittorio Emanuele
☎ (0775) 727053
Open: winter daily 9.30am-12noon, 3.30-5pm. Summer daily 9.30am-12noon, 4-7pm.

Capua
Museo Campano
Palazzo Antignano
Via Roma 68
Open: Tuesday to Saturday 9am-2pm, Sunday 9am-1pm.

Casamari
Abbazia di Casamari
☎ (0775) 333215
Farmacia open: daily 9am-12noon, 4-6pm.
Guided tour: winter daily 3-6pm, summer daily 4-6.30pm.

Caserta
Palazzo Reale
Viale Douher
☎ (0823) 322233/322170
Open: Tuesday to Sunday 9am-
1.30pm.

Cassino
Abbazia di Monte Cassino
☎ (0776) 311529
Open: daily 9.30am-12.30pm, 3.30-
5pm.

Zona Archeologica
Open: daily 9am-1 hour before
sunset.

Cumae
Scavi Archeologico
Open: Tuesday to Sunday 9am,
closes according to season between
2.45 and 6.30pm.

Ercolano
Herculaneum
Corso Ercolano
Open: Tuesday to Sunday 9am,
closes according to season between
2.45 and 6.20pm.

Naples
Castel Nuovo
Piazza Municipio
Open: Monday to Friday 9am-1pm.

Palazzo Reale
Piazza Plebiscito
☎ (081) 413888
Open: November to June, Monday
to Saturday 9am-1.30pm, Sunday
9am-1pm. July to October, Monday
to Saturday 9am-7pm, Sunday
9am-1pm.

Teatro San Carlo
Via San Carlo
☎ (081) 7972332
Visiting hours: Monday to

Saturday 9-10am, 1-3pm, Sunday
9am-1pm. (Visitors are not
admitted during rehearsals).

Chiostro Maiolicati
Santa Chiara
Via Benedetto Croce
☎ (081) 5526209
Open: October to March, daily
8.30am-12.30pm, 4-6pm. April to
September, daily 8.30am-12.30pm,
4-6.30pm.

Cappella San Severo
Via de Sanctis 19
Open: Monday, Thursday to
Sunday 10am-1.30pm and 5-7pm,
Tuesday, 10am-1.30pm.

Museo Nazionale
Piazza Museo
☎ (081) 440166
Open: Tuesday to Saturday 9am-
2pm, Sunday and holidays 9am-1pm.

Cappella San Gennaro
Duomo
Via Duomo
☎ (081) 449097
Open: 8am-12noon

Museo Civico Filangieri
Palazzo Cuomo
Via Duomo
☎ (081) 203175
Open: Tuesday to Saturday 9am-
2pm, Sunday and holidays 9am-
1pm.

Certosa di San Martino
Vomero
☎ (081) 5781769
Open: Tuesday to Saturday 9am-
2pm, Sunday and holidays 9am-1pm.

Galleria Nazionale di Capodimonte
Via di Capodimonte
☎ (081) 7410881
Open: winter, Tuesday to Saturday

9am-2pm, Sunday and holidays
9am-1pm. Summer, Tuesday to
Saturday 9am-7.30pm. Sunday and
holidays 9am-1pm.

Palestrina
*Museo Nazionale Archeologico
    Prenestino*
Palazzo Barberini
☎ (06) 9558100
Open: Tuesday to Sunday 9am-1
hour before sunset.

Pompei
Pompei Scavi
Piazza Marina
☎ (081) 8610744/8611051 (superin-
tendent)
Open: daily 9am, closes according
to season between 2.45 and 7pm.

Pozzuoli
Anfiteatro Flavio
Corso Terracciano
Open: daily 9am, closes according
to season between 2.45 and 6pm.

Useful Information

Alatri
Events and Festivals
August, Folklore Festival.

Tourist Information Centre
Ufficio Turistico
Palazzo Comunale
Via C. Battisti 7
☎ (0775) 45748

Emergencies
Carabinieri (Military Police)
☎ (0775) 450026

Pronto Soccorso (First Aid Service)
☎ (0775) 442161

Anagni
Tourist Information Centre
Pro Loco

Piazza Innocenzo III
☎ (0775) 727852

Emergencies
Carabinieri (Military Police)
☎ (0775) 727005

First Aid Service (Pronto Soccorso)
☎ (0775) 727777

Capua
Tourist Information Centre
Pro Loco
Piazza dei Giudici
☎ (0823) 963930

Emergencies
Polizia Stradale (Traffic Police)
☎ (0823) 961111

Pronto Soccorso (First Aid Service)
☎ (0823) 961280

Caserta
Tourist Information Centre
Ente Provinciale Turismo
Corso Trieste - angolo Piazza Dante
☎ (0823) 321137

Emergencies
Automobile Club d'Italia
Via Nazario Sauro 10
☎ (0823) 321442

Cassino
Tourist Information Centre
Azienda Autonoma di Soggiorno e
    Turismo
Via Condotti 6
☎ (0776) 21292

Transport
Ferrovia (Railway)
☎ (0776) 21107

Emergencies
Vigili Urbani (Town Police)
☎ (0776) 26222

Polizia Stradale (Traffic Police)
☎ (0776) 21025

Pronto Soccorso (First Aid Service)
☎ (0776) 481222

Events and Festivals
29 September, Sagra della Trota
(Trout Festival)

Ercolano
Transport
Ferrovie dello Stato (State Railway)
☎ (081) 327170

Emergencies
Carabinieri (Military Police)
☎ (081) 325108

Ospedale (Hospital)
☎ (081) 231111

Ferentino
Tourist Information Centre
Pro Loco
Piazza Matteotti

Emergencies
Carabinieri (Military Police)
☎ (0775) 244002

Ospedale (Hospital)
(0775) 244653

Naples
Events and Festivals
17 January, Festa d'o' Cippo di
Sant'Antonio (Procession in
memory of St Anthony, protector
of animals).

June, Mostra Oltremare, Fiera
Internazionale della Casa (International trade fair).

May and September, Festa di San
Gennaro (Festival of the patron
saint, St Januarius).

September, La Festa di Piedigrotta
(Neapolitan song festival).

Tourist Information Centres
Ente Provinciale per il Turismo
Piazza dei Martiri 58
☎ (081) 405311

Ente Provinciale per il Turismo
Stazione Centrale
Piazza Garibaldi
☎ (081) 268779

Azienda Autonoma di Soggiorno e
Turismo
Palazzo Reale
Piazza Plebiscito
☎ (081) 418744

Azienda Autonoma di Soggiorno e
Turismo
Ufficio Informazioni
Piazza del Gesu
☎ (081) 323328

Transport
Ferrovie dello Stato (Railway)
Stazione Centrale
Piazza Garibaldi
☎ (081) 5534188

Circumvesuviana (Railway)
Corso Garibaldi
☎ (081) 7792444

Caremar (Ferries)
Molo Beverello
☎ (081) 5513882

Tirrenia (Ferries)
Stazione Marittima
☎ (081) 5512181

Automobile Club d'Italia
Piazzale Tecchio 49d
☎ (081) 614511

Emergencies
Vigili Urbani (Town Police)
☎ (081) 7513177

Polizia Centrale (Central Police)
☎ (081) 7941111

Polizia Servizio Auto Rubate
(Police for stolen cars)
☎ (081) 7941435

Polizia Stradale (Traffic Police)
☎ (081) 293748

Pronto Soccorso (First Aid Service)
☎ (081) 7520696

Guardia Medica (Medical Officer)
☎ (081) 7513177

Palestrina
Tourist Information Centre
Pro Loco
Piazza Santa Maria degli Angeli 2
☎ (06) 9573176

Emergencies
Carabinieri (Military Police)
☎ (06) 9557297

Pronto Soccorso (First Aid Service)
☎ (06) 9558188

Pompei
Tourist Information Centre
Azienda Autonoma di Soggiorno e
   Turismo
Via Sacra 1
☎ (081) 8631041

Emergencies
Polizia Urbana Sezione Turistica
(Local Tourist Police)
☎ (081) 8614098

Guardia Medica (Medical Officer)
☎ (081) 8632627

Pronto Soccorso (First Aid Service)
Clinica Maria Rosaria
☎ (081) 8561811

Pozzuoli
Tourist Information Centre
Azienda Autonoma di Soggiorno e
   Turismo
Via Campi Flegrei 3
☎ (081) 8672419

3

LOWER CENTRAL APPENNINES

This chapter takes the visitor up through the regions of Campania and Molise to the Abruzzo National Park. Comparatively few tourists visit this mountainous, land-locked area of Italy and the visitor can enjoy classical sites, such as *Saepinum*, almost to themselves. The towns, particularly in Molise, are fairly quiet but have a lot of local character. Traditional costume is still worn in many of the villages on the route, and crafts such as lace-making are still practised. The villages inside the Abruzzo National Park, however, are more touristic, as the park gets quite busy in August with Italian holiday-makers, although it is always possible to escape the crowds by heading up into the thickly-forested mountains, which are the preserve of the Marsican brown bear and the Abruzzo chamois.

The region of the Lower Central Appennines has remained relatively unexplored and unexploited because of its harsh terrain and poor communications. Industrial development is virtually non-existent and the stony, thin soil is best suited to sheep farming. Both the Abruzzo and Molise produce excellent *pecorino* (sheep's cheese) including *pecorino con la goccia*, which is soft and quite runny at the edges. Not surprisingly lamb, mutton and kid, are the basis of many of the local dishes, which range from *pezzata* (mutton stew) to *capretto allo spiedo alla Molisana* which is spit-roasted kid, swathed in lard until the last moment when it is removed to allow the skin to cook to a light-golden crisp.

Chapter 3 starts at Benevento, which can be reached either by motorway from Salerno, after visiting the Amalfi coast, or by the SS7 from Caserta, after visiting Naples. Together with chapter 4, it provides an interesting itinerary back to Rome, particularly suitable for visitors who do not wish to continue south of chapter 2 along the Tyrrhenian coast.

Route 3A • Benevento to Saepinum

The provincial capital **Benevento** is situated in a bare and wind-   ☀
swept basin at the confluence of the Calore and Sabato rivers. It has
a population of well over 60,000 and the well-preserved historic
centre is surrounded by an unsightly belt of suburbs. Visitors should
follow signs through the suburbs to *centro*, and park on the large
square, Piazza Orsini, that surrounds the *duomo*. The *duomo* suffered   ⬥
extensive war damage in 1943, but has been well restored and has a
thirteenth-century, Romanesque façade. The interior, however, is
modern, apart from the crypt, which dates from the sixth century.

To visit the rest of the town, head east, past the *duomo's* stout
campanile, which has Roman, carved reliefs built into its lower walls,
along the pedestrianised, main street, Corso Garibaldi. After 200m
(218yd) turn left along Via Traiano to the magnificent, Roman arch,
Arco di Traiano, which stands at the end of the street. It was erected
in AD117, and bears a large inscription dedicated to the emperor
Trajan. It stands to a height of 15m (49ft), and has a single arch which
is remarkably well-preserved and is clad with richly-carved reliefs
on both the inner and outer walls. These impressive works of art
depict scenes of the emperor Trajan's victories in battle.

Return to Corso Garibaldi, and continue eastwards for a further
280m (306yd) to Piazza Matteoti, in which there is an attractive
fountain and obelisk dating from 1808. Along the north side of the
piazza is the church of Santa Sofia with its eighteenth-century bell   ⬥
tower. The church dates from 1668, although parts still remain of the
earlier building that was founded here in AD766, when Benevento
was the capital of an independent Lombard duchy. The church
stands on its original, polygonal ground-plan and the interior contains the remains of eighth-century frescoes in the apse, as well as the
antique columns that were used in its initial construction. In the
former monastery, on the left of Santa Sofia, there is a museum,   🏛
Museo del Sannio, arranged around a charming, twelfth-century
cloister. The collection is wide ranging, one section documenting the
history of ancient Benevento from its earliest origins as a Samnite
city, another displaying art objects, dating from medieval to modern
times. A further section of the Museo del Sannio is housed in the
Rocca dei Rettori, a fourteenth-century castle, 150m (164yd) south-
east of Piazza Matteoti.

Benevento also has an impressive Roman theatre, which is unfor-   𝝥
tunately rather hemmed in by houses, 150m (164yd) south-west of
the *duomo*. It was built in the second century under the emperor
Hadrian, but was enlarged a century later, during the reign of
Caracalla to enable it to hold 20,000 spectators. Two of its original

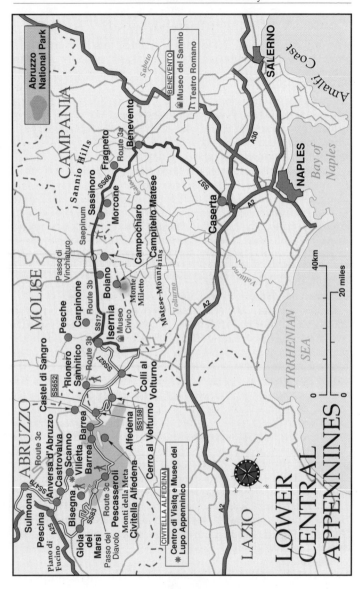

three tiers have been restored and during the summer, opera and drama performances are staged here.

Leave Benevento by heading north of the *duomo* along Corso Vittorio Emanuele. The street leads to the Calore river, where the large, neo-Classical church of Madonna della Grazie can be seen to the left. Cross over the river and continue straight ahead to the station where signs indicate the turning left to Campobasso, out through the town's outskirts, onto the SS88 dei Due Principe. The road passes through a dry, rolling landscape, where tobacco is the

The ancient ruins of Suepinum,
one of Southern Italy's most interesting classical sites

principal crop, and then gradually climbs for over 10km (6 miles), past the village of **Fragneto**, to a summit of 524m (1,719ft). There are good views from here across the Sannio hills of northern Campania, before the road heads down, past the hill villages of **Morcone** and **Sassinoro**, to the River Fratte. Shortly after crossing the river, the road passes into the region of Molise and a few kilometres further on, a track on the left leads under an arch to **Altilia**, a small village built on the ancient ruins of *Saepinum*.

These little-visited ruins have been excellently restored, and in their tranquil setting, stand out as one of the most endearing of Southern Italy's classical sites. *Saepinum* was founded by the ancient Samnites and in the fifth century BC was a place of considerable importance. After being destroyed in 293BC, it became a Roman colony, and enjoyed a stable existence up until the ninth century, when it was sacked by the Saracens. The survivors abandoned the site, moving to higher ground, where the present day village of Sepino now stands.

The ruins are enclosed by a well-preserved wall, which has a circumference of 1,250m (4,100ft), and is built of neatly-cut stones. The theatre, which lies in the north corner of the city walls, is a good point from which to start a tour of the site. Edged by a tidy row of cottages, the lower part of the seating area is well-preserved, as are the stage floor and the lower walls of the stage buildings. Rounded arches lead from either side of the theatre to a walkway which passes between the backs of the cottages and the city wall. Pass through the opening in the city wall, behind the theatre and head to the well-preserved mausoleum of Numisius Ligus. Standing isolated in a field, it has attractive, carved corner stones and a good inscription on its south side. Return to the city wall and follow it southwards, passing below the well-preserved bastions, to the most outstanding of the city's gates, Porta Boiano Terme. Its fine arch bears a long inscription dedicated to Tiberius and Drusus, dating from the fourth century. At either end of the inscription, there stand statues of prisoners with their legs crossed and their hands tied behind their backs, while on the key-stone there is a handsome portrait of a bearded head, thought possibly to be Hercules. Steps lead from inside the gate, on the left, up onto the walls, from where a fine view can be had of the ancient city. Follow the ancient, paved road from the gate, into the city centre, noticing the impluvium on the right, which originally stood in the central courtyard of a Samnite house to collect rain water. At the central crossroads there are the remains of a temple with twenty Ionic columns in peristyle. The road leading off to the right goes to the south city gate, Porta di Terravecchia, while straight ahead lies the forum. Cross over to the forum, where only fragments are left of its surrounding building, and head to the fountain on its east side. The fountain has a lovely, carved relief of a griffin and in the ground to its right there is an impressive drain cover with a grill hewn from a thick slab of stone. Follow the paved road east, beyond the fountain, past the remains of houses to the left, where two more impluviums can be seen as well as the brick-lined recesses of an olive press. Continue along the paved road, through the east gate, Porta di Benevento, which is identical to the west gate, Porta Boiano Terme, but is less well-preserved. Beyond the gate, next to a farmhouse on the left is a circular mausoleum with an inscription dedicated to Ennius Marsus Volmarso. Guarded by a pair of sadly worn lions, its walls are decorated with carved shields and a fasces, while the top is crenellated.

Return through the forum to the central crossroads and turn right. The track leads back to the point where the site was entered.

Route 3B • Saepinum to Alfedena

The route continues north-west of *Saepinum*, towards the Matese mountains, which form a natural boundary between the provinces of Campania and Molise. The road climbs up to Passo di Vinchiaturo (555m/1,820ft) and then traverses the Matese foothills, which are dotted with picturesque villages, some built above deep gorges, others stuck up on rocky spurs. Any of these villages are worth the excursion off the road. One of the more readily accessible villages is **Campochiaro**, where the modest houses are clustered around three ruined towers of a medieval Angevin keep. Some of the older women here still wear their traditional costume. The somewhat larger town of **Boiano**, 5km (3 miles) north-west of Campochiaro, along the SS17, is also worth a visit. It has a characteristic piazza, where locals chat under the trees, while high in the hills above there is an abandoned medieval hamlet. To reach the hamlet, Civita, head up above the piazza and fork right. The road winds up around a series of hairpin bends for 4km (2 miles), to a high spur, along which the hamlet is straggled. On the summit of the hill, above Civita, there are the ruins of a Lombard castle, where, from its high upper courtyard, there is a fine panorama.

The SS17 continues north-west, passing below the highest peak of the Matese mountains, Monte Miletto (2,050m/6,724ft). During the winter the slopes of the mountain are used for skiing, while in the summer it is a good spot for hiking. Those who wish to make the excursion to the mountain, should turn left, following the road for 17km (10 miles) to the resort of **Campitello Matese** from where a chairlift can be taken up to Rifugio Jezza, which lies just below the summit at a height of 1,820m (5,970ft).

The route continues along the SS17, passing the pretty, spired church of Santuario'dell Addorlata, to the left, which was built in the nineteenth century in the mock Gothic style, on the site where two locals had a vision of the Madonna. The road follows the valley, passing below the picturesque hill villages of **Pesche** and **Carpinone**, before reaching the turning off the main road, to **Isernia**, which is signposted Isernia Nord. The road passes through the modern suburb of San Leucio, to the *centro storico*. There is ample parking around the gardens on Piazza Martiri d'Ungheria, from where the centre lies within easy walking distance.

Isernia was heavily bombed in 1943 and most of the town was flattened with the loss of some 4,000 lives. Further damage has since been caused by earthquakes, the most recent of which was in 1984. The narrow streets are now cluttered with timbers which hold up the damaged buildings, but despite this, the town has a lot of character, and its traditional craft, lace-making is still very much in evidence. Women sit outside their houses in the summer, with the 'tombola' resting on their laps, making lace in a technique that originally derived from Spain. The local lace is sold in the town's modest shops, along with the rustic terracotta pottery that is also made in Isernia.

Start a tour of Isernia by heading down the main street, Via Lorusso, to Piazza Celestino, which holds Isernia's finest historic monument, the Fontana della Fraterna. The fountain, built in the fourteenth century, is built from ancient stones, some of which are carved, and has six pretty arches resting on small, antique columns topped by fine capitals. Continue downhill from the fountain, along Corso Marcelli, to the neo-Classical *cattedrale* which dates from 1837. The square on which the cathedral stands, Piazza Andrea d'Isernia, has a fine open view from its west side, and holds the town's only large café. It serves some of the best ice-cream to be found in Southern Italy.

Continue downhill, passing beneath an attractive medieval arch, which supports the cathedral's bell tower and has fine Roman statues standing at each of its four corners. The town's museum, Museo Civico, is a further 400m (437yd) beyond the arch, on the left. It is housed in the former convent of SantaMaria delle Monache, the *campanile* of which, dating from 1015, is still standing while the church is undergoing extensive restoration. The museum is most notable for its excellent documentation of pre-historic Isernia, where evidence of the earliest human genus yet to be discovered in Europe, the *Homo Aeserniensis*, has been found. The excavated finds, which include primitive stone tools, the bones of elephants, rhinoceros, bears and bison, date from the early Stone Age, and are excellently displayed as they were found in situ.

Leave Isernia by heading down to the bottom of the hill and turn right, following signs to Colli al Volturno on the SS627 della Vandra. This small country road winds over gentle hills, past the steep mound of an ancient acropolis on the right bank of the River Nandra. The road continues across the river, and passes through **Colli al Volturno**, which has an attractive old quarter covering a hill to the left, before turning right onto the larger road, SS158. After following the Volturno river valley for 5km (3 miles), the SS158 passes the thirteenth-century church, San Vincenzo al Volturno, which is perched high above the valley, to the left. Originally founded in the eighth century, **San Vincenzo al Volturno** was an important Benedictine monastery. However, it was destroyed during Saracenic

Italian markets are interesting places to visit

raids and only the church and its squat bell tower are left standing. The crypt of San Lorenzo, also escaped destruction, and holds some of the best-preserved examples of early Benedictine frescoes in Italy.

The route forks right at the foot of San Vincenzo al Volturno and follows the SS652, which is signposted to Roccaraso. An impressive viaduct, 826m (2,709ft) long, spans the valley, and offers good views of San Vincenzo al Volturno, as well as the fourteenth-century castle of Cerro al Volturno, which lies in the valley to the right. The SS652 continues, on a series of scenic viaducts, to **Rionnero Sannitico**, from where a pleasant 8km (5 mile) excursion can be made to the town of **Castel di Sangro**. The town lies on a slope, at the confluence of the Sangro and Zittola rivers, just inside the region of Abruzzo. It was largely rebuilt after World War II, but the Baroque church of San Domenico still stands above the main square Piazza Plebiscito, and the remains of a castle lie at the summit of the hill, overlooking the town.

The route continues along the Sangro river valley, on the SS83, to **Alfedena** which lies at the southern edge of the Abruzzo National Park. The village is picturesquely set above the valley, overlooked by the towering ruins of its castle. From here visitors should follow the itinerary through the park on Route 3C.

Route 3C • Alfedena to Sulmona

Route 3C follows the SS83, up above Alfedena, into the mountainous interior of the **Abruzzo National Park**. The park covers an area of 44,000 hectares (10,868 acres), almost half of which is forested, and protects a great variety of Appennine flora and fauna. The park was founded in 1922 with the principal aim of protecting the Marsican brown bear which was then in danger of extinction. There are now estimated to be around seventy to a hundred bears under continual protection, while the park's dense forests of pine, beech and turkey oak also shelter around thirty Appennine wolves, well over six-hundred deer, as well as wild boar, foxes and other more common animals. The park has also rehabilitated the Abruzzo chamois, of which there are estimated to be at least four hundred. These distinctive animals with their black and white markings, and curly horns, tend to inhabit the high remote areas, but are easily spotted when they come down to graze on the open pastures.

The park, is well-equipped for tourism. There are 150 nature trails through the park, which provide plenty of scope for hiking, and in the main tourist centres there are also facilities for horseriding. The rules of the park are to keep to the paths within the indicated reserve areas, and to respect nature. Camping is strictly prohibited except in official sites and fishing is only allowed with a permit.

The first point of interest inside the National Park is the man-made lake, Lago di Barrea, which is 4½km (3 miles) long and has an average width of 500m (546yd). A fine crest of mountains encircle the lake and villages are dotted along its gentle shores. **Barrea**, with its thirteenth-century, ivy-covered castle, lies at the eastern end of the lake, on a rocky spur. The SS83 passes through the village before heading down to the Sangro river which was dammed in 1951 to form the lake and provide hydro-electric power. The road crosses over the river and follows the northern edge of the lake, from where there are good views of **Civitella Alfedena** which lies high above the opposite shore. To reach Civitella Alfedena take the bridge at the western end of the lake and follow the steep and winding road up to the village. This popular resort is a centre for the protection of the Appennine wolf, and is also an excellent point from which to make hiking excursions into the Monti della Meta, the highest mountains in the park, with peaks over 2,000m (6,560ft) high, and to the Riserva Naturale Integrale della Camosciara, the park's largest animal reserve. Information about hiking itineraries is available from the Centro Visito del Parco on via San Lucia. In the museum next door, Museo del Lupo Appenninico, the history of the Appennine wolf is documented. To see the real thing, follow the twenty-minute walking itinerary from Piazzale Santa Lucia to the Area Faunistica del Lupo e Pineta.

The SS83 continues along Lago di Barrea, through the village of **Villetta Barrea**, which lies at the westernmost end of the lake. The road heads west from here, along the Sangro river valley, which has high mountains on either side. **La Camosciara**, signposted on the left, is a regular grazing spot for the Abruzzo chamois. The road ends at a parking area, from where a twenty-minute walk can be made up to a waterfall, the Cascata della Ninfa. For more serious hikers, trails also lead from here into the rugged terrain of the Riserva Naturale Integrale della Camosciara. A steep one-hour hike leads to Rifugio della Liscia (1,650m/5,412ft) which lies at the foot of a range of rocky mountain peaks. The trail continues through the Monti della Meta, passing above Civitella Alfedena.

The SS83 continues to wind between the mountains along the Sangro river valley. A more gentle, but nonetheless scenic hike can be made along the Valle Fondillo, which is reached by turning left, after 6km (4 miles) from Lago di Barrea, and following the track. From the end of the track, it is a 2 or 3 hour hike along the Valico Passagio dell'Orso, to the top of the valley which is 1,672m (5,484ft) high. The SS83 proceeds a short distance further along the Sangro river valley, before climbing up past the hilltop village of **Opi** where there is a refuge for the Abruzzo chamois. The main resort in the park, **Pescasseroli**, lies 5½km (3 miles) further on. It has a well-organised centre, with neat rows of chalets and souvenir shops, and is busy all year round, with facilities for skiing in the winter and hiking in the summer. There is also a nature museum and a small wildlife park, while at the Centro di Visita, lectures, debates and films are held about the park during the summer. The Centro di Visita also sell trail maps of the park which indicate the areas where animals are likely to be seen. One of the most popular hikes from Pescasseroli starts from the southern end of the town and follows the Valico di Monte Tranquillo to the Monte Tranquillo pass, which is at a height of 1,673m (5,487ft). The hike takes just under 3 hours and is very scenic with a fine panorama from the pass.

The SS83 follows the Sangro river from Pescasseroli along a wide valley with pastures at either side. After 5km (3 miles) those who are interested in visiting **Bisegna**, a centre for the Abruzzo chamois, should fork right and continue for 12km (7 miles). The village has a faunistic area where a few species are kept in captivity. It is also a good point from which to go hiking in the Montagna Grande, the rocky range of mountains which rise to the south-east of the village. Details of hiking itineraries are available from the Centro di Visita del Camoscio in the village centre.

The route continues along the SS83, which crosses the Sangro river before climbing up to the Passo del Diavolo pass (1,400m/4,592ft). From the pass, the road winds along a high plateaux, through **Gioia Vecchia**, and across the northern boundary of the park. As the road descends there is a fine view across the vast basin of Piano di Fucino, which holds the massive satellite dishes of a telecommunications centre. After dropping some 700m (2,296ft) in altitude, the SS83 passes through **Gioia dei Marsi**, from where **San Benedetto dei Marsi** can be seen above the cultivated plain to the left. The latter is built on top of *Marruvium*, which was the capital in the seventh century BC of the ancient Marsi, who were amongst the first tribes in Italy to become allied to Rome.

The SS83 continues across the Fucino basin to **Pescina** which lies at its north-eastern rim. Follow signs through the busy centre of this agricultural town, to the A25 *autostrada*. The road climbs up above the attractive rooftops of Pescina's medieval quarter and passes the tall, ruined tower of its castle, before turning left to the motorway toll station. Heading in the direction of Pescara, follow the motorway through the San Domenico tunnel, which is 4,542m (3 miles) long, and leave the motorway by the Cocullo exit, at the other side of the mountain. The road winds down, below the hill-town of **Cocullo** which is well-known for its Processione dei Serpari. This procession, held on the first Thursday in May, is in honour of St Domenico, but the writhing snakes which are paraded around the town, draped over the saint's wooden effigy, hark back to an earlier pagan ritual celebrating the snake healers of the ancients.

Continue downhill from Cocullo, and after passing under the motorway, turn left to **Anversa d'Abruzzo**. As the road winds down through **Casale**. The hamlet of **Castrovalva**, is seen ahead, straggled along the top of a vertical ridge which guards the mouth of the Sagittario gorge. The village of **Anversa d'Abruzzo** lies at the entrance to this gorge and is well-worth stopping by at, to see the church, dedicated to the Madonna delle Grazie which stands on its central piazza. Built of a lovely, warm-coloured stone, the church has an outstanding portal which is decorated with rich carvings of biblical figures and scenes of the *Entombment*, dating from 1540.

A highly recommended excursion of 12km (7 miles) can be made from Anversa d'Abruzzo, up the Sagittario gorge, by following signs from the southern end of the village to Scanno. The road passes through a rock-hewn tunnel and then squeezes between steep rocks below Castrovalva. It is a very scenic drive, albeit on a narrow and winding road, up through the gorge. Two lakes are passed on the way: the first is Lago di San Domenico, a narrow stretch of water, where there is a small hermitage to St Domenic and a picnic and bathing area; the second is the much larger, Lago di Scanno, where there are facilities for boating as well as campsites along its shore.

On a spur, a short distance beyond Lago di Scanno, is the charming town of **Scanno** itself. There are parking spaces at the edge of the village, along Via Napoli, next to the church of Santa Maria della Valle. This attractive church, stands on the site of an ancient pagan temple. Its façade was added during the Renaissance period, while the ornate interior was refurbished in the eighteenth century following damage caused by the earthquakes of 1703 and 1706 respectively.

The steep and narrow streets that extend behind the church have all the character of an Italian medieval hill village, yet the inhabitants of Scanno are thought to be descended from a nomadic tribe that emigrated from the Red Sea or Serbia. Their eastern legacy is most apparent in the traditional costume that is still worn by many of the women, with its characteristic head-dress, known as the *cappellitto*, which is shaped like a fez and is ornamented with silver for spinsters, gold for married women and black for widows. Unless it is a Sunday or a festival, however, a comparatively moderate black headscarf is worn with a long, black, tightly-pleated, skirt under a black apron.

To visit the old centre of the village, head east of Santa Maria della Valle, along Via Abrami, past the eighteenth-century church of

Purgatorio, on the left. The small square opposite the church, on the right, holds the Fontana Sarracco, a fountain, which dates from the sixteenth century and is decorated with a bas-relief of the *Annunciation* (1732). Continue past the fountain along Strada Giuseppe Tanturri, which is the main shopping street. There are numerous shops along here selling local food products, as well as crafts such as lace, and souvenirs including the local costumes. Scanno's most unique handiwork, however, is its jewellery. Silver and gold are twisted into delicate filigree earrings and ornaments.

Strada Giuseppe Tanturri ends at the seventeenth-century church of San Rocca which lies above a small square. On the left of the square is the sixteenth-century Casa Mosca which is ornamented with carved putti. A short distance to its north is the simple fifteenth-century church, Santa Maria di Constantinopoli.

From Scanno visitors should return to Anversa d'Abruzzo, and follow the SS479 to Sulmona which is the starting point of Route 4a.

Additional Information

Places to Visit

Benevento
Museo del Sannio
Piazza Matteoti
Open: Monday to Saturday 9am-1pm.

Teatro Romano
Via Carlo Torre
Open: daily 9am to sunset.

Civitella Alfedena
Centro di Visita e Museo del Lupo Appenninico
Via Santa Lucia
☎ (0864) 89170

Isernia
Museo Civico
Corso Marcelli
☎ (0865) 415179
Open: Tuesday to Sunday 9am-1pm, 3-7pm.

Pescasseroli
Centro di Vista
Viale Santa Luccia

☎ (0863) 910715
Open: daily 10am-12noon, 3-6pm.

Nature Museum
Viale Santa Lucia
☎ (0863) 910405
Open: daily 10am-12noon, 3-6pm

Useful Information

Benevento
Tourist Information Centres
Ente Provinciale per il Turismo
Via Nicola Sala 31
Parco de Santis
☎ (0824) 21960

Ufficio Informazioni
Via Giustiniani 34
☎ (0824) 25424

Transport
Ferrovie dello Stato (Railway)
☎ (0824) 21015

Emergencies
Carabinieri (Military Police)
☎ (0824) 51088/51852

Pronto Soccorso (First Aid Service)
☎ (0824) 71257

Automobile Club d'Italia
Via S. Rosa 24-26
☎ (0824) 21582

Civitella Alfedena
Events and Festivals
2nd Sunday of July, Festa di Santa
Lucia (festival of local patron saint
celebrated with a procession,
games, concert and fireworks).
2nd Sunday of August, Sagra della
Scurpella (Festival of Scurpella), a
local, deep-fried sweet).

Isernia
Events and Festivals
27-29 June, San Pietro delle Cipolle
(Onion Fair)

Tourist Information Centres
Ente Provinciale per il Turismo
Via Farinacci 9
☎ (0865) 3992

Transport
Ferrovia (Railway)
☎ (0865) 50921

Emergencies
Vigili Urbani (Town Police)
☎ (0865) 50044

Polizia Stradale (Traffic Police)
☎ (0865) 412222/413333

Automobile Club d'Italia
Via Kennedy 5
☎ (0865) 50732

Pescasseroli
Tourist Information Centres
Ente Autonomo Parco Nazionale
d'Abruzzo
Viale Sant Lucia
☎ (0863) 910715

Parco Nazionale d'Abruzzo
Ufficio di Zona
Via Consultore 1
☎ (0863) 91955

Emergencies
Carabinieri
☎ (0863) 910716

Scanno
Events and Festivals
13 June, Processione delle Travi (A
procession of children carrying
baskets of bread and flowers, and
oxen pulling cartloads of wood,
which is traditionally donated to
the convent of Sant'Antonio, who
distribute it to those in need during
the winter).
14 August, Il Catenaccio (Re-
enactment of traditional medieval
wedding and folklore display).
11 November, Glorie di San
Martino (Stacks of wood, 15-20m.
50-65ft high, are set alight on the
hilltops surrounding Scanno in
celebration of the patron saint, San
Martino).

Tourist Information Centre
Azienda Autonoma Soggiorno e
   Turismo
Piazza Santa Maria della Valle 12
☎ (0864) 74317

Emergencies
Carabinieri (Military Police)
Via D. Tanturri
☎ (0864) 74319

Pronto Soccorso (First Aid Service)
c/o Municipio
☎ (0864) 747290

Villetta Barrea
Tourist Information Centre
Ufficio Turistico sull'attraversamento
☎ (0864) 89141

4

UPPER CENTRAL APPENNINES

Chapter 4 follows on from chapter 3, through the remote, mountainous region of the Abruzzo, to Lazio, finally ending up in Rome. It takes in the Gran Sasso, the highest massif in the Appennines, and a rival in dramatic beauty to the Alps and Dolomites. The route also passes through the small, but affluent Abruzzo cities, Sulmona and L'Aquila, with their motley architecture and quaint traditions, as well as making excursions to Benedictine monasteries, Roman villas and the leisure gardens of Tivoli. Much of the travelling is on small country roads which wind up and down through the mountains, past remote hamlets and villages. The way of life in these isolated spots is very simple and tourists are few and far between.

Another of the many pleasures of the route, particularly travelling through the Abruzzo, is the region's cuisine. The shepherds in the Abruzzo mountains provide amongst the best *pecorino* (sheep's cheese) in Italy, known as *Pecorino Abruzzese*, which is often used locally instead of Parmesan. The various *caciotta* (cheeses made from ewes' milk) are also excellent. Lamb, mutton and kid feature widely in local dishes, and also a certain amount of pork, which is most commonly used to make sausages, *salami*, and coarse *prosciutto*. Along with pasta, these good and simple ingredients are the basis of the Abruzzo's hearty and flavoursome diet.

The individual character of the Abruzzo, as evidenced in its architecture, crafts and cuisine, is perhaps partly explained by its past; for the region's history is very much a result of its isolation and the harshness of its mountain terrain. Amongst the earliest inhabitants of these remote reaches were the war-like, Italic tribes: the Peligni, the Marsi and the Sabines, to name but a few. Under the threat of ancient Rome, these tribes grouped together to form the

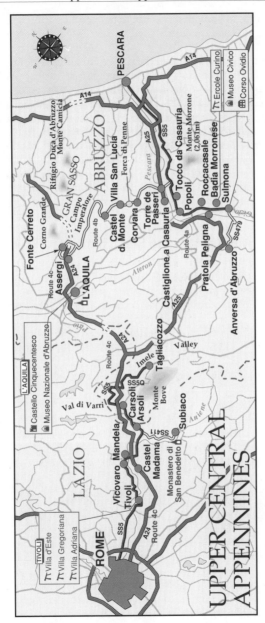

Italic League, a body that was not to be messed with. Their opposition to the Romans eventually led to their defeat in the Social War, between 91 and 82BC. The Abruzzo emerged once more as an independent province, under the rule of Frederick II Hohenstaufen, in the thirteenth-century, and throughout its history within the Kingdom of Sicily and Naples, from the fourteenth century up until Italian independence in 1860, the Abruzzo was the scene of numerous local protests and resistances. L'Aquila's Spanish castle was erected in defiance against a local uprising, to name but one example.

Chapter 4 starts at Sulmona, which is reached from Anversa d'Abruzzo, the last place mentioned in chapter 3, by following the SS479 for a distance of 15km (9 miles). The last section of the route, 4C, follows the A24 motorway from L'Aquila to Rome, with a number of recommended excursions from which the visitor can choose.

Route 4A • Sulmona to San Clemente a Casauria

The elegant city of **Sulmona**, lies in a fertile valley, between two rivers, the Gizio and the Vetta, and is encircled by mountain peaks which are snow-capped most of the year round. The road from Anversa d'Abruzzo approaches the town across the valley floor and crosses the Gizio river at Sulmona's outskirts, after which visitors should fork left. Continue to the northern end of the town, to the Villa Comunale gardens, where there is usually no difficulty in finding a parking space. The gardens stand in front of the town's cathedral, Duomo San Panfilo, which is a good point from which to start a tour of Sulmona.

The *duomo* was built on the foundations of a Roman temple, dedicated to Vespa and Apollo, in the eleventh century. Over the subsequent years, the building has been overly renovated and restored, but the simple Romanesque façade, with its wide belfry incorporated into one end, still holds an elegant Gothic portal. The columns either side of the portal support decorative canopies holding statues, while the lancet arch above the door contains a fresco in its lunette. The only original feature of the interior are the fat columns dividing the central nave, and a Spanish crucifix in the third chapel of the right aisle. The cross, with its grotesque, sinuous figure of Jesus, dates from the thirteenth century and is carved from wood. The cathedral's other feature of interest is its eleventh-century crypt. Stairs lead down from the central nave, to a large vaulted chamber beneath the apse. The vaults of the chamber are supported by fine columns with Byzantine capitals, carved with flat, stylised plant motifs. Also dating from Byzantine times, is the charming bas-relief that rests against the back wall of the crypt. It depicts a quietly smiling *Madonna Enthroned* and dates from the twelfth century. Of the three, wide niches in the apse, the central one holds the episcopal throne, a stone-carved seat, simply decorated with cherubim, which also dates from the twelfth century.

From the *duomo* head south through the gardens and continue into the town centre, which is pedestrianised, following the main street, Corso Ovidio. The town's finest monument, the Annunziata, is 200m (218yd) along Corso Ovidio, on the right. The building is comprised of a palace, known as the Casa Santa, and a church, and was founded in 1320. The structure seen today, however, is a blend of both Gothic and Renaissance, as well as Baroque, architecture. The most obvious Baroque element is the church, which was entirely reconstructed in 1770 to a classic design by C. Fontana, Rome's leading Baroque architect. The palace is more diverse, dating from three different periods, with its major construction taking place in the years 1415, 1483 and 1522 respectively. The three construction phases are clearly exemplified in the façade by each of the portals and their corresponding windows. The portal, on the left, beneath the clock tower and belfry, is the oldest and is richly carved in the Gothic manner. The pointed lunette over the door holds a statue of the *Madonna and Child*, while directly above there is a statue of St Michael. The large, first floor window, to the right of the clock, with its geometric tracery and decorative figures, is also Gothic. The other two portals and their corresponding windows are, however, Renaissance. The larger and more impressive one, that in the centre, was added in 1483 and is typical of the Tuscan architectural style of the period. The entire façade is united by seven ornate pilasters which are topped by statues, depicting the Doctors of the Church, San Panfilo and the Apostles Peter and Paul. Inside the palace, steps lead up from the left side of an inner courtyard, to the Museo Civico. The museum, housed in five spacious rooms of the palace, contains medieval and Renaissance stone carvings, and art works from local churches. Amongst numerous fine religious statues and altarpieces, there is a lovely tabernacle, by the local artist, Giovanni da Sulmona, decorated with a scene of the *Annunciation*, which dates from 1435. The treasury collection is also of interest as many pieces are the work of Sulmonese silver and goldsmiths, who were well-reputed throughout Italy in the fourteenth and fifteenth centuries.

From Annunziata, continue south along Corso Ovidio into the main shopping area. There are many brightly-coloured shops here selling the famous Confetti di Sulmona. The Confetti are sugared almonds or chocolate, wrapped in coloured cellophane and twisted on wires into flower arrangements and other displays. The sugared almonds, the best of which claim to be *senza amido* (without starch) are also sold loose, along with nougat, chocolate and other sweets.

Piazza XX Settembre opens out on the right of Corso Ovidio, just 100m (110yd) south of Annunziata. At the centre of the piazza stands the bronze statue of Ovid, while from the back of the piazza there is a good view of Annunziata's elegant bell tower. Ovid was born in Sulmona in 43BC, and never forgot it. The poet was exiled to the Black Sea in AD8, from where he wrote: *Sulmo mihi patria est* — Sulmona is my country. His words are incorporated into the municipal coat of arms, and Tomi, his place of exile, is now Sulmona's twin town.

Corso Ovidio continues for a further 100m (110yd) to Piazza del Carmine where a Gothic aqueduct, dating from 1256, empties into the Fontana del Vecchio. The fountain was built in 1474 and is typically Renaissance with a single gargoyle spouting water into a simple, white-stone basin. Opposite the fountain, is the fine portal of San Francesco della Scarpa. It was built in the thirteenth century and is surrounded by a multitude of carved bands.

The aqueduct divides Piazza del Carmine from Piazza Garibaldi, a vast open square, where a lively market is held on Saturdays. The market sells everything from household goods, textiles and clothing to fresh fruit and vegetables. It is also a good place from which to buy the local *pecorino* sheep's cheeses that are made in the surrounding mountains. The square is also the venue for a festival which is held on Easter Sunday, and which celebrates the Madonna che Scappa. The festival culminates in a parade on the piazza which follows an effigy of the Madonna, draped in green robes.

Continue straight across Piazza del Carmine, with the aqueduct to the left, and turn right onto Piazza del Plebiscito which holds the church of Santa Maria della Tomba. The church has a fourteenth-century façade, reminiscent in some respects to that of the *duomo*, with its discreet belfry built on one end. The belfry is topped by short, Doric columns, and above the portal there is a fine rose window. The simple, Gothic interior has a few remnants of fifteenth-century frescoes on its walls and a thirteenth-century carved relief of *Adam and Eve* in the presbytery.

Corso Ovidio continues south of Piazza del Carmine to the attractive town gate, Porta Napoli. The gate was constructed in 1315 and has an unusual rusticated façade decorated with small rosettes.

Leave Sulmona by following the road behind the *duomo* and turning right onto via Pescara. The road leads out through the town's suburbs and eventually joins the SS17. Just outside the town, 5½km (3 miles) north of the SS17, is **Badia Morronese**. Located at the foot of

Monte Morrone (2,061m/6,760ft), Badia Morronese was founded in the thirteenth century and was the first seat of the Celestine Order. The Celestine abbey, Santo Spirito, is now a prison, but the site of the hermitage where the Order's founder, Pietro Angeleri, lived, remains isolated, high on a crag above. In 1294, Pietro Angeleri against his better judgement, was removed from his hermitage to take the throne at L'Aquila as Pope Celestine V, a job that he did badly and endured for no more than five months. The road up to the hermitage, Sant'Onofro, leads up past the prison, and ends at a parking area, from where visitors must proceed steeply on foot. The eighteenth-century church, built on the site of the hermitage, contains the original thirteenth-century chapel, complete with its frescoes.

The ruins of an ancient sanctuary, Ercole Curino, can also be reached on foot from the parking area. The footpath zig-zags down, past a belvedere overlooking the ruins and Santo Spirito in the plain below, to a wide terrace where the ancient remains are scattered. For many years the site was believed to have been Ovid's villa and women came here in the superstitious belief that it would cure infertility. However, archaeologists have since proved that the ruins

San Clemente a Casauria, one of Abruzzo's finest monuments

are of a temple, dedicated to Hercules, which dates from the first century BC. Eleven steps lead up to the stylobate, on which the temple once stood. In place of the cella, the inner sanctuary, a hut has been built to protect the geometrically patterned mosaic floor, which is coloured in red, black and white, and has dolphins decorating its border. A sacrificial altar and a fountain can be seen on the lower platform, and large sections of supportive walls, made from polygonal stone, are also in evidence.

Return to the SS17 and head north along the Peligno valley, where white grapes are cultivated to make the local wine, Peligno Bianco, past the attractive town of **Pratola Peligna** and the village of **Roccacasale** which is overlooked by the steeply-stacked ruins of a castle. A short distance further, the road joins the SS5 which is followed to **Popoli**. This small town, guarding the northern end of the Peligno valley, has the ruins of a medieval castle on the hill above, and a pleasant old centre. The church of San Francesco, on the central piazza, has a flight of steps leading up to its fine Romanesque portal. The lower walls of its façade, which are ornamented with statues of Franciscan monks, date from the fifteenth century. The upper façade has an unusual rose window with four distinctive lobes, and was added later in the seventeenth century. Also of interest in Popoli is the Palazzo Ducale on Via G.B. Capponi. It was built in the fourteenth century and has a Gothic façade decorated with coats of arms and mullioned windows.

The route continues north-east of Popoli, either on the A25 *autostrada* or on the SS5 which runs parallel with the right side of the motorway. Eight kilometres (5 miles) on the right, down a rocky valley, is the village of **Tocco da Casauria**, with its turreted castle. The road continues on through **Castiglione a Casauria** to the beautiful church of San Clemente a Casauria which is positioned on a big bend, enclosed by a high wall, at the northern edge of the village.

Rated amongst the Abruzzo's finest monuments, **San Clemente a Casauria** was founded as an abbey in AD871. It was rebuilt in the twelfth century under the Norman rulers of Southern Italy, who favoured the principles of French medieval architecture. The façade of the church is preceded by a gracious portico, comprised of three broad arches of light, clean stone. The arches spring from square pillars which have columns on each of their four sides. The columns are topped by exquisite capitals, deeply-carved with intricate foliage and stylised figures. Corbels decorate the upper edge of the portico, while the fenestrated façade above was added in 1448. Beneath the cross-vaults of the portico three portals pierce the church façade. The central portal has a pair of magnificent bronze doors, with seventy-two decorated panels, dating from 1191, some of which are replaced by wooden panels. Figures flank either side of the portal, and the lunette above holds a richly-carved relief.

The interior has a latin cross ground plan and is divided by pillars into three aisles, with the shallow steps of the presbytery preceding a distinctively rounded, Romanesque apse. In the central aisle, on the right, there stands a magnificent ambo, with four columns supporting a rectangular pulpit, dating from 1180. The foliate carvings on each of its four sides stand out in high relief, while the lectern rests above an eagle and a crouching lion. Opposite the ambo, on the left side of the central aisle, is a paschal candlestick. It stands over 5m (16ft) high and has six twisted columns around the top, with decorated panels of mosaic. In the main apse, the high altar has a paleo-Christian sarcophagus beneath the pyramidal canopy of a ciborium. The ciborium is also richly decorated with carvings. At either side of the presbytery, steps lead down to the crypt which dates from the original church of AD871. The low, cross-vaulted ceiling is supported on a mixed assortment of ancient column fragments. The columns originate from the Roman city that stood on the site of the present day village, *Castrum ad Pischaria*. Other fragments of Roman masonry are dotted about the luxuriant gardens surrounding the church, along with the medieval remains of the monastery buildings that once stood to the right of the church.

Route 4B • San Clemente a Casauria to L'Aquila

From San Clemente a Casauria, Route 4B heads a short way back along the SS5 towards Tocco da Casauria, before turning right onto a small road which leads past the railway station. Pass the station and cross over both the River Pescara and the railway, then turn left and cross over the motorway. The narrow road winds up above the motorway with good views across the valley to the large church and fortifications of Tocco da Casauria. Ahead, high on a ridge lies **Torre de Passeri** with the fine Palazzo Mazzara on its central square. The route heads around the edge of the village onto a small road signposted to Corvara. Continuing up, the road winds along in the lee of a high rocky spur, atop which is the crumbling, stone hamlet of **Pescosansonesco Vecchio** and the shattered ruins of its castle. The road passes through **Pecosansonesco Nuovo**, which lies at the foot of the crag, and then winds on to **Corvara**. This small village with its neat bell tower, is straggled along a precipitous crag, high to the left of the road and commands a fine panorama. Take the left fork, after Corvara, which leads across a high plateau before the road begins to climb. The views are extensive and impressive, especially as the road reaches the Forca di Penne (918m/3,011ft) pass, where there is a ruined tower.

The pass is at the south-eastern most point of the Gran Sasso. This magnificent group of mountains is some 35km (22 miles) long and is the highest massif in the Appennines. The tallest peak, Corno Grande, in the centre of the group rises to a height of 2,912m (9,551ft) and shelters the Appennines' only glacier, the Calderone glacier, which is incidentally the most southerly one in Europe. Hikers are recommended to buy the 1:25,000 scale map, produced by Club Alpino Italiano (Sezione dell'Aquila), Gran Sasso d'Italia, which shows footpaths and refuges as well as a good amount of detail. However, note that the peaks are only snow free from July to September. During the winter there is plenty of scope for skiing, particularly cross-country skiing *(sci di fondo)*, there being some

Gran Sasso, the highest mountain range in the Appennines

20km (12 miles) of high plateau.

From Forca di Penne, the road winds down, with the vast plain, Il Piano, where saffron is cultivated, far below to the left. Known as *zafferano* in Italian, the plant is said to have been first brought here from Spain, by a local priest who was sent away during the Spanish Inquisition. The cultivation of saffron is very labour intensive. The plants lie low to the ground and the flowers, hundreds of which are needed to make even a gram, must be picked before dawn.

After 6½km (4 miles) take the right fork and follow the SS17bis uphill, through the picturesque village of **Villa San Lucia**, following signs to Castel del Monte. The drive to Castel del Monte is the longest and steepest on the route. It climbs, from an altitude of 850m (2,788ft) at Villa San Lucia, gradually up for 14km (9 miles), to **Castel del Monte**, which lies on a bare, rocky mountain top at a height of 1,310m (4,297ft). Castel del Monte has charming, narrow streets and an attractive church with a large belfry, dating from 1346, and during the winter it is centre for *sci di fondo*.

Continue through Castel del Monte and take the right fork. The SS17bis proceeds upwards with an ever-broadening panorama spread below. Eventually, after reaching the summit of Valico di Capa La Serra, at a height of 1,600m (5,248ft), the road starts its descent to **Campo Imperatore**. The *campo* is a huge, grassy plateau, 27km (17 miles) long, at an altitude of 1,800m (5,904ft). Along its north side there rises a stupendous wall of limestone peaks, comprising the main core of the Gran Sasso. The plateau is summer pasture for countless sheep, which provide the Abruzzo with some fine cheeses, including *pecorino* and *ricotta* which is made from the whey. In the summer, fresh lamb is served at the simple, roadside barbecue restaurants which are dotted across the campo, each with its own butcher's (*macelleria*) alongside.

The SS17bis heads west across the plateau, from the foot of Monte Camicia (1,632m/5,353ft) to the hills below Corno Grande. Those who wish to ascend Corno Grande can drive to the foot of it by following the 10km (6 miles) road which turns off right from the SS17bis at the western end of Campo Imperatore. The road, which is to be highly recommended for its excellent scenery, terminates at Rifugio Duca d'Abruzzo (2,388m/7,833ft). From here, those with hiking boots can embark on the fairly demanding trek, which involves scrambling up scree in some parts, to the summit. The view is well worth the effort. On an exceptionally clear day, both of Italy's coasts can be seen. Normally, however, as long as the sky is fairly clear, it is possible to see the Adriatic with the Gargano peninsula jutting out into it, with the Tremiti islands just offshore, and of course all the surrounding mountains of the Gran Sasso. A less demanding hike from Rifugio Duca d'Abruzzo can be made to Rifugio Garibaldi (2,230m/7,314ft). The hut is positioned on a ridge, south-west of Corno Grande, and offers a good view of Corno Grande itself. A half-hour's walk south of Rifugio Duca d'Abruzzo takes the visitor to the Albergo di Campo Imperatore, where Mussolini was held captive in 1943. He remained here for less than three months, before being airlifted to safety by the German air-force. The Albergo's interior is closed for restoration, but nearby is the small church of Madonna della Neve, the highest altitude church in Europe, and an observatory, adjoined to which is a botanical garden with more than four-hundred species of Appennine flora.

The SS17bis continues along the foot of Monte Cristo (1,930m/6,330ft), before gradually winding down to **Assergi**. This small village lies on the edge of the Gran Sasso massif, above a wide river valley. On a rocky lump, overlooking the river, is the church of Santa Maria Assunta which dates from the twelfth century. The village, however, is mainly passed by, by skiers and hikers on their way to **Fonte Cerreto** (4km/2 miles north-west), from where a *funivia* (cable railway) ascends the Gran Sasso. The Funivia del Gran Sasso makes the dramatic ascent from an altitude of 1,007m (3,303ft) at the Fonte Cerreto station, to the Albergo di Campo Imperatore which is at a height of 2,112m (6,927ft). The distance from station to station is 3km (2 miles) and the journey takes no more than a few minutes, however the cable car is only in operation during the winter skiing season.

The route continues to L'Aquila, the capital of Abruzzo, on the A24 motorway which heads south, crossing high above the hills on a series of high viaducts. Leave the motorway at the **L'Aquila Est** junction and follow the road from here down into the broad valley basin that surrounds the city. The road leads through **L'Aquila's** outskirts to the castle which lies in the north-west corner of the city walls. It is best to look for a parking space around the castle; otherwise it is necessary to drive into the centre, where the streets are narrow, and try to park on one of the small piazzas.

The castle, which is a good starting point for a tour of the city, was built in 1534 under the Spanish Viceroy, Don Pedro of Toledo. It stands at the centre of a busy public gardens and is excellently-preserved. It is well defended: the stark walls, 10m (33ft) thick in places, have sturdy bastions and are surrounded by a vast, dry moat, 23m (75ft) wide and 14m (46ft) deep. The only bridge across the moat is on the south-east side where there is an ornate portal, which is decorated with the arms of Charles V. The portal gives access to the Museo Nazionale d'Abruzzo, housed in the extensive buildings that surround the castle's inner courtyard. The museum has both a pre-historic and archaeological section, as well as an excellent collection of sacred art, mainly by artists of the Abruzzo School. One of the most impressive exhibits on the ground floor, housed in the castle's east bastion, is the massive skeleton of an elephant, which was found just outside the city and is believed to date from more than one-and-a-half million years ago. The collection of sacred art, on the first floor, includes: an important group of polychrome, terracotta and wooden statues, dating from the thirteenth to seventeenth centuries, by local artists; a notable, fifteenth-century polyptych depicting the *Stigmata of St Francis* and the *Life of John of Capestran*; as well as a number of detached frescoes, paintings and crucifixes, among the latter is a fine processional cross by Nicola da Guardiagrele, dating from 1434.

Head south of the castle, along Via Sinzio, which heads towards the *campanile* of San Bernardino, one of L'Aquila's grandest churches. It was constructed between 1454 and 1472 to house the mortal remains of the Franciscan preacher, San Bernardino da Siena. Its tall façade, added in 1527, to a design by the Renaissance architect, Cola dell'Amatrice, has three storeys of twinned columns. It is preceded by a monumental staircase, the Scalinata San Bernardino, which affords a magnificent vista of the distant, often snow-capped mountains. The main portal, at the top of the steps, has a carved relief in its lunette by the local sculptor, Silvestro d'Aquila, who trained under the Florentine master, Donatello. The interior was recon-structed in the Baroque style, after a terrible earthquake in 1703, which brought down much of L'Aquila. The central nave is covered by a highly decorative, gilt ceiling, which holds paintings by the Neapolitan, G. Cenatempo, dating from 1720, and has the mono-gram of San Bernardino at its centre. In the second chapel in the right aisle there is a large, enamelled terracotta altar piece by A. della Robbia which depicts the *Resurrection* in the lower part and the *Coronation of the Virgin* above. The third chapel in the right aisle holds a venerated statue of the *Madonna* by Silvestro d'Aquila. The same sculptor made the mausoleum of San Bernardino, which contains the saint's glass coffin, in the fifth chapel in the right aisle. It dates from 1505. The finely-carved, eighteenth-century choir stalls which line the deep apse behind the main altar are also noteworthy.

From San Bernardino, head west along Via di San Bernardino to the crossroads, Quattro Cantoni. Turn left at the crossroads and follow the attractively arcaded, shopping street, Corso Vittorio Emanuele, to Piazza del Duomo. This spacious piazza holds a centuries-old, large and busy market every morning until 1pm. Many of the stalls sell local Abruzzo crafts, including copper, lace, ceramics and textiles, as well as culinary objects such as pasta cutters. The local pasta, *maccheroni alla chitarra*, is cut by a novel device which takes its name from the strings that are stretched across it, like those of a guitar. Towards lunchtime, long queues form at the delicatessen vans which serve crusty rolls, *panini*, filled with *porchetta*. The *porchetta* is a whole suckling pig, stuffed with wild fennel and garlic, that has been slowly roasted. It is served warm and sold by the *etto* (100g/3oz), as well as in rolls. Another speciality of L'Aquila, but only to be found in restaurants, is *stracci*, a mixture of meat, vegetables, cheese and bechamel sauce, baked in the oven. Those with a sweet tooth will also find L'Aquila's nougat, *torrone*, which is soft and chocolate-covered, quite irresistible.

Piazza del Duomo was built in 1257, but most of the buildings surrounding it were destroyed in the earthquake of 1703. The cathedral, San Massimo, which lies at the western end of the piazza has a rather unremarkable, neo-Classical façade dating from the nineteenth century. The church façade of Suffragio on the south side of the piazza is more interesting. It dates from the eighteenth century and was designed by Carlo Buratti, who was the pupil of Rome's influential Baroque architect, Carlo Fontana.

L'Aquila's remaining two monuments lie in the city's outskirts, one near the west walls, the other near the east. It is easiest, therefore, to visit these sites by car. Santa Maria Collemaggio, the more important of the two, lies 400m (437yd) east of the city walls, on the road to Popoli. It was founded in 1287 and shortly afterwards witnessed the crowning of the Celestine monk, San Pietro Morrone, who became Pope Celestine V here in 1294. The wide façade of the church, clad in pink and white diaper stone work, is pierced by three portals, each with a beautiful, Gothic rose window above. The central portal, which was added in the fifteenth century, has rows of small niches at either side, a few of which still hold their original statues. The rose window above the central portal is the largest and most elaborate. It is placed in the upper wall of the façade which is divided from the lower by a sculpted frieze. This, and another characteristic of the façade, the flat roof, were the prototype features from which the Abruzzo church style subsequently evolved.

The interior has been excellently restored, and is complete with the attractive pink and white stone floors that were laid in the fourteenth century. Octagonal stone columns, supporting lancet arches, divide the church into three aisles. The central aisle is the widest and is covered by a very high, timbered ceiling. The right aisle has a series of point-arched niches set in its wall some of which hold fifteenth-century frescoes. The first niche has a lovely fresco of the *Madonna di*

Loreto with *Sant'Agnese and Sant'Apollonia*. The second has the *Dormitis Virgini* and *Coronatio*, while the third holds a *Crucifixion*. The left aisle also contains a niche with a fresco, depicting the *Madonna and Child* and thought to date from the early sixteenth century. By contrast to the simplicity of the main body of the church, the transepts and dome are decorated in a Baroque style. There is a Baroque altar at either end of the transepts, the right hand one supporting a sixteenth-century, terracotta statue of the *Madonna and Child*. To the right of the main altar are the remains of San Pietro Celestine in a glass coffin, within the Renaissance-Lombard mausoleum designed by Girolana da Vicenza in 1517. The festival in honour of San Pietro Celestine, Perdonanza Celestiniana, which takes place from the twenty-third to the twenty-ninth of August, culminates in a procession, on the evening of the twenty-eighth, to Santa Maria Collemaggio. The congregation is admitted through the Porta Santa, the holy door, on the left side of the church, and blessed and pardoned for all sins, according to a decree granted by Celestine at his coronation on the twenty-ninth of August, 1294.

To reach L'Aquila's final monument, from Santa a Maria Colle-

The tiled façade of Santa Maria Collemaggio , L'Aquila

maggio, head due west along Viale di Collemaggio. At the end of the road, turn right and follow Via XX Settembre to the western side of the town. From here, take the small road left, which winds down the hill to the city's south-western walls, just inside of which is the Fontana delle 99 Cannelle. This unusual fountain, set on the left side of a small piazza, has low rectangular basins on two levels, surrounding three sides of a paved courtyard. Water spouts from ninety-nine, carved heads, representing animals such as horses and lions, as well as portraits of monks and women, arranged in a neat line above the upper basin. Legend recounts that the ninety-nine spouts allude to the ninety-nine communities that were grouped together under Frederick II, in 1240, to found L'Aquila, a city thereby large enough to defend itself against the Pope. Indeed, ninety-nine is a number that appears in various forms in L'Aquila, there being ninety-nine churches, ninety-nine streets and even a bell on Piazza Palazzo that strikes ninety-nine times at dusk each day. According to the inscription, the fountain was started in 1272 by Tancredi of Pentina. The south side, however, on the right, was added during the Renaissance, in 1582. The inscription also bears the date of the fountain's restoration in 1744.

Leave L'Aquila by continuing beyond the fountain, passing through Porta Riviera, the city's south-west gate. Turn right, and proceed along the city walls on Via Santa Maria della Ponte, passing the railway station to the left. From the station, head north, continuing along the walls, on Viale della Stazione. Turn left at the end of the road and follow signs along the SS17 to the A24 *autostrada*.

Route 4C • L'Aquila to Rome

Route 4C leaves L'Aquila on the A24 motorway, in the direction of Rome. There are good views as the road climbs between thickly-forested hills, to the Raio river valley. The road continues to climb to Valico di San Rocco (1,100m/3,608ft) from where a tunnel, 4km (2 miles) long, pierces the high range of mountains that divide Abruzzo from Lazio. At the other end of the tunnel, the road gradually descends the mountains' south face and passes through further tunnels before reaching the Val di Varri flood plain. From here, those with time may wish to make the excursion to **Tagliacozzo**.

To reach this charming, medieval town, leave the motorway at the Tagliacozzo junction, and follow the SS5quater for 15km (9 miles). The town lies on a spur above the Imele Valley, on the rocky foothills of Monte Bove, at an altitude of 730m (2,394ft). The central square, Piazza del'Obelisco, is surrounded by fourteenth- and fifteenth-century houses, and has, as its name suggests, an obelisk at its centre which is surmounted on a fountain. Situated at the top end of the town is the imposing Palazzo Ducale. It was first built by the powerful Orsini family in the fourteenth century, and later enlarged by the Colonna, a noble, Roman family. There is a Gothic loggia at the right end of the façade, which is decorated with fifteenth-century frescoes by Lorenzo da Viterbo. The church of San Francesco, also at the top end of the town, is notable for the Gothic rose window in its façade, and its simple adjoining cloisters which hold remnants of frescoes and a Renaissance well.

The route continues to follow the A24 motorway, through a hilly landscape which is sprinkled with hilltop villages. One such village, **Carsoli**, to the left of the road is crowned by the remnants of its overgrown castle. Just past Carsoli an excursion can be made to the earliest centre of Western monasticism, Subiaco. To make this excursion take the Carsoli-Oricola junction and follow the SS5 south for 9km (5 miles) to the small hill-town of **Arsoli**, which lies just inside the region of Lazio. It has a well preserved, sixteenth-century castle, Castello Massimo, which contains frescoes by the Zuccari brothers. Continue through the town and head down hill for 2km (1 mile), before turning left onto the SS411. The road follows the Antiene river valley, for a further 16km (10 miles) to **Subiaco**.

This small, medieval town is ensconsed by steep, wooded hills and surrounded by a wall. At its western edge stands the fourteenth-century church of San Francesco, which has an impressive triptych by A. Romano, dating from 1467. There are also frescoes, in the third chapel on the left, which are attributed to the Sienese painter, Sodoma (1477-1549). The town's cathedral, dedicated to St Andrew was erected in 1766 and is of little interest, although the surrounding streets are pleasant to wander through.

The main purpose of the excursion to Subiaco, however, is to see the laura, or hermitage, where St Benedict lived. St Benedict was born in the Umbrian town of Norcia, in AD480, of a pious family. He was sent as a young boy to be educated in Rome, but at the surprisingly young age of fourteen, he rejected his way of life in Rome and retired in solitude, to the cave, above Subiaco. After three years the monks of the nearby monastery at Vicovaro, elected him as their abbot, but soon regretted it. The severity of the reforms he imposed on them led to their rebellion and their attempted poisoning of him. Legend recounts that the chalice which contained the poison, shattered when St Benedict made the sign of the cross over it. After this the saint had the sense to return to his cave, taking an entourage of disciples along with him.

Over the thirty-five years that St Benedict spent at Subiaco, he fastidiously worked to create the Rule of Benedict. It defined how one should live, and encompassed every aspect of monastic life, from the hours and times of prayer, to the admission procedure and disciplinary measures (which included corporal punishment), as well as setting out the basic vows of poverty, chastity and obedience. He emphasised too the importance of denying privacy, possessions and leisure. By the eighth century, the Rule of Benedict was followed by most monks in the West, while his basic philosophy, *Ora et Labora* (*Prayer and Work*) has been the foundation of Western monasticism.

St Benedict left Subiaco altogether after a local priest filled with rancour, sent a troop of prostitutes up to the hermit's lair. Benedict and his disciples withdrew to an even more remote and inaccessible spot, away from such trials, and founded the monastery of Montecassino, in AD529. He left behind him at Subiaco some thirteen monasteries, only one of which remains today. Called the Monastero di Santa Scolastica, after the saint's twin-sister, it lies 3km (2 miles) to the east of Subiaco. From the town, follow signs to *monastero* along the road to Valle Pietra. Just before the bridge of San Mauro, turn left and follow the steep gorge of the Antiene river up to the monastery walls.

Most of the complex dates from the period when the monastery was at its cultural and artistic zenith, between the eleventh and thirteenth centuries. Construction was continued, however, during the Renaissance, when the monastery had in 1464 Italy's first printing press. The monastery is neatly grouped around a large *campanile*, which has five layers of mullioned openings, and dates from 1052. The monastery building surrounds three cloisters, the first of which is the most recent, and was built in 1580. The second cloister is Gothic and contains architectural fragments of a Roman villa which was built for the emperor Nero, in the first century, on a site just below the monastery. The villa was said to rival Hadrian's at Tivoli in the magnificence of its water gardens, which were created by damming the River Antiene. The third cloister of the monastery, the oldest, dates from the thirteenth century and has beautiful, Cosmatesque decoration. The church also dates from the thirteenth century, although the interior is neo-Classical from the eighteenth century.

The road continues to wind steeply up the valley gorge for a further 2km (1 mile) beyond Monastero di Santa Scolastica, to St Benedict's lair, Sacro Speco, the Holy Cave. The Monastero di San Benedetto, clinging precariously to a vertical cliff, grew up around the hermit's cave, in the thirteenth and fourteenth centuries. A tree-lined path leads up from the carpark to the monastery entrance. The corridor that leads from the entrance to the church is covered in frescoes by the Umbrian school, dating from the fifteenth century. The church, erected in the mid-fourteenth century, also contains a wealth of frescoes. In the first chapel, where there is a thirteenth-century, marble pulpit, there are frescoes by the Sienese school dating from the thirteenth and fourteenth centuries. The second and third chapels are decorated by artists of the Umbrian-Marche school and date from 1430. Steps lead down from the altar to the lower church which was originally built over the hermit's cave. The fresco cycle, depicting the *Life of St Benedict*, which covers the walls, is the work of a Roman painter, Maestro Consolo, and is dated 1280. The chapel, Cappella San Giorgio, also contains frescoes, including a portrait of St Francis, which dates from 1223 and is said to be the earliest picture of the saint. Sacro Speco, is entered from the foot of the stairs and contains a statue of St Benedict, dating from 1657, by A. Raggi, who was a pupil of the Baroque polymath, Bernini.

Route 4C continues along the A24 motorway, passing several, lovely, hilltop villages, such as **Mandela**, before reaching **Vicovaro**. The latter is a short and easy diversion, being just 3km (2 miles) from the Vicovaro-Mandela junction. This attractive town, founded as *Varia* by an Italic tribe, the Aequi, still has remnants of its ancient cyclopean walls around it. Its centre, however, is distinctly medieval, and dates from 1191, when it passed into the hands of the Orsini family. The church of San Giacomo, built in 1454, stands on an octagonal ground plan and bears the Orsini coat of arms in the tympanum above the main portal. The site of the Orsini palace is now taken by the eighteenth-century Palazzo Cenci-Bolgnetti, although two towers and parts of the walls of the older building still remain.

After the Vicovaro-Mandela junction, the A24 proceeds towards the Vicovaro tunnel. Just before entering the tunnel, on a hill to the left is the large Benedictine monastery of San Cosimato, the site of a large villa in Roman times. The rock on which it stands is riddled with hermits' caves. After the tunnel, Vicovaro is glimpsed through the trees to the right, as the road continues south, past Castel Madama. Visitors should leave the motorway at the Castel Madama junction and follow the SS5 to **Tivoli.**

Known in Roman times as *Tibur*, modern day Tivoli has considerable traffic congestion. It has been a popular, even fashionable, place to live since 340BC, when the Romans, attracted by the natural waterfalls on the Antiene river and its relatively cool summer climate, started to build the villas and gardens for which Tivoli is famous today.

Due to its popularity as a resort, there are several carparks dotted around the town, most are fee-paying. The area around the castle, at the southern side of the town, is the best place to head for, as there are three fairly large carparks there. The castle is also a useful reference point for finding one's way about the town. Known as Rocca Pia, the castle was built on the site of a Roman amphitheatre in the fifteenth century, under Pope Pio II, and, with its four crenellated towers still intact, is fairly well preserved.

One of Tivoli's main attractions, Villa d'Este, lies 350m (383yd) to the north-west of the castle. Its entrance is on Piazza Trento, in the corner of the square, to the right of the sixteenth-century church of Santa Maria Maggiore. The villa was built in 1550 for Cardinal Ippolito II d'Este on the site of a former Benedictine monastery. From the main door, a series of rooms lead through to an inner courtyard. A door from the right side of the courtyard leads into a grand suite of apartments with frescoes by the Zuccari brothers, amongst others, decorating the ceilings and walls. The rooms look out over the villa's most outstanding feature, its beautiful gardens. Created in 1576, the gardens are centred around an extravagant cascade of water, which flows from one terrace to the next. At the bottom of the steps, which lead down from the villa into the gardens, is the first of the many fountains. Known as the Fontana del Biccierone, the fountain has a shell-shaped bowl and was probably built to a design by Bernini. The main pathway through the park, the Viale del 100 Fontane, leads off from here, passing the many statues and water spouts on the way. To the right of the pathway is Fontana dell'Ovato, a semi-circular fountain, and to the left the Rometta, a minute reproduction of antique Rome. The pathway continues down to the Fontana dei Draghi, to the right of which is the Fontana dell'Organo Idraulico. This ingenious fountain was designed by a Frenchman, C. Venard, to play music. The pathway ends at the Rotonda dei Cipressa, a gracious folly surrounded by cypress trees.

To reach Villa Gregoriana it is necessary to cross over to the other side of the town. This can be done by car or by a pleasant walk through the narrow, cobbled streets of the old centre. Take the alleyway, Via Edoardo Taner, from the west side of Piazza Trento. Then turn left and immediately right, heading uphill to Piazza Plebiscito, where there is a daily fruit and vegetable market. Pass through the piazza and follow the main pedestrian, shopping street, Via Palatina, from the north corner, for 100m (110yd). Pass straight through Piazza Palatina, onto Via Ponte Gregoriana and Piazza Rivarola, from where the bridge should be taken across the river. From the north side of the bridge, the Roman Temple of Vesta, with its circle of columns, can be seen perched high at the edge of a cliff above the water. The gardens of Villa Gregoriana, in which the temple stands are entered through the large gates, 150m (164yd) beyond the bridge, on the left.

Villa Gregoriana has no villa as such, but many fountains, follies and Roman ruins, set in a magnificent park that was created in 1835 for Pope Gregory XVI. The River Antiene flows through the centre of the park, while the excess flow was diverted, as a precaution against flooding, through two underground, rock tunnels to the east. A footpath leads the visitor up through the park to the Grande Cascata, where the water from the tunnels cascades over a 108m (354ft) drop, down into a shady pool below. Along the rocky river channel are a number of caves. One, into which the river flows is known as the Grotta della Sirene, another, from which it emerges, as the Grotta di Nettuno. The Temple of Vesta, at the west side of the park was built in the second century BC and has finely-carved Corinthian capitals, topping ten of the eighteen columns that originally stood here. The rectangular temple next to it, Tempio di Sibilla, dates from the same era and was used as a church up until medieval times.

From Piazza Rivarola, those with time may wish to make the pleasant stroll along Via San Valerio. The street leads from the north-west corner of the piazza to the *duomo*. Erected in the seventeenth century, the *duomo* stands on the foundations of an earlier Romanesque church, all that remains of which is the *campanile* with its pyramidal top and mullioned openings. The interior of the *duomo* dates from the eighteenth century and is uninspiring. However, in the last chapel on the right, there is an important wooden sculptural group, the *Deposition*, which was carved in the thirteenth century.

Via Colle, a picturesque street, lined with medieval houses, continues past the *duomo* to San Silvestro. Dating from the eleventh and twelfth centuries, this fine Romanesque church contains notable frescoes in its apse, from the same period. From here either head back to the town centre by following the steep steps and narrow alleys around the high walls of Villa d'Este, or return the same way.

Tivoli's most outstanding villa, the Roman Villa Adriana, lies outside the town, 6km (4 miles) to the south-west. To get there, continue towards Rome along the SS5, which winds downhill from Tivoli, through olive groves, to the industrial suburb of **Villa Adriana** in the plain below. Continue through the suburb, until the Pirelli tyre factory on the left. Take the first left turn after the factory, and follow its walls, before forking right. The road then continues for a further 1km (½ mile) through residential suburbs to the villa gates, where the modern developments are thankfully left behind.

From the ticket office at the gate, a driveway leads through the trees for 300m (328yd) to a carpark, from where visitors must

The ancient Temple of Vesta, in the idyllic park at Villa Gregoriana, Tivoli

proceed on foot. Before heading off to the ruins, , it is worth taking a look at the scale model of the villa which can be seen in the refreshments area on the south side of the carpark. The villa was built between AD118 and 130 for the Emperor Hadrian's retirement, on the site of an earlier villa dating from the first century BC. Hadrian ruled the Empire when it was still in its heyday and concerned himself mainly with uniting the far-reaching territories under a common yoke of law and administration. He achieved this by travelling throughout the Empire lands, mainly on foot, implementing the necessary reforms in person. In doing so, Hadrian, probably more than any other Roman emperor, spent a great deal of his reign, contemplating the cultures, architecture and natural phenomena of distant lands. At Villa Adriana, he tried to conglomerate his experiences by reproducing the most impressive of the sites he had seen.

The footpath leads from the refreshment area to a large, rectangular pool, the Pecile, which is surrounded by porticoes, similar to the Poikile of Hadrian's beloved Athens. In the north-east corner of the Pecile, is Villa dell'Isola, the most romantic of the site's ruins. Statues and colonnades encircle an island which is surrounded by a moat and holds the ruins of a small villa, thought possibly to have been baths. The footpath continues south, past the ruins of a Nymphaeum, to a large baths complex, comprised of the Piccole Terme with its small, elliptical bath, and Grande Terme, where there is a spacious sports area. Continuing along the footpath, beyond the baths is the Canopo, an artificial canal, which, originally lined with statues, represented the Egyptian town of Canope, and had a Temple of Serapim at the southern end. Make a circuit of the canal and return through the ruins of the Pretorio (behind Terme Grande). The Pretorio, originally three-storeys high, was used as a store-house. Follow the path northwards from here, around the back of the same Nymphaeum as passed earlier, and turn right to the ruins of Hadrian's palace, the Palazzo Imperiale, which are spread over an area of 50,000 hectares (12 acres). The palace complex includes the Piazza d'Oro, a finely porticoed square at the south-east extremity, and the library at the north-western end. The library, surrounding a courtyard, contains remnants of mosaics. From the north-east corner of the library courtyard, the footpath continues uphill to the Terrazza di Tempe. This forested terrace offers fine views across the ruins, and there are the ruins of a Nymphaeum next to the eighteenth-century Casino Fede. It is possible to continue still further from here to the remains of a theatre, the Teatro Greco.

Rome lies just over 20km (12 miles) west of Tivoli and is best reached by the A24 motorway, which avoids congestion in the suburbs.

Additional Information

Places to Visit

Badia Morronese
Ercole Curino (Archaeological Site)
Open: daily 9am-1pm, 3-8pm.

Castiglione a Casauria
San Clemente a Casauria
Open: daily 9am-3pm.

L'Aquila

Museo Nazionale d'Abruzzo
Castello Cinquecentesco
Open: daily 9am-2pm
☎ (0862) 64043

Subiaco
Monastero di Santa Scolastica
Open: winter, Monday to Saturday
9am-12noon, 3.30-6.30pm; Sunday
and holidays 8-9.45am, 11am-
12noon, 3.30-6.30pm. Summer,
Monday to Saturday 9am-12noon,
4-7pm; Sunday and holidays 8-
9.45am, 11am-12noon, 4-7pm.

Monastero di San Benedetto
Open: winter, daily 9am-12noon, 3-
5.30pm. Summer, daily 9am-
12noon, 3-6.30pm.

Sulmona
Museo Civico
Annunziata
Corso Ovidio
☎ (0864) 210216
Open: Tuesday to Saturday
8.30am-12.30pm. Sunday and
holidays 9am-12noon.

Tivoli
Villa d'Este
Piazza Trento
☎ (0774) 22070
Open: daily except Monday 9am-
6.40pm.

Villa Gregoriana
Via Quintilio Varo
Open: October to March daily
9.30am-4.30pm. April to May daily
9.30am-6pm. June to August daily
10am-7.30pm. September 9.30am-
6.30pm.

Villa Adriana
☎ (0774) 530203
Open: daily except Monday 9am-1
hour before sunset.

Useful Information

Fonte Cerreto
Transport
Stazione Funivia Gran Sasso
d'Italia (Cable Car)
☎ (0862) 606143
Open: daily 8.30am-5pm.
Operates on every half hour except
at 1.30pm.

L'Aquila
Events and Festivals
July and August, Festival of
Musical Concerts 23-29 August,
Perdonanza Celestiniana
(Opening of the Porta Santa at
Santa Maria di Collemaggio and re-
enactment of the coronation of
Pope Celestine V, historical
pageant, exhibitions and entertain-
ments).

Tourist Information Centres
Ente Provinciale Turismo
Piazza Santa Maria Paganica 5
☎ (0862) 410808

Azienda Autonoma Soggiorno e
  Turismo
Via XX Settembre 8
☎ (0862) 22306

Centro Turistico del Gran Sasso
Corso Vittorio Emanuele 49
☎ (0862) 410859

Transport
Stazione Ferrovia Statale (Railway)
Piazzale della Stazione
☎ (0862) 419290

Emergencies
Vigili Urbani (Municipal Police)
Piazza Palazzo
☎ (0862) 414000

Pronto Soccorso (First Aid Service)
☎ (0862) 22333

Automobile Club d'Italia
Via Bone Novelle 6
☎ (0862) 29555

Subiaco
Tourist Information Centre
Azienda Autonoma Soggiorno e
    Turismo
Via Cadorna 59
☎ (0774) 85397

Emergencies
Carabinieri (Military Police)
☎ (0774) 85508

Pronto Soccorso (First Aid Service)
☎ (0774) 85517

Sulmona
Events and Festivals
Easter Day, La Madonna che
Scappa in Piazza (Procession with
a statue of the Madonna and a re-

enactment of the Resurrection).
July and August, fair of Abruzzo
and Molise crafts.

Tourist Information Centre
Azienda Autonoma Soggiorno e
    Turismo
Via Roma 21
☎ (0864) 53276

Transport
Ferrovie dello Stato (Railway)
☎ (0864) 210377

Emergencies
Vigili Urbani (Municipal Police)
☎ (0864) 52322

Polizia Stradale (Traffic Police)
☎ (0864) 52345

Pronto Soccorso (First Aid Service)
☎ (0864) 5491

Tivoli
Tourist Information Centres
Azienda Autonoma di Turismo
Piazza Nazioni Unite
☎ (0774) 293522

Azienda Autonoma Soggiorno
    Tivoli
Giardino Garibaldi
☎ (0774) 21249

Emergencies
Carabinieri (Military Police)
☎ (0774) 20030/25765

Pronto Soccorso (First Aid Service)
☎ (0774) 20086

5

THE TYRRHENIAN COAST

Chapter 5 follows the Tyrrhenian coast, south of Naples, visiting many of the beautiful spots along the Sorrento peninsula, the Amalfi coast and the Cilento peninsula, all of which lie within the province of Campania, before travelling down the mountainous interior of Calabria. The absence of large cities, with the exception of Cosenza, and the friendliness of the local people, both in the more remote areas where tourists are seldom seen, and along the coast in the busy resorts, make it a relaxing tour.

The route ends at Villa San Giovanni, at the toe of Italy, from where visitors can either cross over to Sicily, and tour it following routes in chapters 6 and 7, or continue round the Calabrian coast in chapter 8. Those not visiting Sicily, or wishing to tour the Calabrian coast, can cut across the neck of the peninsula from the plain of Sant'Eufemia to join chapter 8 at Catanzaro. Visitors travelling with caravans should be warned that sections of the A3 *autostrada* south of the Sant'Eufemia plain are not passable in high winds. However, the motorway is highly recommended, as it is very scenic and toll-free.

Route 5A • Castellamare di Stabia to Paestum

A tour of the Sorrento peninsula starts at **Castellamare di Stabia**, which is 30km (19 miles) south of Naples, down the A3 *autostrada*. The town is large and somewhat chaotic, but by following the ring road to Sorrento, it is possible to avoid the worst of the traffic. The road passes through a series of tunnels before emerging at the medieval Castello Revigliano, which looks back across the bay to Vesuvius and Naples. The road from here heads down, past the town's large industrial docks, to the cliff-edged coast which is dotted with narrow, crowded beaches. On the cliff tops ahead, high above its little beach, stands the popular resort of **Vico Equense** with its

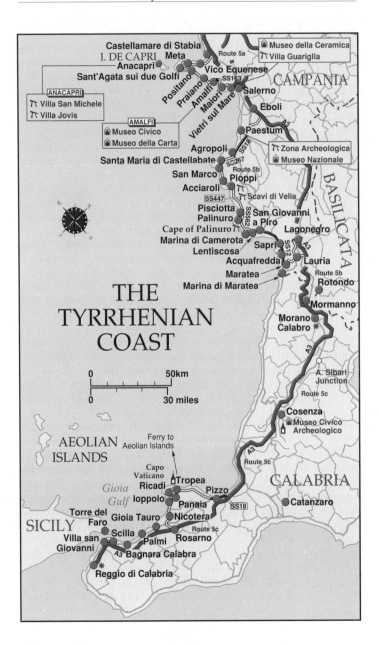

THE TYRRHENIAN COAST

Castellamare di Stabia
I. DE CAPRI   Meta   Route 5a
Anacapri
Sant'Agata sui due Golfi   Vico Equenese
SS163
ANACAPRI   Positano   Amalfi   Salerno
Praiano   Maiori
𐄂 Villa San Michele   Vietri sul Mare
𐄂 Villa Jovis
AMALFI   Agropoli
Museo Civico   SC267
Museo della Carta   Santa Maria di Castellabate   Route 5b
San Marco   Pioppi
Acciaroli
SS447   Scavi di Velia
Pisciotta
Palinuro   SS562   San Giovanni
Cape of Palinuro   a Piro   Lagonegro
Marina di Camerota   Sapri
Lentiscosa   Acquafredda   Lauria
Maratea   Route 5b
Marina di Maratea   Rotondo

Museo della Ceramica
Villa Guariglia
CAMPANIA
Eboli
Paestum
Zona Archeologica
Museo Nazionale
BASILICATA

THE
TYRRHENIAN
COAST

0   50km
0   30 miles

Mormanno
Morano
Calabro

A. Sibari
Junction
Route 5c

AEOLIAN   Ferry to
ISLANDS   Aeolian Islands

Cosenza
Museo Civico
Archeologico

Capo   Route 5c
Vaticano   Tropea
Ricadi   Pizzo
Gioia   Ioppolo
Gulf   Panaia   SS18
Torre del   Gioia Tauro   Nicotera   Catanzaro
Faro   Scilla   Route 5c
SICILY   Villa san   Palmi   Rosarno
Giovanni   A3   Bagnara Calabra
Reggio di Calabria

CALABRIA

tiled domed church. The main road by-passes the town and continues along the peninsula, from where there are fine views across the
Bay of Naples. After passing through **Seiano**, which is strewn with
villas, the road heads down through **Meta** where intarsia woodwork
is made. Lifts give access to the two small beaches far below.

From Meta, a right fork leads through **Sant-Agnello**, passing
nearby the Museo Correale di Terranova, which houses a collection
of local decorative arts in a fine eighteenth-century villa, to **Sorrento**.
The town is excellently positioned, with a backdrop of citrus groves
and mountains, atop sheer crags that drop vertically to the sea below.
In season, it is packed with tourists and parking can be a problem.
However, despite the crowds and the souvenir shops, the old centre
of Sorrento has retained a certain charm. From the west side of the
central square, Piazza Tasso, follow Corso Italia passing the fifteenth-century loggia of the Sedile Dominova with its green and
yellow majolica-tiled dome, on the right, to the *duomo*. The unusual
bell-tower of the *duomo* is stacked like a wedding cake on top of four
antique columns. The *duomo* itself was modified earlier this century,
but the attractive side portal, carved from marble, dates from 1479.
Inside, the first chapel on the right contains carved bas-reliefs dating
from the fourteenth and fifteenth centuries, while the choir stalls in
the main apse are a fine example of Sorrentine intarsia work.

Return to Piazza Tasso and head north to the public gardens, Villa
Comunale, from where there is a fine panorama along the coast,
taking in Naples with the cone of Vesuvius to the right, and the island
of Capri to the left. At the entrance to the park, the Baroque church
of San Francesco has a lovely thirteenth-century cloister with Arabic
style arcades, carved from tufa, along two of its sides. Below the park
is a marina where bathers swim from wooden piers that have been
built out from the base of the cliffs. The port at the east end of the
marina is a point of embarkation for ferries and hydrofoils to Capri.

The island of **Capri**, like Sorrento, attracts great numbers of
tourists. Its main attractions are tours by boat of the numerous
grottoes that dot the island's rocky shore, and the two main villages,
Capri and **Anacapri**, both of which have picturesque cobbled streets
and are good bases from which to go walking. The island is also of
interest for the liberally-strewn, Roman remains which date from the
first century BC. When Tiberius retired here in AD27, the island was
already a popular and well-developed leisure spot. The Emperor
built no less than twelve villas, the best-preserved of which is Villa
Jovis. Situated at the north-east tip of the island, the ruins of the villa,
which include rock-hewn cisterns, baths, and the imperial apartments where there are remains of mosaics, can be reached on foot in

just under an hour from Capri. Villa San Michele, to the north-west of Anacapri, was built on the site of another of Tiberius' villas. It was the home of a Swedish doctor from 1857 to 1949 and the building is now open as a museum, containing the doctor's private collection of eighteenth-century furniture as well as antiquities.

The route continues by crossing over the tip of the peninsula from Sorrento to the resort of **Sant'Agata Sui Due Golfi**, which takes its name from its unique position on a hilltop, 391m (1,282ft) above sea level, from where both the gulf of Naples and Salerno can be seen simultaneously, either side of the peninsula. The road gradually winds down towards the coast, offering magnificent views on the way, with the picturesque group of islets, li Galli, a short distance offshore. After 6km (4 miles) the SS163 is joined and the precipitous, but extremely scenic, journey along the Amalfi coast begins. There are occasional lay-bys from which to stop and admire the view, otherwise the road is barely wide enough to accommodate both lanes of traffic. Overtaking is difficult as there is rarely a straight stretch of road long enough to see safely ahead, however, this does not stop the locals, so drive with caution.

Positano, the first village on the Amalfi coast, appears to be almost impossibly stacked on dozens of narrow terraces up either side of a deep cove. A warren of alleyways and steps lead down, between the neat white houses with their luxuriant gardens, to a small beach in the harbour, which is guarded by medieval towers.

The SS163 continues to wind along the deeply creviced coast, high above tiny pebble coves and far below the towering mountain peaks, to **Praiano**. This picturesque village has a large church, San Gennaro, with an impressive majolica dome, as well as a good beach with a medieval tower, which can be reached by steps down from the road. The road continues through a series of tunnels carved in the rock and crosses over two gorges, those of Furore and Conca, before passing the entrance to Grotta di Smeralda. This large, water-filled cavern with its eerie stalactites and stalagmites, is reached by a lift down from the roadside, and then by boat.

The road continues through **Conca Marina**, which has two busy beaches at the foot of the cliffs, to **Amalfi** where visitors can park on the piazza at the sea front. Surrounded by steeply-terraced citrus groves, Amalfi fills the deep, sheltered bay of the Valle dei Mulini, and is guarded by a tenth-century watch tower high on the hill above. Probably due to its easily-defensible location, Amalfi was one of the earliest cities to emerge from the Dark Ages. In the sixth century, after successfully resisting Saracen attacks, Amalfi was established as the first sea republic in Italy. By the ninth century it was a major sea-trading power and minted its own coin, the Tari. Its downfall, however, came when the Pisans attacked in 1130 and left the city in ruins. Its decline was further enhanced in 1343 when an earthquake struck and the city was virtually washed out to sea. Despite all this, Amalfi's lovely, ninth-century *duomo*, stands remarkably intact. It is positioned on Piazza Duomo, at the centre of the town, and has a tall flight of steps leading up to its elegant façade. The decorative patterning of the façade dates from 1203, while the bronze doors were cast in Constantinople in 1066. The attractive *campanile* to the left of the façade was constructed between 1180 and 1276. The interior is also well-restored, and the crypt, which is entered from the fourth chapel on the right, holds relics of the Apostle St Andrew, whose head was brought from Constantinople in 1204. Back in the main body of the church there is a fine, medieval ambone and paschal candlestick, attractively decorated with mosaic inlay. Also of interest are the pair of antique columns, originating from Paestum, on either side of the choir.

Set along the left side of the *duomo* is the Chiostro del Paradiso. This beautiful cloister, surrounded by Arabic style arcades, was built in 1266 as a burial ground for the local nobility, and now houses a good collection of Roman and medieval architectural fragments. Other remains of medieval Amalfi can be seen in the small Museo Civico in

The wild and dramatic Amalfi coast, one of the most beautiful areas in Europe

the Municipio. To reach the museum, return to Piazza Duomo and follow Via Roma from its south-east corner, along the sea front, for 100m (110yd). Amongst the most important exhibits in the museum are the *tavole Amalfatini*, the maritime law codes that were drawn up during the Amalfi Republic and were used up until 1570. Another small museum, documenting the history of Amalfi's paper mills, can be visited in the Valle dei Mulini. The valley extends inland behind the town, and contains some of the oldest papermills in Europe.

The SS163 heads downhill from Amalfi and through a tunnel to **Atrani**. This picturesque village, just 1km (½ mile) east of Amalfi, lies on a rocky spur. During the times of the Amalfi Republic it was a wealthy residential quarter. The most important of its churches, of which there are thirty in all, is that of San Salvatore de'Bireto, which was originally built in AD940 for the capping of Amalfi's doges. It was reconstructed in 1810, but has retained its original doors (1086), which like those seen in Amalfi, were cast in Constantinople. The 1800s also saw Atrani connected by road for the first time, under the Bourbons, having been only accessible by boat prior to this. A 7km (4 mile) excursion can be made from the SS163, just beyond Atrani, up into the mountains to **Ravello**. This smart resort town was founded under the Amalfi Republic, but maintained independence from 1086 until 1813, during which time many fine buildings, particularly those in the Norman-Saracen style, were erected. The town's most beautiful monument to this era is Villa Rufolo which was started in the eleventh century. The villa was home to numerous French kings including Charles of Anjou and Robert the Wise, as well as Pope Adrian IV, the only English pope. The luxuriant gardens in which the villa stands inspired Wagner's magic garden in the *Parsifal*, and a Wagner season is staged here every summer. The interior houses a collection of sculptures and antiquities, and there is an excellent terrace, 339m (1,112ft) long, from where there is a splendid panorama.

Just to the north of Villa Rufolo, in the central square, Piazza Duomo, stands Ravello's attractive *duomo*. Originally founded in 1086, it was re-modelled in 1786, although the original antique columns, and the bronze doors cast in 1179 by Barisano da Trani, remain in situ. The interior has also retained many of its original features, including two attractive ambones, the larger one being decorated with Byzantine-style mosaics and sculpted to a design by Niccolo da Foggia in 1272, and the smaller one having a lovely mosaic of *Jonah and the Whale*, which dates from 1130.

The SS163 continues to follow the tortuous coast, through the steeply terraced citrus groves, and down past the busy beach resorts of **Minori** and **Maiori**, respectively. Minori lies in the mouth of the Reginuolo valley and has a steeply sloping sand and gravel beach which is well-maintained and suitable for children. The resort also contains the ruins of a first-century Roman villa. Maiori is larger and straggles along a 1km (½ mile) sand and gravel beach at the mouth of the Tramonto valley. Dominating the resort is the church of Santa Maria a Mare which dates from the twelfth century and has an attractive majolica tiled dome.

The road then heads up to the craggy cape, Capo d'Orso, and down through a tunnel, after which the sprawling city of Salerno comes into view. Continuing down, the road crosses over the Erchie valley, before reaching the colourful fishing village of **Certara** which has a majolica domed church at the edge of its harbour. The road winds up through the centre of the village and twists along the coast to **Vietri sul Mare**, a large resort with crowded beaches at the foot of its cliffs. There are many shops in the town selling the local ceramics, which are decorated with brightly coloured seascapes and floral motifs. There is also a small museum, the Museo della Ceramica, where Vietri's history of ceramic-making is documented from the seventeenth century to the present day.

From Vietri Sul Mare follow signs to the A3 *autostrada* and head south in the direction of Reggio Calabria. The motorway by-passes **Salerno**, which apart from having a fine, Norman cathedral holds little to attract the visitor, and heads towards the wide plain, Piana del Sele, from where Route 5B continues to Paestum.

Route 5B • Salerno to Morano Calabro

The first point of interest south of Salerno is **Paestum**, which, with its beautiful, ancient Greek temples, lies at the northern edge of the Cilento peninsula. The site is well-signposted from the Eboli exit on the A3 *autostrada*, first on a minor road, then on the SS18, across the richly-cultivated plain, Piana del Sele. The modern day town that surrounds the archaeological zone of Paestum has grown up to cater for the large numbers of tourists who visit the site, and during peak season it may be difficult to find a parking space. Most people park on the main road that runs alongside the site, otherwise there are several small, private carparks, most of which belong to hotels and restaurants.

Paestum, originally called *Poseidonia*, the city of Neptune, was founded in the early sixth century BC by Greek colonists from *Sybaris*. The best remaining structures, the three temples, date from this period. The buildings added by the Romans, who took the city in 273BC, are by comparison insignificant. The Roman city, plagued by malaria, dwindled until it was wiped off the map in AD877 by Saracen raids, and it was not until 1750, when a new road was being constructed, that Paestum was, by chance, once again brought to light.

The archaeological zone, enclosed by railings, covers a large and well-kept grassy area. There are several entrances, but the main gate is at the southern end of the site, opposite two of Paestum's great temples. The larger and more impressive one, the Temple of Neptune, is one of the finest, ancient Greek, Doric temples in existence. It was built in 450BC and, remarkably, is still complete with its thirty-six fluted columns, surmounted by an impressive, carved frieze and entablature, with grand pediments at either end.

The smaller temple, the Temple of Hera, flanking its southern side, was one of the earliest temples to be built at Paestum and is also excellently-preserved. It dates back to 565BC and has all fifty of its tapered columns, although the frieze decorating the entablature only remains in parts and neither of the pediments have survived.

Via Sacra, the ancient paved road through the city, leads north to the forum, or market place, which was built in Roman times on the site of the Greek agora. Once surrounded by baths and temples, now only low walls and foundations of buildings are visible. A footpath leads through the forum to the remains of the Roman amphitheatre, part of which lies buried beneath the modern day road.

Paestum's third temple, the Temple of Ceres, lies about 500m (547yd) north of the forum. Its columns, thirty-four in all, are well-preserved and demonstrate an unusually early (500BC) blending of the Doric and Ionic styles.

Provided it is not a Monday (closing day), the ticket to the site also gives admission to the excellent museum which is on the opposite side of the main road, between the amphitheatre and the Temple of Ceres. It contains an outstanding collection of locally-excavated finds, including a series of thirty-three metopes that originally decorated the entablature of the Temple of Hera, carved with figures depicting Homeric and mythical legends. There are also many fine tombs, the showpiece being the Tomba del Tuffatore, the Tomb of the Diver, which is decorated with rare and excellently-preserved Greek murals, dating from 480BC.

From Paestum follow signs to **Agropoli** on the SS267. The long, sandy beach to the north of this town is crowded with holiday accommodation, however, the medieval centre, signposted *centro storico*, is worth visiting. Park near the hilly promontory, on which the old town is clustered, and head for the town gate. Just through the gate and on the right, a narrow, flag-stoned street, winds up to the castle which stands at the summit of the promontory. A private

house has been built inside, but the castle is open to the public and there are fine views to be had by climbing up onto its sturdy walls, which date from Byzantine times. During the summer, on weekends, a small stage in the inner courtyard is used for concerts and theatrical performances.

Leave Agropoli on the SS267 and continue south, through the hills to the popular resort of **Santa Maria di Castellabate**. The old part lies at the southern end of the bay, and is centred around a brightly-painted church which stands on the edge of a sandy beach. Just north of the beach there is a colourful fishing harbour and a well-restored, sixteenth-century castle with a strongly-fortified turret. The narrow streets around the castle are pleasant to walk through, being lined with elegant stone houses and small restaurants.

The town of **Castellabate**, with its fine medieval castle, is perched

(Opposite) The ancient Greek temples of Paestrum are among the finest to be found in Southern Italy

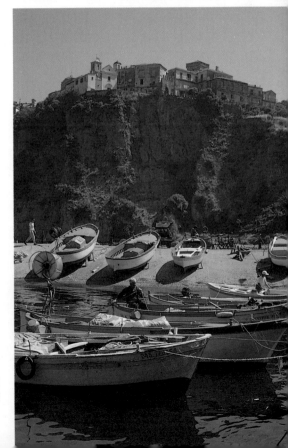

Fishing boats moored at Agropoli

high above the resort but can only be reached by a 4km (2 mile) drive up a very winding road. Continuing south along the SS267, a vast, sandy and well-kept beach stretches ahead as far as the next resort, **San Marco**. The remains of a breakwater, hewn from rock in Roman times, still protects the harbour of San Marco and fragments of Roman walls have survived amongst the holiday homes. The Licosa peninsula, which juts out, just south of San Marco, was the setting for an ancient legend. The peninsula is named after the siren Leucosia who, having failed to bewitch Ulysses, allegedly threw herself into the sea from Punta Licosa, the peninsula's tip.

The SS267 crosses the neck of the peninsula, and then winds high above the shore before heading down to the long sandy beach that extends as far as **Acciaroli**. This small resort, built on a promontory, has a peaceful fishing harbour which is defended by an ancient tower. Next to the tower is the Parrochiale d'Annunziata, a twelfth-century church with a ceramic-tile scene of the Annunciation decorating its bell-tower.

From Acciaroli, the SS267 winds up to the top of a headland, from where there is a fine panorama extending as far south as the cape of Palinuro. On descending, the road passes through the town of **Pioppi**, and then crosses the flat and built-up area in the Alento river bed. The ruins of ancient Greek Velia lie in the hills above and are reached by turning left after crossing the Alento river. There is a parking area on the left, from where visitors should head on foot under the railway bridge to the site entrance.

Velia, named *Elea* by the Phoenician refugees who founded the settlement in 540BC, was amongst the most important cities of *Magna Grecia*. It spawned the Eleatic school of philosophers, which included such well-known figures as Xenophanes and Parmenides. The ruins seen today are spread over a wide area, extending from the southern city walls, which are just beyond the site entrance, to the northern walls which are at the top of the hill. An ancient paved road leads up to the northern walls, past the agora, to Porta Rossa, an excellently preserved gate that dates from the fourth century BC.

The acropolis, with its medieval tower, lies to the west. The footpath starts about 50m (55yd) downhill from Porta Rossa and passes along the shoulder of the hill. In late spring, the hillside is covered in wild asparagus, while the ruins are idyllically set amongst a grove of giant olive trees. Of the two twelfth-century chapels on the hill, the lower one contains a collection of finds excavated at the site. The tall tower, which was built under the Angevin rulers, stands on the foundations of a temple that dates from the fifth century BC. There is a fine panorama of the coast from the lookout point behind the tower.

From Velia the SS447 winds up and down, along the Tyrrhenian coast, passing through the remote hill towns of **Ascea** and **Pisciotta** before eventually heading down to a long, sandy bay which extends from **Caprioli** right up to the cape of Palinuro. The popular resort of **Palinuro** spills out along the beach, but the original fishing village, positioned in a secluded bay at the end of the headland, has remained remarkably unspoilt. It is Virgil's *Aeneid* that gives the village its name, for it was here that the spirit of the drowned Palinurus, Aeneas' helmsman, appeared to his master in a dream, asking to be given a rightful burial. A strenuous hike around the headland will be rewarded by further remnants of classical times with the scant remains of *Molfa*, an ancient port which was once connected to Velia. A more leisurely trip can be made by boat, taking in the Grotta Azurro and other caves that dot the headland, many of which were inhabited in prehistoric times.

Continuing by road, the SS562 crosses the neck of the cape to its south side where tall rocks with natural arches stand within swimming distance of secluded sandy beaches. The road is partly channelled through the natural rock, and after passing through a rock tunnel, there are more gently sloping, sandy bays before the small resort of **Camerota**. The shoreline beyond Camerota is so steep and rocky that it is only accessible by boat. The SS562, therefore, heads inland, snaking up a tortuous road, lined with caves, above the resort, to the mountainous interior.

At **Lentiscosa**, a small town straggled along the mountain side, the road squeezes between the houses, before continuing up still further. As the road climbs, the vista across the mountains, which are densely covered with olive groves, gradually widens until the sea is in sight. On its winding course back down, the road passes through the town of **San Giovanni a Piro**, which is a good base from which to go hiking on Monte Bulgheria (1,225m/4,018ft). There are also the remains of an abbey founded by Basilian monks in AD980, 1km (½ mile) from the centre of the town.

The SS562 continues its descent through the foothills of Monte Bulgheria to the seaside resort of **Scario**, where there is a long, pebble beach. Continuing for a further 4km (2 miles) beyond Scario, the SS18, a larger road, is joined. It crosses the Bussento river and enters the town of **Policastro Bussentino** which lies at one end of the Policastro gulf. Those who wish to visit the old part of the town, the *centro storico*, where there is an attractive twelfth-century church, should turn off left. Otherwise the road continues through the town's modern outskirts and follows along the flat and busy shore of the gulf, to **Sapri**, at its opposite end. Once an ancient Greek, and later Roman, port, Sapri is now a rather low-key resort, pleasantly positioned at the foot of Monte Olivella (1,026m/3,365ft), with a sheltered gravel beach and a children's park at its centre.

Continuing south there are magnificent views looking back along the coastline before the SS18 leaves both the Cilento peninsula and the region of Campania.

The next stretch of coast, the Costa Maratea, is exceptionally scenic and offers some breath-taking views from dizzy heights above the shoreline. After passing through a tunnel, just inside the region of Basilicata, the road winds down through the village of **Acqua Fredda**, and then climbs up high along a cliff top to **Cersuta**. From here, as the road winds back down again, the enormous, white statue of the Redeemer, designed by Innocenti in 1965, comes into view on the summit of the sugar loaf hill, high above the town of **Maratea**. To visit the *centro storico*, the medieval quarter of Maratea, turn left at the town outskirts and head uphill. Those who wish to climb up to the belvedere on which the Redeemer's statue stands should continue up beyond the town to Monte San Biagio, where there is also a small sanctuary.

Continuing along the coastal road, south of Maratea, small islets are seen offshore, before the road reaches the fortified headland, Torre Caiano, which marks the boundary between the regions of Basilicata and Calabria. The Calabrian coast from this point on is largely built-up and unattractive, and the route turns inland, following the SS585 up the wide Castrocucco river valley towards the A3 *autostrada*. This can be joined either by turning right onto a steep and winding road via the town of **Lauria**, or by continuing on the SS585 via **Lagonegro**, which is a slightly longer but easier route.

The A3 *autostrada* is probably one of the best ways of getting to see the interior of the upper Calabrian peninsula, as the road soars high above valleys, offering magnificent views in all directions. After passing by the mountain village of **Mormanno**, which is glimpsed briefly between two tunnels on the left, the road continues south across the Campotenese, a high mountain plateau at an altitude of 900m (2,952ft).

Hikers may be interested in making the excursion from the Campotenese exit to **Monte Pollino** (2,248m/7,373ft), the highest peak in Southern Italy. From the junction, follow the road to Rotonda for 3km (2 miles) before turning right onto a narrow lane that winds up to Rifugio de Gasperi. A fifteen-minute walk from here can be made to a panoramic viewing point. However, the trail to Monte Pollino, starts from further along the track, at the summit of the hill, at Colle dell'Impiso. The trail, which is marked by red splashes of paint on the rocks, is steep and strenuous, and at least five hours should be allowed. The views, however, are stupendous, taking in three of Italy's seas. The flora too is outstanding, while amongst the fauna, which is sadly still hunted, are the Golden Eagle and the Appennine Wolf.

A short distance further south along the A3 *autostrada*, after a series of tunnels, a pleasant, 6km (4 miles) excursion can be made from the Morano Calabro-Castrovillari junction, to the picturesque hill town of **Morano Calabro**.

The road crosses the valley basin, to the hill on which Morano Calabro is steeply stacked. At the edge of the village, the road passes the church of San Bernardino. Founded in 1452 by the local feudal lord, Antonio Sanseverino, the church is a rare example of fifteenth-century Calabrian architecture and is well-preserved, complete with its fine interior woodwork. The façade is preceded by a portico with four arches and has a simple, fifteenth-century, carved portal. The interior is comprised of a single nave which is covered by a coffered, wooden ceiling. The Moranese, from the sixteenth to the eighteenth century, were known throughout Italy for their marquetry, and local craftsmen, over the centuries, have beautified the church interior with their skill. The inlaid pulpit and choir stalls date from the seventeenth century, while the choir lectern, which is made of walnut, dates from the fourteenth century. A fifteenth-century, wooden crucifix, is suspended above the altar, but the altar painting, a fine polyptych, by the important Venetian artist, B. Vivarini in 1477, is temporarily in the custody of Cosenza, having recently been recovered from a theft.

Continue uphill, and park at the Villa Comunale gardens. Nearby is the ornate dome, vividly patterned with blue and terracotta tiles, of the Calabrian-Baroque church of Collegiata della Maddalena. Continue on foot, heading up narrow alleys and stairways, to the domed church at the top of the village, Chiesa dei Santi Pietro e Paolo. The church holds many fine statues, including two works by Pietro Bernini, the father of Rome's great Baroque artist, Gianlorenzo Bernini.

A narrow road continues up above the church to the ruins of a castle. Originally the site of a Roman watch-tower, the Normans built a fortress here in the 1100s. The fortress had an eventful history, coming under attack from the Aragonese in 1285, and eventually falling into the hands of Antonio Sanseverino, who had it reconstructed in 1514. The design to which the feudal lord had the castle rebuilt was meant to resemble that of Castelnuovo in Naples, with rectangular walls guarded by cylindrical towers and a moat. It was not completed until 1545, and then only stood for less than two centuries before its destruction in 1733. The crumbling walls of its towers and the remnants of the Norman keep are all that now remain, although the magnificent panorama, across the Coscile valley to the Pollino chain of mountains warrants the climb alone.

Route 5C • Morano Calabro to Villa San Giovanni

Route 5C continues south on the A3 *autostrada*, through a landscape that gradually flattens out, becoming at the Spezzano A. Sibari junction, a wide, cultivated plain which extends all the way to the Adriatic coast. Twelve kilometres (7 miles) further south, the motorway passes along the fertile bed of the Crati river to the outskirts of **Cosenza**.

Once the capital of the Bruttians, an ancient Italic tribe, Cosenza lies at the confluence of the Crati and Bussento rivers. Today, nothing remains of the ancient city, and as a provincial capital and seat of a university, Cosenza is a mixture of the modern and the medieval. The modern takes the form of an unsightly sprawl of suburbs which fills the Crati valley floor. The medieval part covers a hillside above the river, and has probably changed little since the Angevins and the Aragonese fought for its possession. Indeed, there remains something of a medieval way of life, trapped in the very narrowness of the streets, where old-fashioned stores are dimly lit, children run up and down alleyways, and rubbish is strewn liberally outside doorways. The narrow streets also make for difficulty in parking, or even driving around, and it is best, therefore, to park near the river in the new town, along one of its wide, busy thoroughfares and approach the old city on foot.

The busy market area on Piazza Campanella, which lies at the foot of the old city, is a good point from which to start a tour. Take note of San Domenico, with its lovely rose window dating from 1448, which is set below street level on the east side of the piazza, before setting out across the stream of traffic to the bridge. From the bridge, the pretty dome and cupola of San Domenico can be seen above the rooftops behind, while on the opposite bank, to the left is San Francesco di Paola with its square bell-tower, and directly ahead San Francesco d'Assisi. On the other side of the bridge, cross over to the far left corner of Piazza Valdesi and follow Corso Telesio up the hill. This medieval thoroughfare, hemmed in by tall, balconied houses, leads steeply up to the *duomo*, which stands at the top of a cobbled piazza.

The *duomo*, consecrated in the presence of Frederick II in 1222, is built of an attractive warm stone in the Gothic-Cistercian style, and has a graceful, façade with three simple rose windows corresponding to three portals below. The spacious interior is divided by square pillars into three aisles and has a raised presbytery. At the top of the presbytery steps, on the left, is the monument of Isabella of Aragon who died in 1271. The stone carving is the work of a French sculptor and shows the Madonna and Child with two queens kneeling at either side, set within a Gothic surround. On the right side of the presbytery, just before the steps, there is a well-preserved Roman sarcophagus, decorated with finely-carved hunting scenes.

From the piazza on the left side of the *duomo* there are good views across the Crati river valley, while at the back of the *duomo* are the remains of the cloisters. Just above the cloisters is Piazza Gian Parrasio, from where Corso Telesio continues uphill before opening out into the large Piazza XV Marzo. At the centre of this piazza is a statue of the sixteenth-century philosopher, B. Telesio, who was born in Cosenza. The buildings surrounding the piazza include an attractive theatre, at the right side of which is the Accademia Consentina, where local archaeological finds, dating from early Bruttian Cosenza, are housed. The city's public gardens, Villa Comunale, continue up the hill to the left of the theatre.

Head back down Corso Telesio, and after passing the *duomo* take the first steps on the left, up Via del Seggio, to San Francesco d'Assisi, which stands above a warren of medieval alleyways. The church dates from the thirteenth century, but only its portal and a small vaulted chapel have survived from this period. The chapel, which is in the right transept, is lined with wooden choir stalls dating from 1505, and has the mummified body of the Franciscan monk, Beato Giovanni da Castrovillari (1480-1530), displayed at the altar. The decoration of the rest of the church is fairly bland, apart from the elaborate, wood-carved panelling and paintings in the Cappella Santa Caterina, which was completed in 1705.

Back outside the church, from its left side, a fine view can be had across the city rooftops to San Domenico on the far side of the river. The steps back down to Corso Telesio, however, lead from the right side of the church.

Route 5C continues south along the A3 *autostrada*, passing through a hilly landscape to the wide bed of the Savuto river which the road follows along to the coast. After heading down the coast for 16km (10 miles) the road skirts inland around the edge of the Sant'Eufemia plain, which lies at the narrowest point of the Calabrian peninsula. The plateau that rises from the left side of the plain was the site of the Battle of Maida, in 1806, where the British expelled the French from Calabria. At the southern edge of the plain, leave the motorway at the Pizzo exit, first taking the SS18, then turning off right onto the Pizzo

Litoreana, the coastal road. The road winds above a sandy shoreline crowded with hotels and restaurants, passing the Chiesetta di Piedgrotta, a small church hewn from tufa rock at the water's edge, before entering Pizzo. **Pizzo** is a lively resort with plenty of local character to be found in a warren of narrow streets. A ruined castle, built in 1486 by Ferdinand I, looks down over the large marina.

The coast to the south of Pizzo is largely built up and there is an unsightly concentration of industry around **Vibo Marina**, although visitors may wish to stop to take one of the daily motorboat tours that operate from the port here, to the Aeolian islands. Otherwise, press on to the lovely resort town of **Tropea**, a further 25km (15½ miles) south.

The old medieval centre of Tropea, which is excellently positioned on a headland, is pedestrian only and visitors should park outside the walls. Porta Nuova, the town gate, leads onto Corso Vittorio

(Opposite)
The delightful village
of Scilla, clustered on a
headland at the end of
the Violet Coast

A local fruit and
vegetable shop,
Cosenza

Emanuele, the main street, which is lined either side with small shops. At Piazza Ercole, midway along Corso Vittorio Emanuele, turn right, following Via Roma to the *duomo*. This attractive building, built in the eleventh and twelfth centuries is Sicilian-Norman in style, with tall and slender blind arcades decorating the outer walls, typical of the Gothic era. The prettily-decorated apse stands on a panoramic terrace, perched high above the town's docks, while the façade looks onto a courtyard, edged by arcades along two sides and with a squat bell tower in one corner. Inside, tall arches divide the church into three aisles, each of which ends in a rounded apse. The right apse holds a statue of the *Madonna and Child* by G.A. Montorsoli (1555); the main apse has a fourteenth-century Byzantine image of the *Roumanian Madonna* set in a silver frame; and the left apse contains a sixteenth-century marble ciborium. Also of interest is the black, wooden crucifix, dating from the sixteenth century, in the second chapel of the right aisle.

Return to Corso Vittorio Emanuele and continue to head downhill to the railings at the end of the street which look down onto a sandy beach far below. The beach extends for a total of 6km (4 miles) and although it slopes quite steeply, it is suitable for children. At the edge of the sand there rises a sheer rock, which was once an island, at the top of which stands the sanctuary, Santa Maria dell'Isola. Originally built by Benedictine monks in medieval times, the sanctuary has been reconstructed numerous times since.

Leave Tropea by following signs to Capo Vaticano, which is the tip of the promontory, some 10km (6 miles) to the south. From here, head inland and up through the hill villages of **Ricadi** and **Panaia**, from where there are good views of the coast and the Aeolian islands. The road then descends through **Coccorinello** and winds along a dramatic cliff edge, from where there are also excellent views. Continue along this scenic part of the coast through **Ioppolo**, before climbing higher still above the shore to the town of **Nicotera**. This large and sprawling town has a picturesque *centro storico* where there is a Baroque cathedral and fine views overlooking the Gioia gulf.

From Nicotera head inland to the modern town of **Rosarno**, which lies at the edge of a vast and well-cultivated plain, and join the A3 *autostrada*. The motorway crosses the plain, passing the industrial town of **Gioia Tauro** at its southern edge. After crossing the Petrace river, the road climbs up into the foothills of the Aspromonte, Calabria's southernmost mountain range, the interior of which is preserved as a National Park. A series of tunnels then carry the road gradually down to what is known as the Costa Viola (Violet Coast). Here, viaducts cross over deep inlets with resorts such as **Bagnara**

Calabra and **Favzinna** clustered at the water's edge far below. Sea food is a speciality of the Violet Coast and Bagnara Calabra is the home of Pesce Spada, a dish of swordfish cooked with peppers, capers, lemon, garlic and herbs. **Scilla**, marks the southern end of the Violet Coast, and is an easy and worthwhile excursion off the motorway. The village sits on a headland looking out over the fateful crag described in Homer's *Odyssey* where so many boats were doomed to crash. The castle built on top of the crag dates from the thirteenth century and guards the Straits of Messina which divide the mainland from Sicily, which is just four nautical miles off shore.

The A3 *autostruda* continues along the shore of the straits with the Torre del Faro, the lighthouse tower at the easternmost tip of Sicily easily within sight. From **Villa San Giovanni**, **Messina** is close enough to be able to distinguish its buildings, and visitor's who wish to follow chapters 6 and 7 around Sicily should either embark from the port here, or continue to the port of **Reggio di Calabria**. Rebuilt after a devastating earthquake in 1908, Reggio di Calabria is a modern, provincial capital. It holds little of interest for the visitor apart from its excellent museum, the Museo Nazionale, which holds the famous Bronzi di Riace, a series of bronze statues of nude warriors which date from the fifth century BC. The 3km (2 mile) promenade along the sea front, **Lungomare Giacomo Matteotti**, is also attractive, and has a fine view across the straits. At the southern end of the promenade there are traces of the ancient Greek walls and the remnants of a Roman baths, Terme Romane. Reggio di Calabria is also of interest for its production of oil of bergamot. It has world monopoly over the product and hosts a major international trade fair of bergamot in March.

Additional Information

Places to Visit

Amalfi
Museo Civico
Municipio
☎ (089) 871066
Open: Monday to Friday 8am-2pm, Saturday 8am-12noon.

Museo della Carta
Valle dei Mulini
Open: Tuesday, Thursday, Saturday 10am-1pm.

Grotta di Smeraldo
Conca dei Marina
Open: daily March to May 9am-5pm. June to September 8.30am-6pm. October to February 10am-4pm.

Villa San Michele
☎ (081) 8371428
Open: winter daily, except Tuesday, 10.30am-3pm. Summer daily 9.30am-6pm.

Capri
Villa Jovis
Open: Tuesday to Sunday 9am-1
hour before sunset

Cosenza
Museo Civico Archeologico
Accademia Consentina
Piazza XV Marzo
☎ (0984) 73387
Open: Monday to Friday 9am-1pm.

Paestum
Zona Archeologica
Open: daily 9am-1 hour before
sunset

Museo Nazionale
☎ (0828) 811023
Open: Tuesday to Saturday 9am-
1.30pm. Sunday and holidays 9am-
12.30pm.

Ravello
Villa Rufolo
Open: October to May daily
9.30am-1pm, 2-4.30pm. June to
September daily 9.30am-1pm, 3-
7pm. (Thursdays, free entrance)

Duomo (Cathedral)
Piazza Duomo
Open: September to June daily
(except Monday) 9am-1pm. July to
August daily (except Monday) 3-
8pm.

Reggio di Calabria
Museo Nazionale
Piazza de Nava
Open: Winter, Tuesday and
Thurday 9am-2pm.
Saturday 9am-1pm, 3-6pm.
Summer, Tuesday to Saturday
9am-1pm, 3-6pm.
Sunday 9am-1pm.

Sorrento
Museo Correale di Terranova
Via Correale 50
☎ (081) 8781846
Open: winter, Monday to Saturday
(except Tuesday) 9am-12.30pm, 3-
5pm; Sunday 9.30am-12.30pm.
Summer, Monday to Saturday
(except Tuesday) 9.30am-12.30pm,
4-7pm; Sunday 9.30am-12.30pm.

Cattedrale
☎ (081) 8782248

Velia
Scavi di Velia
Open: daily 9am-1 hour before
sunset

Vietri sul Mare
Museo della Ceramica
Villa Guariglia
Open: Tuesday to Sunday 9am-
1pm (summer, also open Thursday
and Saturday 5-7pm).

Useful Information

Agropoli
Tourist Information Centre
Pro Loco
Via San Marco
☎ (0974) 824885

Transport
Ferrovie dello Stato (Railway)
(0974) 823239

Emergencies
Pronto Soccorso (First Aid Service)
☎ (0974) 823179

Amalfi
Events and Festivals
July-August, open-air ballet, prose
and folk performances, and
concerts in the Chiostro Paradiso.

Tourist Information Centre
Azienda Autonoma di Soggiorno e
  Turismo
Corso Roma 19
☎ (089) 872619/871107

Emergencies
Polizia Municipale (Municipal
  Police)
☎ (089) 871066

Guardia Medica (Medical Officer)
☎ (089) 872785

Anacapri
Events and Festivals
1 and 6 January, Folk dancing on
Piazza Diaz. 13 June, Sant'Antonio
di Padova (Festival of patron saint,
procession with statue of
Sant'Antonio di Padova).

Ariacapri
Tourist Information Centre
Azienda Autonoma di Cura
  Soggiorno e Turismo
Via G. Orlandi 19/a
☎ (081) 8371524

Transport
Seggiovia del Monte Solaro (Chairlift)
Via Caposcuro 10
☎ (081) 8371428
Open: November to March daily
(except Tuesday) 10.30am-3pm.
April to October daily 9.30am until
sunset.

Emergencies
Vigili Urbani (Municipal Police)
Via G. Orlandi
☎ (081) 8371012

Carabinieri (Military Police)
Rio Caprile 5
☎ (081) 8371011

Unita Sanitaria Locale No 37
(Sanitary Unit)
Via Caprile 30
☎ (081) 8372091

Atrani
Tourist Information Centre
Informazioni
Municipio
☎ (089) 871185

Capri
Events and Festivals
1 and 6 January, folk dancing on
Piazza Umberto I. 14 May, San
Costanza (Festival of patron saint,
procession with statue of San
Costanza).

Tourist Information Centre
Azienda Autonoma di Cura
  Soggiorno e Turismo
Piazza Umberto I
☎ (081) 8370686

Transport
Funicolare (Cable Car)
Marina Grande
☎ (081) 8370420

Gruppo Motoscafisti (Motorboats)
Marina Grande
☎ (081) 8370286
Boat tours of the island and Grotta
Azzura depart from Marina
Grande, June to September daily
9am.

Aliscafi Alilauro (Ferry)
☎ (081) 8376995
Aliscafi SNAV (Ferry)
☎ (081) 8377577
Caremar (Ferry)
☎ (081) 8370700
Navigazione Libera del Golfo
(Ferry)
☎ (081) 8370819

Emergencies
Polizia (Police)
Via Roma 70
☎ (081) 8377245/8377246

Vigili Urbani (Municipal Police)
Piazza Umberto 1
☎ (081) 8370688

Ospedale Capilupi (Hospital)
☎ (081) 8370585/8370014/8378762

Pronto Soccorso (First Aid Service)
☎ (081) 8378149

Cosenza
Events and Festivals
Spring, every two years, Festival of
Calabrese Costume.

Tourist Information Centres
Ente Provinciale per il Turismo
Via Pasquale Rossi
☎ (0984) 30595

Azienda Provinciale Turismo
Viale Trieste 50
☎ (0984) 27821

Direzione del Parco Nazionale
della Calabria
Ufficio Amministrazione di
Cosenza
Viale della Repubblica 26
☎ (0984) 26544

Transport
Ufficio Informazioni Stazione
Ferrovia Statale
(Information Office for State
Railway)
☎ (0984) 482640

Emergencies
Polizia Urbana (Town Police)
Piazza dei Bruzi
☎ (0984) 26802

Ospedale Civile dell'Annunziata
(Hospital)
☎ (0984) 6811

Automobile Club d'Italia
Via Tocci 2a
☎ (0984) 74381

Maratea
Tourist Information Centre
Azienda Autonoma di Soggiorno e
Turismo
Piazza del Gesu 32
Santa Venere
☎ (0973) 876129

Paestum
Events and Festivals
July-August, occasional concerts,
ballet performances and classical
plays, held in the *zona archeologica*.

Tourist Information Centres
Azienda Autonoma di Soggiorno e
Turismo
di fianco alla Chiesa
dell'Annunziata
☎ (0828) 811016

Transport
Stazione Ferrovia Statale (Railway)
☎ (0828) 722171

Emergencies
Polizia Urbana (Town Police)
☎ (0828) 843035

Carabinieri (Military Police)
☎ (0828) 843040

Guardia Medica (Medical Officer)
Capaccio Scalo
☎ (0828) 843224

Palinuro
Tourist Information Centre
Pro Loco
Di Fronte alla Chiesa
☎ (0974) 931121

Ravello
Events and Festivals
Summer, Wagner Season in
gardens of Villa Rufolo.

Tourist Information Centre
Azienda Autonoma di Soggiorno e
    Turismo
Piazza Duomo 10
☎ (089) 857096

Emergencies
Polizia Municipale (Municipal
    Police)
☎ (089) 857498

Guardia Medica
☎ (089) 872785

Sorrento
Events and Festivals Good Friday,
Venerdi Santo
(Religious procession through the
streets of Sorrento in traditional
hooded costumes).

Tourist Information Centre
Azienda Autonoma di Soggiorno e
    Turismo
Via Luigi de Maio 35
☎ (081) 8782229/8781115

Transport
Ferrovia Circumvesuviana
(Vesuvius Railway)
☎ (081) 8782100

Ferrovia Stato (State Railway)
☎ (081) 264644

Caremar (Ferry)
Marina Piccola
☎ (081) 8781282

Consorzio Partenopeo di
    Navigazione (Ferry)
Marina Piccola
☎ (081) 8781861

Emergencies
Polizia (Police)
☎ (081) 8781438/8781727/8781110

Vigili Urbani (Municipal Police)
☎ (081) 8781048

Polizia Stradale (Traffic Police)
☎ (081) 8781113

Ospedale (Hospital)
☎ (081) 8771488/8783496

Tropea
Tourist Information Centre
Associazione Turistica Pro Tropea
Piazza Ercole
☎ (0963) 61475

Emergencies
Vigili Urbani (Municipal Police)
☎ (0963) 61221

Polizia (Police)
☎ (0963) 603189

Carabinieri (Military Police)
☎ (0963) 61018

Ospedale Civile (Hospital)
☎ (0963) 61366

6

NORTHERN SICILY

The island of Sicily, called *Trinacria* by the ancient Greeks due to its triangular shape, lies just over 30km (19 miles) from mainland Italy. Despite its proximity to the mainland, Sicily has a separate identity, and offers the visitor a range of new sights and experiences. The coast, which is 2,000km (1,240 miles) long, is well-endowed with the ruins of classical temples and ancient cities, while the deep blue Mediterranean waters lap at the Sicilian shore. In the towns and cities there is a mingling of Saracen, Norman and Spanish Baroque architecture. The pace of life here is slow, the Sicilians are caring and gracious people, and seem to have all the time in the world.

During July and August, the temperatures on the island soar up to 45˚C (113˚F), a fact exacerbated by the hot Scirocco wind which often blows from Africa. Yet, even at the end of a scorching summer, Sicily is lush and verdant. The landscape is crowded with citrus groves, prickly pears, palms and abundant flowering shrubs, such as bourgainvillea and oleander. In the cities, the people cool down in shady parks and outdoor cafés with a *gelato* or a refreshing sorbet, which come in lemon, orange blossom or watermelon flavours. Some Sicilians even start the day with an icecream, having a *cornetti con gelato* for breakfast, the customary brioche, but crammed with the icecream of your choice.

The simplest and most economical way to reach Sicily with a car, is by ferry, from Villa San Giovanni to Messina. There are car-ferries every ten minutes with the private Caronte company, and also with the state-run ferries which operate in conjunction with the *ferrovia* (railway). Chapter 6 starts at Messina and travels along the northern coast of Sicily to Palermo. Where possible, visitors are recommended to use the motorways, which charge tolls, but are preferable to the poorly-surfaced, and often congested, state highways. From

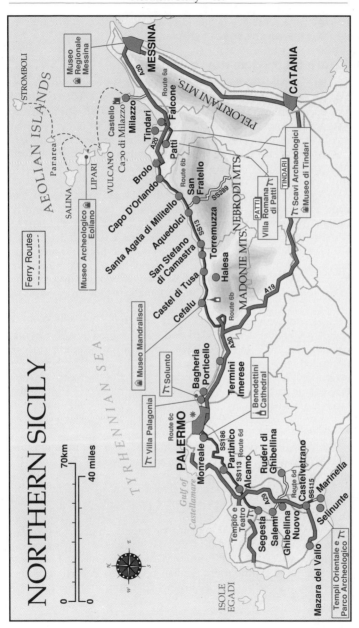

Palermo, the route heads inland to ancient *Segesta* and Selinunte, which is the starting point of chapter 7.

Route 6A • Messina to Tindari

The city of **Messina** lies at the foot of the Peloritani mountains, around a sickle-shaped harbour. In the days of the ancient Greeks it was a prosperous trading colony, later to be fortified by the Saracens, who held it until the Crusaders, heralding the start of the Norman era, landed in 1060. However, despite its long history, Messina has few historical relics, for in 1908 an earthquake caused a 6m (20ft) high, tidal wave to sweep over the city, taking with it some 80,000 lives.

The *duomo*, which was founded by the Norman ruler Roger II, has been painstakingly reconstructed to its original twelfth-century design. It stands at the centre of the harbour, 200m (218yd) from the water's edge, on Piazza del Duomo. The façade is typically Roman-esque and has an attractively-carved, Gothic portal, which was added in the fifteenth century. The interior has a high central nave with an ornately-painted, open beam ceiling. Mosaics decorate the dome and apses, although the only originals are those in the left apse depicting the *Madonna with Santa Lucia*.

Piazza del Duomo also contains the largest clock tower in Sicily. It stands to a height of 60m (197ft), and was designed by a Strasbourg company in 1933. The clock face, which is on the south side, is decorated with symbols of the zodiac. On the west side there are a series of gilded statues, representing the days of the week, the four ages of man and religious figures, all of which move into action as the clock chimes at midday. The fountain on Piazza del Duomo, the Fontana di Orione, was sculpted by a pupil of Michelangelo, G.A. Montorsoli, in 1547.

The only other place of interest in Messina is the museum, the Museo Regionale, which is at the northern end of the city. The museum has a notable collection of Sicilian art, ranging from Byzan-tine icons and mosaics, to large, eighteenth-century oil paintings by Messinese artists. Amongst the most prestigious works, are two paintings by Caravaggio: *The Raising of Lazarus* (1609), and *Adoration of the Magi* (1604). Also of note are the polyptych of *St Gregory*, by Antonello da Messina (1430-1479), who was one of Sicily's greatest painters, and the fifteenth-century *Madonna and Child* by Francesco Laurana, another important Sicilian artist. The collection of six-teenth-century sculpture is noteworthy too, and includes G. Montorsoli's *Scilla* 1557.

Leave Messina by following the A20 *autostrada* signs in the direction of Palermo. The motorway is joined at the top of Viale Boccetta, from where it skirts along the foothills of the Peloritani mountains, above the city and harbour, before heading through a series of tunnels to the Tyrrhenian coast. Travelling westwards on the A20 along the coast, on a clear day it is possible to see the Aeolian Islands (Isole Eolie), which can be visited from **Milazzo**. This fine old town, 34km (21 miles) west of Messina, lies on a narrow peninsula, which is unfortunately flanked by heavy industry on either side. Apart from being the nearest point from which to make an excursion to the Aeolian Islands, the town also has a good castle. The main street, Via Umberto, ends at Piazza Roma, from where Via Impallomeni heads uphill to the castle walls. Head on foot up to the gate which pierces the eastern wall, and continue up the cobbled footpath to a second gate where there is a vaulted entrance hall. The castle was built, on the site of the ancient Greek acropolis, by Frederick II in the thirteenth century. It was later enlarged by the Hapsburg Emperor, Charles V, and further altered in the seventeenth century under the Spanish. Inside the castle's well-preserved walls, the central keep and the Duomo Vecchio, the former town cathedral, are still standing. During the summer a stage is installed in the main courtyard for drama and musical productions.

The road continues beyond the castle to **Capo di Milazzo**, the tip of the peninsula, which is 6km (4 miles) further north. There are fine views from here of the Aeolian Islands, which were named by the ancient Greeks after the God of Wind, Aeolus, who according to legend kept the winds in caves here. Due to their volcanic origin, the islands also provided the ancient Greeks with a rich source of obsidian, which they traded throughout the Mediterranean.

Those who wish to visit the **Aeolian Islands** should head to Milazzo's port, which is at the neck of the peninsula on the east side. There are regular ferries during the summer to the islands of Vulcano and Lipari, but in peak season it is necessary to book well in advance, as the islands are a popular destination for Italian holiday-makers. There are seven islands in all, only two of which, Lipari and Salina, permit cars. It is possible, however, to leave vehicles in a garage in Milazzo. Most people visit the islands to swim and sunbathe. The surrounding water is clear and deep, particularly suitable for scuba diving, and the secluded beaches have either black volcanic sand or white pumice pebbles.

The exclusive island of **Vulcano**, 1½ hours from Milazzo, boasts one of the archipelago's finest beaches. It faces onto the dramatic rock stacks, known as the Faraglioni and has fine black sand. The water is very warm and fizzes slightly with volcanic gases, and there is a pool of sulphurous mud. Bathers cake themselves with the mud, although this is not recommended for children or pregnant women as it is slightly radioactive. The largest volcanic crater on the island, which the ancient Greeks believed to hold Vulcan's forge, still omits an occasional plume of yellow smoke, although it has not erupted since 1890. The island's smaller crater, the Vulcanello, has lain dormant for a much longer time, and is now well-known to hikers as the Valle dei Mostri, as the crater has formed a valley lined with fantastic, eroded shapes.

Lipari is 1km (½ mile) north of Vulcano. It is the largest of the islands, and is a convenient base from which to make excursions to the rest of the archipelago. The town of Lipari is crowned by a sixteenth-century, Spanish castle, which was built on the site of the ancient Greek acropolis. Inside the castle walls there is an excellent museum, the Museo Eoliano, which documents the history of the Aeolian Islands from Neolithic to Roman times, and houses a fine collection of ancient Aeolian ceramics. Of particular note are the figures vases dating from the fourth century BC, and the Greek masks made of terracotta.

There are regular bus services to the island's resorts, namely **Canneto, Campobianco** and **Porticello** where there are white, pumice-stone beaches. Those keen on hiking may wish to visit **San Calogero**, at the western side of the island where there are the scant remains of a Mycenean site and the ruins of a Roman baths that were built over a natural hot spring.

Salina, named after its salt lagoons, is just under 4km (2 miles) north-west of Lipari. It is the greenest of the Aeolian Islands, being well-endowed with natural springs, and has two volcanic peaks: Monte dei Porri (860m/2,821ft), and Monte Fossa delle Felci (962m/3,155ft) which is the highest in the archipelago. A panoramic road links the five main villages on the island: **Santa Maria di Salina**; **Lingua**; **Malfa**; **Leni**; and **Pollara**, which is located in the crater of Monte dei Porri.

The island of **Stromboli** is visited for its highly-active volcano which regularly emits showers and sparks. Guided tours to the rim of the crater, which is 924m (3,031ft) above sea level, involve a stiff 2 or 3 hour hike. Alternatively, there are boat trips to the cascade of lavic rock which plunges from the crater rim down to the water's edge. Either way, the volcano's activity is most impressive after dark.

Boat trips can also be taken to **Strombollichio**, a vertical stack of basalt rock which lies just over a kilometre (1 mile) from Stromboli. A staircase, with over 200 steps, climbs the sheer rock face to the lighthouse at the summit, from where there are fine views of Stromboli and its volcano.

Back on mainland Sicily, the route continues west along the A20 motorway, for 21km (13 miles) to **Falcone** from where the Santuario Madonna church can be seen atop the sheer and rocky outcrop ahead. Follow the SS113 del Tindari up through the village of **Tindari**, to a small carpark, which is on the right, beneath a grove of olive trees.

Proceed on foot, past the umpteen souvenir stalls that sell hazel-nuts strung like rosaries and painted tambourines, to the sanctuary. The sanctuary was built in the 1960s to house the venerated statue of a black Madonna which is placed in a glass case on the high altar. It is carved from a dark, oriental wood, and dressed in golden robes, and is thought to be Byzantine in origin. The Madonna is revered,

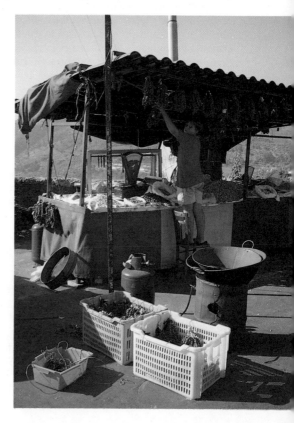

A hazel-nut stall at Tindari

however, for her ability to perform miraculous deeds, such as when she saved a young boy who was falling over the cliff edge.

The sanctuary is built on the site of ancient Greek *Tyndaris*, which was founded by Dionysius I (430-367BC) in order to defend the north coast of Sicily. To visit the ruins of the city, follow the footpath from the sanctuary, past more souvenir stalls, to the site entrance, which is on the right. The ruins are delightfully set, amongst cactus plants and eucalyptus trees, overlooking the Tyrrhenian Sea. On the left of the entrance, there is a collection of local finds, displayed in five modest rooms. Amongst the most interesting exhibits are a stone-carved mask of King Priam, a colossal head of Augustus, and a scale model reconstruction of *Tyndaris* theatre buildings.

The path continues down to the *decumanus*, the main artery through the ancient city, which dates from the fourth century BC. Turn right, and follow the *decumanus*, past the remnants of housing on the left, to the grand façade of the basilica. Constructed with hefty blocks of soft stone, the main arch in the façade leads through to a spacious hall which is lined with pilasters along either side. In ancient times traffic would have passed through here to the agora which once lay beyond. On days of public meetings, however, the hall was closed off at either end and the traffic to the market was diverted through the narrow side arches that can be seen at either side.

Return along the *decumanus* and continue to the opposite end of the city, to the theatre which is on the left. The theatre is harmoniously positioned, in the typical Greek tradition, on a hill side, looking out to sea. The Romans altered the building somewhat, and added a wall around the stage floor for gladiatorial spectacles. Today, a season of theatrical performances are staged here during the summer.

Route 6B • Tindari to Solunto

From Tindari, follow the SS113 which winds between olive groves and cactii, high above the sea, through **Mongiove**, to the outskirts of **Patti**. The sombre, red-roofed cathedral of this busy town, contains the mausoleum of Adelasia, who was wife of the Norman conqueror, Roger I. The main sight of interest in Patti, however, is the Villa Romana which is reached by turning right at the edge of the town and following signs to the *autostrada*. Follow the road down towards the coast, pass under the motorway, and turn right onto Via Giovanni XXIII. Park immediately on the right, under the motorway, and proceed on foot to the entrance to the **Villa Romana di Patti**.

The villa was accidentally uncovered in 1973 during the construction of the motorway and excavations since have revealed it to be one of the largest of its kind in Sicily. It covers an area of 20,000sq m (215sq ft), and is lavishly paved throughout with mosaics, similar in style to those at Piazza Armerina. A small museum at the site entrance provides information about the villa's history as well as displaying many of the local finds. The footpath from the museum leads to the nucleus of the villa which is in the form of a large peristyle, measuring 33½m (110ft) by 25m (82ft). Protected by temporary roofing, a series of walkways lead the visitor around the peristyle which is edged by apartments. Many of the apartments contain remnants of their original mosaic floors which have finely detailed geometric designs. One of the finest mosaics is that in the three-apsed hall, along the south side of the peristyle, which has a series of octagonal medallions containing depictions of animals. To the north-east of the peristyle there is a thermal baths complex, but only the foundations are visible.

From the villa, follow signs to the A20 *autostrada*, and proceed along the coast, past the village of **Brolo**, which surrounds a bay and is guarded by a square tower. After a short distance the road passes a parking area at **San Gregorio Nord**, from where there are good views of the promontory, **Capo d'Orlando**, with its ruined, thirteenth-century castle. On the east side of the promontory is the popular beach of **San Gregorio**, where in 1299, King Frederick II of Aragon was defeated by a group of local barons.

The A20 continues along the foothills of the Nebrodi mountains, which are covered in olive groves, to the large resort of **Sant'Agata di Militello**. The motorway finishes here and the route continues on the SS113. Just after Sant'Agata di Militello, visitors may wish to make an inland excursion to the Nebrodes, which lie at the heart of the Sicilian Apennines, and culminate in the peak of Monte Soro (1,847m/6,058ft). To reach Monte Soro, take the SS289 through the small, Norman town of **San Fratello**.

The route, however, continues on the SS113 along the coast, through **Aquedolci**, where the cave, Grotta di San Teodoro, may be visited. Beyond Aquedolci, there are pebble beaches, backed by gently sloping olive groves and citrus orchards, up until **San Stefano di Camastra**, which covers an attractive headland. The town is known for its ceramics, and the main street is lined with pottery shops, which offer a wide range of ware, from traditional majolica and terracotta, to highly-glazed ceramics with pictorial designs.

Continuing west of San Stefano di Camastra, the road crosses the Torrente San Stefano river, and passes through the industrial area of **Villa Margi**, before reaching **Torremuzza**, which is named after its defense tower. To the west of Torremuzza, narrow pebble beaches are fringed by steep hills, up until the fortified headland of **Castel di**

Tusa. The ancient site of *Halesa* is 3km (2 miles) inland, but the ruins, which date from the fifth century BC, are very scant.

The SS113 continues west, criss-crossing back and forth over the railway, and passing small, rocky bays and pebble beaches. At the resort of **Finale** there is a prominent headland, which is guarded by a well-restored defense tower. The road continues along the coast towards the next headland. On the eastern side of the headland, the ruined tower, **Torre Caldura**, looks across a wide bay lined with hotels. On the western side of the headland is the charming town of **Cefalu**, which is spread at the foot of a magnificent limestone cliff.

There is ample parking on Piazza Cristoforo Colombo, which is next to the lido at the western side of the town. The historic centre is within 400m (437yd), and can be reached by following Via Amendola to Corso Ruggero. At the corner, on the left, is the twelfth-century tower of the Osterio Magno, which is all that remains of the supposed residence of Roger II, under whom Cefalu reached its zenith. Head north of the tower, along Corso Ruggero, which is lined with fine Renaissance and Baroque buildings, for 200m (218yd) to Piazza del Duomo.

The *duomo* lies along the east side of the piazza, at the top of a flight of steps, in the shadow of the limestone cliff. The cathedral was started by order of Roger II, in 1131. It was not consecrated, however, until 1267, and even then it was never completely finished. The façade is flanked by imposing square towers, which are typical of the Norman era, but the triple-arched porch between them, is a later addition, and was designed by the Northern Italian architect, Ambrogio da Como, in 1471.

The interior of the cathedral has a lofty, central nave, with a decorative, open-beamed ceiling. The clerestory is supported on pointed arches, derived from Arabic architecture, which spring from smooth columns with Roman and Byzantine capitals. The artistic focus of the cathedral, however, are the beautiful, gold-ground mosaics, dating from 1148, that decorate the central apse. *Christ Pantocrator* looks down from the dome of the apse, with *Madonna and Archangels* and the *Apostles* covering the wall below. The walls either side of the apse are decorated with mosaics depicting the *Fathers of the Church*, each of whom is identified by an inscription in Greek or Latin. Those on the right are *Martyrs and Prophets*, those on the left are *Deacons and Prophets*.

From the piazza, head west down the narrow, cobbled street, Via Mandralisca. After 100m (110yd) the local museum, Museo Mandralica, is passed on the left. It houses a small collection of art and archaeology, ranging from antique Sicilian coins and Byzantine icons to Renaissance oil paintings. Amongst the prize exhibits is a black and red Greek vase, dating from the fourth century BC, which is beautifully decorated with the scene of a tuna fish seller. Also of note is the *Portrait of an Unknown Man* by Antonello da Messina, dated 1470.

Continue down to the end of Via Mandralisca and turn left onto Via Vittorio Emanuele. The shops and restaurants lining the west side of this picturesque street have fine views out to sea, as does the Lavatoio, an ancient wash-house, 50m (55yd) along. A wash-house has stood on this spot since antiquity, but most of the structure seen today dates from the sixteenth century, although parts of an earlier, Arabic building have been incorporated.

Those with time and energy may wish to hike up to the Rocca, the fortress, which is perched on the crag top above the town at a height of 269m (882ft). Steps lead up from Piazza Garibaldi, at the southern end of the main street, Corso Umberto I. After a steep twenty-minute climb the ruins of a fifth-century BC temple, dedicated to Diana, are passed to the right. The path continues upwards to the medieval walls and the scant remains of the Norman castle, from where the views alone warrant the climb.

A more relaxing way to end a tour of Cefalu is to return to the

The austere façade of Cefalu cathedral,
one of the most exquisite buildings in Sicily

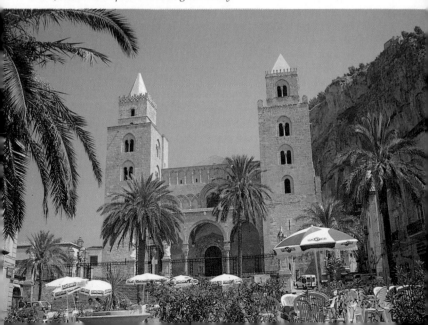

carpark and head for the lido, a well-kept, sandy beach that is 500m (547yd) long. There are good views from here of the town and cathedral, and the beach is backed by a pleasant promenade, Lungomare Cristoforo Colombo, which is lined with hotels and restaurants.

From Cefalu, the A20 motorway is rejoined. It continues along the coast, beneath the rocky peak of Monte San Calogero (1,326m/ 4,349ft), to the town of **Termini Imerese**. The town is surrounded by industry, but the old centre remains intact on a relatively peaceful headland. The large *duomo*, which sits on the summit of the headland was reconstructed in the seventeenth century and has a typically Baroque interior with an attractive, fifteenth-century crucifix suspended in the main apse. Termini Imerese also has a few remnants of the spa resort that stood here in Roman times. The best remains, which include part of an amphitheatre, are in the gardens of Villa Palmieri. The gardens are 350m (383yd) west of the *duomo*, next to the town gate, Porta Palermo.

Continue along the motorway for a further 14km (9 miles) to **Casteldaccia**, from where an excursion can be made to the ancient ruined city of *Solunto*. To reach the ruins, turn right at the outskirts of Casteldaccia and follow the SS113 Riviera, which winds along the coast for 3km (2 miles), to the resort of **Porticello**. Take the first turning on the left and follow the tortuous road up to the site carpark. From here, a footpath leads up to the ticket office which is inside a small museum. The museum has a modest collection of local finds which date from the city's foundation in the mid-fourth century BC up to the Roman era. Amongst the more interesting exhibits are carved capitals which were removed from the courtyards of Hellenistic housing, fragments of statues, and a painting of a theatrical mask on a small piece of stucco.

From the museum, continue up the ancient paved road, Via dell'Agora, which turns sharply right at the top of the hill. The street continues through the centre of the city, with open views to the coast along one side, and a wealthy housing district on the other. The housing covers the terraced slopes of Monte Catalfano, ancient *Solus*, and is arranged on a grid plan. Some of the houses have remnants of their colonnaded courtyards, with fragments of mosaic and stucco in the surrounding rooms.

The street ends at the agora, where the remains of nine recesses can be seen along the west side. At the northern end of the agora there is a large cistern filled with the bases of columns that would have supported a roof. Built into the slope of the hill, above the agora, are the scant remains of the theatre. Parts of the foundations of the stage floor are visible, but the seating, which would have held an audience of over 1,000 people, is overgrown.

From *Solunto*, the route proceeds along the motorway, past **Bagheria**. This once-grand town was a popular residential area for the wealthy Palermese in the seventeenth and eighteenth centuries. The town has become an unsightly suburb, but one of the old palatial villas, Villa Palagonia, which was built in 1715 for the Prince of Palagonia, is open as a museum. The façade is preceded by a monumental staircase. Inside, there is a series of lavishly decorated apartments and a hall of mirrors, the Salone degli Specchi. The villa, however, is best known for the grotesque statues dotted about the gardens. The prince, who was hunch-backed, commissioned two-hundred statues to be made of deformed creatures, which caused the German poet, Goethe, who visited the villa in 1787, to describe it as a 'sanctuary of madness'.

Palermo is a further 15km (9 miles) west of Bagheria and is covered in Route 6C.

Route 6C • Palermo

Palermo, the capital of Sicily, is a city of bygone splendour and romantic decay. Cars squeal over narrow, flag-stoned streets which are lined with crumbling façades and grimy *palazzi*, while the city's shops are generally small and down-at-heel. The city's monuments, however, are testimony to a glorious history. In the days of the Saracens there were said to be over five-hundred mosques in the city, and as the capital of the Norman kingdom, it boasted one of the greatest courts in Europe. Frederick II, who grew up in the Norman court and became Emperor in 1220, made Palermo an unrivalled centre of culture and learning. The most impressive monuments all date from the Saracen and Norman periods, although the Spanish, who dominated Palermo in later years, also endowed the city with some attractive architecture.

The principal sights in Palermo can be seen in a day, and are all within reasonable walking distance of the centre. Those with cars are recommended to visit Palermo as a day excursion from somewhere outside the city, as parking and driving are difficult. There is a regular train service along the coast and the central railway station is close to the city centre. The best option for drivers is to park in a private garage, such as the one behind the central railway station, or try to find a space on one of the city piazzas. One of the largest is Piazza Marina, near the port, which tends to be less busy at lunchtimes.

The best place from which to start a tour of the city is at the central crossroads, the Quattro Canti. The curved façades, which decorate

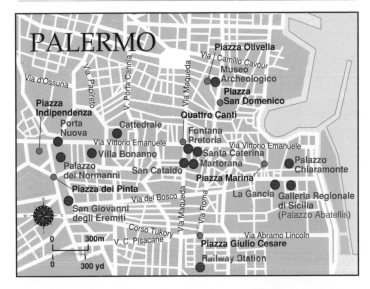

each corner of the crossroads date from 1609, when the city was under Spanish rule. From the south-west side of the crossroads, follow Via Maqueda, and take the steps up on the left to Piazza Pretoria. Filling the centre of this piazza, is the elegant, Renaissance fountain, Fontana Pretoria. The fountain was originally designed for a Florentine villa, but was shipped, piece by piece, to Palermo in 1574. The ample, circular basin is raised on a plinth, enclosed by wrought-iron railings, and is adorned with fine statues of gods, nymphs and sea creatures. The church of Santa Caterina, along the east side of the piazza, dates from the same era as the fountain, and is topped by a large, slate dome.

Head from the south-west corner of the piazza, past Santa Caterina, to the adjoining flag-stoned square, at the far side of which is the **Martorana**. A Baroque façade clads the north transept of the Martorana, but the proper entrance to the church is up the steps to the right. The steps lead up to a secluded courtyard, where the apse of the tiny Norman church of San Cataldo is on the right, and the ponderous bell tower of the Martorana is on the left. The church entrance, which is built into the base of the bell tower, leads into an atrium. This is divided from the main part of the church by a few shallow steps, at the top of which is a row of columns. The second column from the right has an inscription in Arabic. The column probably came from the mosque that stood here before George of

Antioch had the Martorana erected in 1143. George of Antioch was a wealthy Admiral, under the Norman King Roger I, and he spared no expense in decorating his church with beautiful, golden mosaics. In the first niche on the left, at the top of the atrium steps, there is a mosaic of the Admiral kneeling to the Virgin. On the opposite side of the steps, the mosaic in the first niche on the right, shows Roger I

The cloisters of San Giovanni degli Eremiti, Palermo

being crowned by Christ.

The main body of the church is laid out on a Greek cross plan with an assortment of ancient columns along the central nave, and a dome with transepts at either side. The dome is the central focus of the church, and has an excellent mosaic of *Christ Surrounded by Angels and Apostles*. Other mosaics clad the transepts, although the main apse and other parts of the church have Baroque frescoes.

Return to the Quattro Canti crossroads and head south-west along **Via Vittorio Emanuele**. Formerly known as the Cassaro, this now dilapidated street, with its bedraggled shops selling second hand books and military uniforms, is the oldest thoroughfare in the city. After 600m (652yd) a grand square, edged by marble balustrades, opens out on the right, with the city's **cathedral** along one side. The cathedral was erected in 1185 under an English archbishop, Walter of the Mill, who was known in Italian as Gualtiero Offamiglio. The Norman building was, however, re-modelled at various stages, between the fifteenth century and the eighteenth century, and the towers at each corner of the building are one of the few remaining original features. The main portal, which is on the south side was added in 1426 while the vast dome, awkwardly surmounting the eastern end, was built to a design by the Florentine architect F. Fuga in the late-eighteenth century. Fuga was also responsible for the neo-Classical decoration of the interior. The presbytery, however, still holds the twelfth-century episcopal throne, and in the treasury, which is to the right of the choir, there are further Norman relics as well as the tiara of Constance of Aragon. The Norman imperial tombs, boldly carved of red porphyry, are in the first chapel on the right. There are four in all: the front right belongs to Henry VI (1197), the back right to Constance (1198), the back left to Roger II and the front left to Frederick II. Also of interest in the cathedral are the sixteenth-century statues and sculptures by the Gagini family, including the water stoups in the central nave, and the relief panels and statues of the Apostles in the presbytery.

Continue to head south-west along Via Vittorio Emanuele, past the palm-filled gardens of the Villa Bonanno to the sixteenth-century gate, Porta Nuova. The **Palazzo dei Normanni**, the next sight of interest, is on the left, but to reach the entrance it is necessary to go through Porta Nuova, turn left at the gardens on Piazza Independenza, and proceed, for a further 150m, (164yd) alongside the palace walls. The gate is on the left, from where steps wind up to the palace entrance.

The palace dates from the ninth century when Palermo was ruled by a Saracen Emir. However, the Normans greatly enlarged the building in the twelfth century, and further modifications were made by the Spanish between the sixteenth and eighteenth centuries. Today it is the seat of the Sicilian Parliament, but the Norman chapel, Cappella Palatina, and some of the royal apartments are open to the public. From the entrance, a pink marble staircase leads up to the first floor, which surrounds an inner courtyard. On the left side of the courtyard is the **Cappella Palatina**. This tiny chapel is one of the most popular tourist sights in Palermo. In peak season there are long queues to see the outstanding mosaics that bejewel the walls of the excellently-preserved interior. The chapel was built for Roger II in 1132 and decorated in a style that was most certainly fit for a king. The floors are covered by Cosmatesque paving, the wooden ceiling is sculpted into geometric stalactites, with minutely painted details on every facet. Of the wealth of astounding mosaics, those decorating the dome and apses are the oldest and were probably done by Byzantine artisans from Constantinople. In the presbytery, the walls are decorated with scenes of the Evangelists, and along the walls of the nave there are mosaics depicting the Old and New Testament, including the story of Saints Peter and Paul. The original paschal candlestick, which is 4m (13ft) high, can still be seen in the presbytery, and to its right, there is a Norman ambone, beautifully-carved from marble with griffins and rich foliage. The King's throne is built against the back wall of the chapel and is finely inlaid with Cosmatesque, geometric mosaic designs.

To visit the palace apartments, return to the staircase and continue up to the second floor. The guided tour includes the Sala Gialla which was formerly a ball-room, and the Sala Rosso, named after the red damask that lines the walls. Both of these rooms are used during parliamentary sittings. The highlight of the tour, however, is the Sala di Ruggero. This charming room lies on one side of a former tower and is decorated with its original Norman mosaics. The mosaics depict hunting scenes and symbolic animals, such as the lions beneath palm trees, which represent freedom, and the eagle holding a rabbit between his talons, representing the submission of the populace to the King.

From Palazzo dei Normanni, continue to Piazza dei Pinta, which is at the southern end of the palace. Cross over the piazza and follow Via dei Benedettini for a short distance further south to **San Giovanni degli Eremiti**, which is on the right. This delightful church and cloister is set in a luxuriant garden, filled with exotic flowering shrubs and cactus plants, and shaded by lime, palm and fig trees. It tends to be overcrowded in peak season, but is a sight not to be missed. The cloister, which is edged by pairs of dainty columns, is passed on the right, while the church is further on, on the left. The distinctive red domes remain from the mosque that stood here before Roger II had it converted to a church in 1132. The interior, now bare of its furnishings, resembles a mosque in having an open square plan covered by two main domes.

The museums in Palermo are at the opposite end of the city, but can be reached on foot from the Quattro Canti crossroads. The **Museo Archeologico Regionale** is in the north-eastern quarter of the city. To get there, continue north-east from the Quattro Canti, along Via Vittorio Emanuele, for 200m (218yd) to the intersection with Via Roma. Turn left along Via Roma, and continue for a further 250m (273yd) to Piazza San Domenico with its eighteenth-century Domenican church. Take the left turn, Via Montelleone, and proceed along this narrow street for 300m (328yd) to Piazza Olivella where the entrance to the museum is found on the right.

The museum is housed in the former Philippine convent which was built in 1590. From the ticket office, which is on the left, one enters the first of the convent's two cloisters, the Chiostro Minore, which dates from the eighteenth century. It is surrounded by ancient anchors found on the sea bed off Sicily and stone-carved fragments, and has an elegant sixteenth-century fountain at its centre. The next cloister, the Chiostro Grande, is also filled with ancient finds, including a collection of Roman statues. The most important collections in the museum are, however, in the rooms off the east side of the cloister. In the first room there is a well-displayed collection of pottery, dating from the sixth century BC, arranged in reconstructed barrow tombs. Those interested in the site of Selinunte may wish to watch the film which is screened in the room next door. Beyond, is the Sala Pirro Marconi, which has a remarkably complete collection of water spouts carved with lion's heads, which date from the fifth century BC and were found at the ancient Greek city of *Himera*. Straight ahead there is a good collection of Etruscan relics, but the museum's prime exhibits are in the Salone di Selinunte, on the left. This room holds an unequalled collection of carved reliefs from the temples of Selinunte. On the left and right there are a series of friezes dating from the sixth century BC. Against the back wall, there are four metopes, which were carved in 450BC. From left to right, they are of *Heracles Fighting an Amazon*, the *Marriage of Zeus and Hera*, *Actaeon Savaged by Dogs*, and *Athena and the Titan*.

The rest of the museum's collection is on the first floor, which is reached by the stairs up from the Chiostro Minore. Not to be missed is the Sala dei Bronzi which has the beautiful Hellenistic statue of the *Ram of Syracuse* as well as the Roman copy of the Pompeian statue of

Hercules Subduing a Stag.

The **Galleria Regionale di Sicilia** is in the south-eastern quarter of the city. To get there, return to Vittorio Emanuele and continue to head north-east for 450m (492yd) to Piazza Marina, which is on the right. Head through the gardens, which fill the centre of the piazza, to the façade of Palazzo Chiaramonte. This fine, medieval *palazzo* was built in 1307 for the feudal Chiaramonte lords, and served as the prototype for many subsequent *palazzi* built in Sicily. Head to the right of Palazzo Chiaramonte to the church, La Gancia, and turn left along Via Alloro. The gallery, which is housed in Palazzo Abatellis, is a short distance along this street, on the right. The *palazzo* was built in 1495 and is a successful blend of Gothic-Catalan and Renaissance architectural styles. It surrounds an inner courtyard, on the left side of which is the entrance to the gallery. The ground floor rooms contain sculptures, which range from wooden polychrome statues to marble *Madonnas* by Antonello Gagini. In room 2, however, there is a large painting of the *Triumph of Death* by an unknown artist which dates from the fifteenth century.

On the first floor, which is reached by stairs from the back right hand corner of the inner courtyard, there is a more extensive collection of paintings. This ranges from small, jewel-like Byzantine icons

A traditional way to tour around Sicily

to fifteenth-century triptyches by Sicilian masters. One of the most famous paintings in the collection is the *Annunciation* by Antonello da Messina.

Route 6D • Palermo to Selinunte

Route 6D leaves Palermo on the SS186 to **Monreale**. The road heads along the wide valley of the Conca d'Oro for 5km (3 miles), to a sharp fork on the right, from where a series of hairpin bends wind up the slopes of Monte Caputo, to the outskirts of Monreale. Follow signs to the large carpark at the southern side of the town. From here it is a steep, but short walk to Monreale's Norman cathedral, which lies at the heart of the historic centre, on Piazza del Duomo. The cathedral was started in 1174, under the last of the Norman Kings, William II. It was built to rival the cathedral in Palermo, but lost the contest with the demise of Norman power, which followed William II's death in 1189. This turn of events left Monreale's cathedral untouched, and today it ranks amongst the most pristine examples of Norman architecture in Southern Italy.

The seventeenth-century portico, with its three tall arches, is one of the few later additions that were made to the cathedral. It is flanked by stout towers at either side, although that on the left is incomplete. Beneath the portico, a finely-inlaid portal frames a splendid pair of bronze doors which are covered by relief panels depicting biblical scenes. They were cast in 1185 by Bonanus Pisano, to whom the doors of Pisa cathedral are also attributed.

Inside, the cathedral has a traditional basilica ground-plan, with three aisles, divided by antique columns, which support a high clerestory. The most outstanding feature of the vast interior, however, is the golden mosaics which cover a total area of 6,340sq m (68,208sq ft). They cover all the upper walls, including the clerestory, the presbytery and the three apses, and were done by artisans from the eastern Byzantine Empire during the twelfth and thirteenth centuries. Perhaps the most impressive mosaic is that of *Christ Pantocrator* which fills the semi-dome of the main apse. The hand alone measures 2m (7ft), while the entire head and shoulders are 20m (66ft) high. The wall below has *Saints and Angels*, arranged in rows, with the *Virgin Enthroned* at the centre of the upper row. At either side of the deep arch, preceding the apse, there is a mosaic of *William II Crowned by Christ* and *William II Offering the Church to Mary*. Below each mosaic there is a throne: the one on the left was the Archbishop's, and the one on the right belonged to the King.

The Kings' sarcophagi were removed from Monreale to Palermo cathedral at the end of the Norman era. However, the right transept still has two porphyry sarcophagi, one of which belongs to William II and the other to William I. In the right apse, beyond the sarcophagi, there is a large mosaic of *St Peter*. In the left apse there is another grand mosaic of *St Paul*, while the left transept holds tombs of local dignitaries.

The other mosaics in the cathedral are arranged along the clerestory, and in the side aisles. The cycle of mosaics on the clerestory walls depict scenes from the *Old Testament* and are to be read in a clockwise direction, starting from the right side of the altar. The mosaics in the side aisles depict the *Teachings of Christ*, but are poorly illuminated

To visit the cathedral's cloisters, the Chiostro dei Benedettini, return to Piazza del Duomo. The ticket office is in the corner of the piazza, to the right of the cathedral. The cloisters are edged by two-hundred or more, pairs of decoratively-carved columns, and an arcade of pointed arches with inlaid designs. At the centre of the cloisters there is a garden full of cactii, and in the south-west corner there is an unusual fountain, made up of a chunky column.

Monreale has many other interesting corners to explore, including the lively Piazza Vittorio Emanuele which runs alongside the cathedral. A spot not to be missed, however, are the shady gardens at the Belvedere. This is reached via the archway on the right side of Piazza del Duomo, next to the post office. The arch leads through to a courtyard which is surrounded by an eighteenth-century convent, and has a children's playground at its centre. The Belvedere is a short distance beyond, perched at the edge of a cliff, with excellent views of the Conca d'Oro valley.

From Monreale, return to the SS186 and continue south-west for 21km (13 miles) to **Partinico**. A historic campaign against the Mafia took place here in the 1950s, led by the social reformer, Danilo Dolci. The town is rather grim and the route follows the ring road which eventually joins the SS113. **Alcamo**, 15km (9 miles) south-west of Partinico on the SS113, holds more of interest for the visitor. It was founded by Frederick II in the thirteenth century and is overlooked by a fine castle. There are several churches dotted along the main street, Corso 6 Aprile, most of which contain sixteenth-century sculptures by the Gagini family.

The route continues along the SS113 for a further 13km (8 miles) to the ancient site of **Segesta** which is dominated by its imposing temple. A narrow road winds up to the site, where there are two parking areas; an upper and a lower. From the upper parking area, steps lead up to the city's finest remaining monument, the temple which looms on the hillside above. It was started in 424BC, but never completed. Despite this it is excellently-preserved, having all its columns intact with the entablature, which is decorated with triglyphs, as well as the shallow pediments at either end. The roof was never constructed, neither was the cella, and the fat columns with their simple Doric capitals were left unfluted. The stylobate, or platform, on which the temple stands, has three steps, most of which still have the protruding stud which enabled the stones to be lifted and placed, but would normally be removed on completion.

To visit the theatre, the only other major surviving monument at Segesta, head for the lower parking area, from where a bus service is available. Alternatively, take the footpath which involves a steep 1km (½ mile) hike. The theatre is built into the north slope of Monte Barbaro, at a height of 400m (1,312ft), and looks out across hills and valleys to the Gulf of Castellamare. It was constructed during the Hellenistic era, although additions were made in Roman times, including the sustaining wall along the top.

From Segesta, head down to the motorway, and follow the A29 in the direction of Mazara del Vallo. The road heads through one of the areas worst hit in the 1968 earthquake, which left some 50,000 people in the region homeless. In **Salemi**, which is 30km (19 miles) south of Segesta, almost a third of the town's inhabitants lost their homes. Those that make the excursion to the town will find the old centre, however, has survived mostly intact, although the castle on the hilltop above is strapped together with wooden planking.

Ruderi di Ghibellina which lies in the opposite direction from Salemi, 20km (12 miles) east of the motorway, was completely flattened. A large cemetery stands on the site, and amongst the rubble a theatre has been built to stage a series of classical drama which is held in remembrance of the disaster.

The A29 motorway continues south, past **Ghibellina Nuova**, the new town that was erected to re-house Ghibellina's surviving population. It is still not marked on most maps, but it is clearly visible from the motorway with its monumental, 5-petalled flower, built of concrete. At **Castelvetrano**, which is a further 17km (10 miles) south, leave the motorway and proceed along the SS115 to Selinunte. This outstanding archaeological site, beautifully located on the coast, is in two parts, the first of which, the Templi i Orientale, is on the right at the outskirts of the resort, **Marinella**. From the carpark, head through the subway, to the three eastern temples of **Selinunte**. They were constructed in the city's heyday, before the devastating attack of the Carthaginians in 409BC. The most impressive remaining, is the southernmost one, Temple E, which was re-erected in the late 1950s. It has all thirty-eight of its original fluted columns, each of which is over 10m (33ft) high, and is topped by a Doric capital. Parts of the entablature have also survived with their triglyphs.

To the right of Temple E, are the plundered remains of Temple F, which was built in the mid-sixth century BC. A solitary column, 9m (30ft) high, stands amongst the debris of column bases and fragments. Next to Temple F is the northernmost of the three temples, Temple G. This temple is also strewn on the ground apart from one column, but it is exceptional for its vast size. It ranks amongst the largest temples in the ancient Greek world, which include the Artemision at Epheseus in Turkey, and the Zeus Temple at Agrigento. Each column was over 16m (52ft) high, and was made of

The impressive ruins of Temple E at Selinunte

individual sections, now tumbled on the ground, each of which weighs 100 tons. Some of the columns were left unfluted as construction was still underway when the Carthaginians attacked.

The other part of Selinunte, the acropolis, is reached by following signs to the *parco archeologico* where there is a carpark at the foot of the acropolis hill. From here, proceed on foot to the ticket office which is on the left and continue up the roadway. On the right there are some well-preserved sections of the acropolis wall before reaching the custodian's house at the top of the hill, on the left. From here, turn right and continue up, past the foundations of two temples, Temple O and Temple A respectively, on the right. The bases of these temples are strewn with blocks of stone and segments of columns. Temple A, the better-preserved of the two, dates from 490BC and was originally surrounded by thirty-six columns. A short distance beyond, there is an intersection with the main east-west thoroughfare. On the right is the largest and oldest temple at Selinunte, Temple C, which has twelve of the original forty-two columns left standing amongst a confusion of fallen stones. It was from this temple that the beautifully-carved metopes, now in the Palermo museum, were removed. It was built in the early sixth century BC, and stands at the highest point of the acropolis, from where there are fine views of the long sandy bay that extends either side of Marinella.

Head west of Temple C to the central crossroads where the main north-south artery intersects. Follow this well-paved road northwards, past Temple D, which is on the right. This temple was started in 570BC, and completed in 554BC, but is now reduced to a heap of fallen stones and column fragments. The street continues northwards, through a housing district which was built in the fourth and third centuries BC, to the city gate. It was built after the Carthaginian attack of 409BC along with a well-defended wall which was 4 ½m (15ft) thick and enclosed an area of 100 hectares (247 acres). The fortifications, defending the city wall, were built with the stones from the abandoned, outlying city. The deep trench outside the gate was roofed over by rows of temple columns, which now lie on the ground to the north. Columns are also built into the curved wall of the outer fortification. It is worth climbing up onto this wall for the fine views north, across the Manuzza plateau where the original city was once spread, and south to Temple C, with its columns outlined on the horizon.

From here, visitors can either return back through the city the way they came, or follow the rough path along the eastern city wall which leads back towards the carpark.

Additional Information

Places to Visit

Bagheria
Villa Palagonia
Piazza Garibaldi
☎ (091) 903522
Open: daily 9am-12noon, 2-5pm.

Cefalu
Duomo
Piazza del Duomo
☎ (0921) 21141
Open: daily 9am-12noon, 4-6pm.

Museo Mandralisca
Via Mandarlisca 13
☎ (0921) 21547
Open: daily 9am-12.30pm, 3.30-6pm.

Lavatoio
Corso Vittorio Emanuele
Open: daily 8.30am-1pm, 4.30-8pm.

Lipari
Museo Archeologico Eoliano
Via del Castello
☎ (090) 9880175
Open: Monday to Saturday 9am-2pm, Sunday and holidays 9am-1pm.

Messina
Museo Regionale Messina
Via della Liberta 275
☎ (090) 358605
Open: Monday to Saturday 9am-1pm, 3-7.30pm, Sunday and holidays 9am-12.30pm, 3-7.30pm. Closed: first and third Sunday afternoon of each month.

Milazzo
Castello
Visit by guided tour only: October to February 9am, 10am, 11am, 12noon, 2.30pm, 3.30pm. March to May 10am, 11am, 12noon, 3pm, 4pm, 5pm. June to August, 10am, 11am, 12noon, 5pm, 6pm, 7pm. September 10am, 11am, 12noon, 3pm, 4pm, 5pm.

Monreale
Duomo
Piazza del Duomo
☎ (091) 586122
Open: daily 8.30am-12.30pm, 3.30-6.30pm.

Chiostro dei Benedittini
Piazza del Duomo
☎ (091) 6404403
Open: winter, Monday to Sunday 9am-1.30pm. Summer Monday to Saturday 9am-7pm, Sunday 9am-1.30pm.

Palermo
Martorana
Piazza Bellini 3
☎ (091) 6161692
Open: Monday to Saturday 8.30-1pm, 3.30-5.30pm. Sunday and holidays 8.30am-1pm.

Cattedrale
Corso Vittorio Emanuele
☎ (091) 334373
Open: daily 7am-12noon, 5-7pm.

Palazzo dei Normanni
Piazza Indipendenza
☎ (091) 6561111
Open: Monday, Friday and Saturday 9am-12.30pm. 15 August to 15 September daily 9am-12.30pm.

Cappella Palatina
Piazza Indipendenza
☎ (091) 488449
Open: Monday to Friday 9am-
12noon, 3-5pm. Saturday, Sunday
and holidays 9-10am, 12noon-1pm.

San Giovanni degli Eremiti
Via dei Benedettini
☎ (091) 426900
Open: Monday, Thursday and
Saturday 9am-2pm. Tuesday,
Wednesday and Friday 9am-1pm,
3-7pm. Sunday and holidays 9am-
1pm.

Museo Archeologico Regionale
Piazza Olivella
☎ (091) 587825
Open: Monday to Saturday 9am-
2pm, Tuesday and Friday also 3-
6pm. Sunday and holidays 9am-
1pm.

Galleria Regionale di Sicilia
Palazzo Abatellis
Via Alloro 4
☎ (091) 6164317
Open: Monday, Tuesday and
Friday 9am-1pm, 3-6pm. Wednesday, Thursday and Saturday 9am-
1pm. Sunday and holidays 9am-
12.30pm.

Patti
Villa Romana di Patti
☎ (0941) 361593
Open: daily 9am-1 hour before
sunset

Segesta
Tempio e Teatro
Open: daily 9am-1 hour before
sunset.
Bus service to theatre from carpark
every half hour.

Marinella
Selinunte *(Templi Orientale e Parco
    Archeologico)*
Open: daily 9am-2 hours before
sunset.

Porticello
Solunto (Zona Archeologico)
Via Porticello
Frazione Solunto
☎ (091) 904557
Open: daily 9am-2 hours before
sunset.

Tindari
Scavi Archeologici
☎ (0941) 22202
Open: daily 9am-1 hour before
sunset

Museo di Tindari
☎ (0941) 369023
Open: Monday to Saturday 9am-
2pm. Sunday and holidays 9am-
1pm.

Useful Information

Cefalu
Events and Festivals
Estate di Cefalu (Summer festival,
international folk competition,
regatta, concerts, puppet theatre
shows).

Tourist Information Centre
Azienda Autonoma di Soggiorno e
    Turismo
Corso Ruggero 77
☎ (0921) 21050

Transport
Stazione FFSS (Railway)
☎ (0921) 22506

Emergencies
Vigili Urbani (Municipal Police)
☎ (0921) 21226

Polizia (Police)
Via Stanislao
☎ (0921) 21104

Carabinieri (Military Police)
Via Santa Barbara
☎ (0921) 21205

Ospedale Civico G. Giglio
(Hospital)
Via Moro 1
☎ (0921) 21121

Ghibellina Nuova
Events and Festivals
July to September, season of
classical drama

Tourist Information Centre
Ente Provinciale per il Turismo
Viale Segesta
☎ (0924) 67123

Lipari (Aeolian Island)
Events and Festivals
24 August, Festa di San Bartolomeo
(Festival of St Bartholomew).

Diving
Centro Nautico Eoliano (Subaqua
  Centre)
Salita S. Giuseppe 8
☎ (090) 9812110

F. Vajarelli (Subaqua Centre)
Via F. Crispi
☎ (090) 9812771

Dive School (Subaqua Centre)
Via Marina Garibaldi
Canneto
☎ (090) 9880088

Tourist Information Centre
Azienda Autonoma di Soggiorno e
  Turismo
Corso Vittorio Emanuele 233
☎ (090) 9880095

Transport
Navigazione Generale Italiana
  (Ferry)
☎ (090) 9811955

Societa Eolie di Navigazione (Boat
  excursions)
Via Vittorio Emanuele 247
☎ (090) 9812341

Societa Navigazione Basso Tirreno
  (Boat excursions)
Marina Corta
☎ (090) 9812592

Emergencies
Vigili Urbani (Municipal Police)
☎ (090) 9811330

Carabinieri (Military Police)
☎ (090) 9811333

Pronto Soccorso (First Aid Service)
☎ (090) 9811010

Guardia Medica (Medical Officer)
☎ (090) 9812739/9811230

Messina
Events and Festivals
3 June, Processione della Madonna
della Lettera (Procession in honour
of city's patron saint).

24 June, Processione della Varetta
(Procession with the *varetta*, a silver
casket containing holy relics).

12-13 August, Passegiata dei
Giganti Mata e Grifone (Parade
with giant plaster effigies of Mata
and Grifone, the mythical founders
of Messina).

15 August Processione della Vara
(Procession celebrating Ascension
Day. A column is paraded about
the town with a statue of Christ.
Excellent firework display in the
evening).

Tourist Information Centres
Azienda Autonoma di Soggiorno e
  Turismo
Piazza Cairoli 45
☎ (090) 694780/2933541

Azienda Autonoma Provinciale
  Turistico
Via Calabria 301
☎ (090) 675356/7770731

Transport
Aliscafi S.N.A.V. (Hydrofoil)
Via Cortina Porto
☎ (090) 364044

Traghetti F.S. (Ferry)
☎ (090) 675234

Traghetti Caronte (Ferry)
☎ (090) 44982

Traghetti Tourist Ferry-boats
☎ (090) 41415

Stazione Centrale (Railway)
☎ (090) 675234/5

Emergencies
Vigili Urbani (Municipal Police)
☎ (090) 771000

Carabinieri (Military Police)
Via Monsignor D'Arrigo
☎ (090) 42801/57251

Ospedale Piemonte (Hospital)
☎ (090) 2221

Ospedale Regina Margherita
(Hospital)
Viale della Liberta
☎ (090) 3651

Milazzo
Events and Festivals
Second Sunday after Easter, Festa
di San Francesco di Paola (Festival
in honour of St Francis of Paola).
First Sunday of September, Festa di

San Stefano (Festival in honour of
St Stephen).

Tourist Information Centre
Azienda Autonoma di Soggiorno e
  Turismo
Piazza Dullio 10
☎ (090) 9222790

Transport
Navigazione Generale Italiana
  (Ferry)
Via dei Mille 26
☎ (090) 9283415

Siremar Traghetti (Ferry)
Via dei Mille 28
☎ (090) 9286020

Siremar Aliscafi (Hydrofoil)
Via dei Mille 57
☎ (090) 9221812

Aliscafi Covemar (Hydrofoil)
Via L. Rizzo 9
☎ (090) 9287728

Aliscafi S.N.A.V. (Hydrofoil)
Via L. Rizzo 14
☎ (090) 9284509

Emergencies
Ospedale Generale di Zona
☎ (090) 92901

Palermo
Events and Festivals
15 July and 4 September, Festa di
Santa Rosalia (Torchlit procession
to Santuario Santa Rosalia, on
Monte Pellegrino, in honour of
city's patron saint).

Tourist Information Centres
Azienda Autonoma di Turismo per
  Palermo e Monreale
Via Belmonte 43
☎ (091) 540122

Azienda Autonoma Provinciale
Piazza Castelnuovo 34
☎ (091) 583847/6110977/6111180

Transport
Stazione Ferroviaria (Railway)
Piazza G. Cesare
☎ (091) 6165914

Emergencies
Vigili Urbani (Municipal Police)
Via Dogali
☎ (091) 222890

Polizia Stradale (Traffic Police)
Piazza Turba
☎ (091) 422524

Pronto Soccorso (First Aid Service)
Ospedale Civico Regionale
   Generale
Via Carmello Lazzaro
☎ (091) 6061111/484544

Guardia Medicale Turistica
(Medical Officer for Tourists)
Via Sferracavallo 146
☎ (091) 532798

Patti
Tourist Information Centre
Pro Loco
Piazza M. Sciacca
☎ (0941) 21327

Emergencies
Ospedale Circoscrizionale Barone
   Romeo (Hospital)
☎ (0941) 21154

Salina (Aeolian Island)
Events and Festivals
17 July, Festa di Santa Marina
(Festival of St Marina at Santa
Maria Salina).

23 July, Festa di Maria Santissimi
del Terzito (Festival of Maria
Santissimi del Terzito at Leni).

10 August, Festa di San Lorenzo
(Festival of St Laurence at Malfa).

Diving
Centro Nautico Aqua Sub
(Subaqua Centre)
Leni
☎ (090) 9809033

Tourist Information Centre
Ufficio Informazione (open
summer only)
Santa Maria Salina
☎ (090) 9843003

Transport
Navigazione Generale Italiana
   (Ferry)
Santa Maria Salina
☎ (090) 9843003

Follone e Zavone (Boat excursions)
Via Colombo
Santa Maria Salina
☎ (090) 9843143

Emergencies
Vigili Urbani (Municipal Police)
Santa Maria Salina
☎ (090) 9843021

Carabinieri (Military Police)
Santa Maria Salina
☎ (090) 9843019

Pronto Soccorso (First Aid Service)
Santa Maria Salina
☎ (090) 9843337

Vigili Urbani (Municipal Police)
Leni
☎ (090) 9809125

Guardia Medica (Medical Officer)
Leni
☎ (090) 9809186

Vigili Urbani (Municipal Police)
Malfi
☎ (090) 9844008

Guardia Medica (Medical Officer)
Malfi
☎ (090) 9844005

Stromboli (Aeolian Island)
Diving
La Sirenetta Diving Centre
☎ (090) 986025

Walking
Guide C.A.I. - C.N.S.A. (Hiking
    Guides)
☎ (090) 986263/986211/986175

Tourist Information Centre
Ufficio Informazione (open
summer only)
Ficogrande
☎ (090) 986285

Transport
Mandarano (Boat Hire)
☎ (090) 986003

Emergencies
Carabinieri (Military Police)
☎ (090) 986021

Guardia Medica (Medical Officer)
☎ (090) 986097

Tindari
Events and Festivals
8 September, Festa di Madonna
Nera (Festival of the Black
Madonna).

Vulcano (Aeolian Island)
Tourist Information Centre
Azienda Autonoma di Soggiorno e
    Turismo
Via Porto di Ponente
(open summer only)
☎ (090) 9852028

Transport
Navigazione Generale Italiana
    (Ferry)
☎ (090) 9852401

Societa Eolie di Navigazione (boat
    excursions)
Via Vittorio Emanuele 247
☎ (090) 9812341

Societa Italiana per il Turismo (boat
    excursions)
☎ (090) 9852226

Emergencies
Carabinieri (Military Police)
☎ (090) 9852110

Guardia Medica (Medical Officer)
☎ (090) 9852220

7

SOUTHERN SICILY

Route 7a • Selinunte to Enna

Route 7a continues east of Selinunte on a minor road which follows the Riviera Naturale Orientale. The gentle, red-earthed slopes of the riviera are thickly covered in vines, cactus plants, and eucalyptus trees, through which there are occasional glimpses of the sea. After 15km (9 miles) the new town of **Menfi**, which was rebuilt after the 1968 earthquake, is passed to the left. The road continues along the scenic riviera for a further 22km (14 miles) to the outskirts of **Sciacca**, where visitors should fork right and follow signs to *centro*. Old Sciacca is entered through the town's west wall, where there is a fine, sixteenth-century gate, Porta San Salvatore. Chiesa del Carmine, facing the gate, was also built in the sixteenth century, and has a brightly tiled dome. Follow Via F. Incisa, along the right side of Chiesa del Carmine, passing the richly-carved portal of Santa Margherita on the right. The reliefs of biblical scenes, which decorate this portal, were sculpted by Francesco Laurana in 1468. After a further 150m (164yd), turn right to Piazza Rossi where there is ample parking. The town's main square, Piazza Scandaliato, is a short distance south-east. It has a fine position, looking out above the port, and is surrounded by cafés and restaurants. Follow Corso Vittorio Emanuele, the main street through the town, from the eastern end of the piazza, to the *duomo* which is on the left. The façade dates from the eighteenth century, but inside, there are a number of sixteenth-century sculptures by the Gagini family, and in the fourth chapel on the right there is a *Madonna* by Francesco Laurana (1426).

Sciacca also has a number of thermal establishments which are at the eastern end of town and operate from April to November. The facilities are modern and treatments involve a twelve to fourteen day course of steam inhalations and mud baths. Cures are offered for osteoarthritis and rheumatism, as well as metabolism, respiratory and gynaecological problems. The waters are sulphureous and have a temperature of 54°C (129°F).

Leave Sciacca, following signs to Agrigento, on the SS115. The road winds along the coast to the wide, citrus-filled plain of **Ribera**, which is a centre for growing Washington oranges and is known as the *Citta delle Arance* (City of Oranges). Continue through the citrus orchards for a further 12km (7 miles), and after crossing the Platani river, take the first turning on the right to visit the ruins of **Eraclea Minoa.** Follow signs to the *zona archeologica*, where there is a parking area at the end of an unsurfaced track. The ruins are dramatically set, on top of high white cliffs, overlooking one of Sicily's most impressive sandy beaches. The city was founded in the fifth century BC, and like Selinunte was attacked by the Carthaginians in 409BC.

On the right of the entrance gate there is a small museum which has a collection of amphorae, terracotta figurines of Sicilian goddesses, and fragments of black and red ceramics, all of which were found locally. A footpath, lined with sections of ancient columns along either side, leads from the museum to the city wall, inside which is the theatre. The theatre was built in the fourth century BC of a soft sandstone, which is now protected from erosion by a plastic covering, and enjoys a magnificent view across the Ionian sea. The auditorium is divided into nine segments, with special reserve seats, carved with arms and back rests, at the centre of the bottom row.

To the south and west of the theatre there is a large residential quarter, which dates from the same era, and is laid out on a grid plan. In most parts only the foundations of the houses remain, but in some there is evidence of black and white mosaic flooring, and fragments of plaster on the walls. On the hilltop, above the theatre, a sanctuary has been discovered, and also the remnants of potteries. The views merit the climb, even though the ruins are scant. A footpath can be followed along the hilltop back to the carpark.

Those that wish to go to the beach should return back along the unsurfaced track, and follow signs to the *zona balneare*. The route, however, continues south-east along the SS115 for 30km (19 miles), past the industrial port of **Porto Empedocle** to **Agrigento**. This sprawling provincial capital lies along a ridge top and has a skyline which is dominated by concrete apartment blocks. However, it is not the modern city that one comes to see, but ancient Greek *Akragas* which is famous for its beautiful temples. Follow signs, below Agrigento, to Vale dei Templi, the Valley of the Temples, as the site is now called. A carpark is provided on the left of the road, from where the ancient ruins can be explored on foot in two separate excursions.

The first, and the most impressive part of the site, is reached by crossing over the road and following the wide avenue up the hill. To the right, is the **Tempio di Ercole** (Temple of Hercules) which had eight of its original thirty-eight columns re-erected in 1923, although the rest of the temple remains tumbled on the ground. The avenue continues up, past the necropolis on the left, to **Tempio della Concordia** (Temple of the Concord), which is amongst the best-preserved temples in the ancient Greek world. It was erected in 440BC and has thirty-eight Doric columns, carved from soft tufa stone. The entablature is complete with its carved triglyphs and the pediments are both intact at either end. Perhaps, the most remarkable feature of the building, however, are the interior walls which remain with their elegant arcades and columns along either side. Here, one can see the prototype for the early Christian basilica, with its three aisles divided by columns and arches.

The avenue continues up for a further 650m (710yd) to **Tempio di Giunone** (Temple of Juno), which is perched high on the ridge ahead. This temple was built between 460BC and 440BC and has twenty-five of its fluted, Doric columns still standing. The columns rest on a tall, stepped stylobate and parts of the entablature remain.

Return to the carpark, and head for the western part of the city, which is entered through the gate on the left. A sandy path leads from the ticket office to the scant remains of the **Tempio di Giove Olimpico** (Temple of Olympian Zeus). Once known as the Eighth Wonder of the World, the temple competed in size with the Artemision of *Epheseus* (Turkey) and Temple G at Selinunte. It measured 113m (370ft) by 56m (184ft) and was encircled by columns that were 20m (65ft) high. The façade had four telamones, giant statues, supporting the pediment, one of which lies on the ground here.

Continue along the footpath, which heads down to a vast flat area, at the far side of which, are the ruins of the **Tempio di Castore e Polluce** (Temple of Castor and Pollux). The four columns left standing amongst the debris of this temple were re-erected in 1832 and have traces of the white plaster with which they were once covered. To the right of the temple, the foundations can be seen of a sanctuary, dedicated to the divinities of the underworld and dating from the sixth century BC.

Return to the carpark and follow the road towards Agrigento for 1km (½ mile), past the small, Gothic church of San Nicola, on the right, to the **Museo Archeologico**, which is on the left. This modern

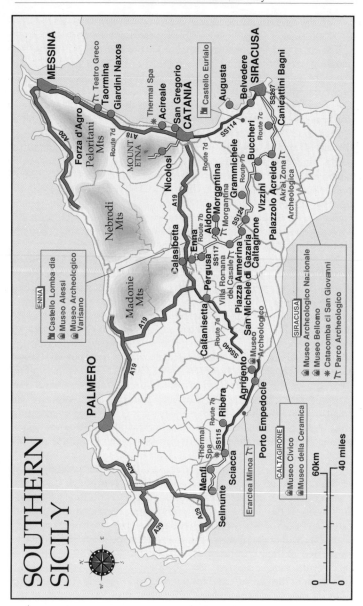

Tempio della Concordia, one of the best preserved temples from the ancient Greek world, Agrigento

The picturesque village of Calasibetta, seen from Enna

museum has an excellent collection of archaeological finds from the Agrigento area. Of particular interest is the black and red vase collection in Room 3 which is arranged in chronological order, ranging from the sixth century BC up to the third century BC. In Room 4 there are sculpted lions' heads which served as gutters along temple roofs; and in Room 6 there is a model reconstruction of the Temple of Olympian Zeus, as well as copies of the telamones that decorated its façade.

From Agrigento, follow the SS640, which passes below the Tempio della Concordia, before heading through vine-covered slopes to **Caltanisetta**. To avoid this large industrial town, fork left at its outskirts and follow the ring road to the A19, which is 14km (9 miles) north. Take the A19, in the direction of Catania, and after a series of long tunnels, turn off at the exit for **Enna**. Follow the SS121 up to Enna which is dramatically situated on a rocky ridge at an altitude of 931m (3,054ft). It is the capital of an agricultural province which has supplied the mainland with grain since Roman times, when Demeter, the goddess of grain, had a very important shrine here. The shrine is located at the far eastern end of the town, next to the castle, which is a good point from which to start a tour of Enna.

There is a carpark at the foot of the castle walls from where the visitor should proceed on foot to the shrine, which is known as the Rocca di Cerere. Rock-hewn steps lead up to a natural stone platform where a temple was built in 480BC. There are no significant remains of the temple, only basins and ledges cut into the rock, but the views are outstanding. To the north, the picturesque village of **Calasibetta** towers above the landscape on a high terraced ridge, while in the distance beyond are the peaks of the Nebrodi and Madonie mountains. To the east, on a clear day it is possible to see Mount Etna.

Return to the castle and head to its entrance which is up the steps, on the north-west wall. The castle, Castello di Lombardia, was built by Frederick II, and is one of the largest in Sicily, covering an area of over 25,000sq m (29,900sq yd). It is well-preserved with all six of its original towers standing, the tallest of which is the Torre Pisana, from where there is a magnificent panorama. The well-defended walls, which are built onto the natural rock, contain three inner courtyards. The main courtyard holds a theatre which is used during the summer for concerts. It is also possible to visit the apartments of Frederick III of Aragon.

From the castle, head down Via Roma, to the *duomo* on Piazza Mazzini. The *duomo* was first built, under Queen Eleanor or Aragon, in 1307, but it has been reconstructed many times since. The façade is Baroque and has a ponderous bell-tower that dates from 1600. The interior has a Renaissance elegance, with black, alabaster columns topped by finely-carved capitals along either side of the central aisle. Set in niches, at either side of the door, are white marble statues of the *Annunciation*. In front, there are marble fonts, sculpted in the sixteenth century by the Gagini school. The ceiling is beautifully coffered and the presbytery, which is raised on alabaster steps, holds a fifteenth-century, painted crucifix, and a handsome marble pulpit which is inlaid with coloured stone.

Back on Piazza Mazzini, walk around to the apse of the *duomo*, next to which is the entrance to the Museo Alessi. This small museum is appointed in the house of the former Canon G. Alessi (1774-1837). On the ground floor there is a collection of oil paintings, dating from the fifteenth century, which includes nineteenth-century oils by Ennese painters. On the first floor is the cathedral treasury and on the mezzanine floor, there is a collection of ancient coins and terracotta figurines, all of which date from the Greek and Roman eras.

On the south side of Piazza Mazzini, there is another museum, the Museo Archeologico Varisano. Housed in an elegant *palazzo*, the museum has a collection of local finds dating from Neolithic to Roman times.

There are no other major places of interest in Enna, but it is worth continuing to stroll along the flag-stoned street, Via Roma, past Palazzo Pollicarini on the right which has a fine, Gothic-Catalan portal, dating from the fifteenth century. Via Roma ends at Piazza Vittorio Emanuele which contains the church of San Francesco and offers a fine panorama. Another prime viewing spot is the Torre di Federico, which is in the suburbs, to the south of the town. This octagonal tower was built by Frederick II as part of the town's defensive wall and is now surrounded by a public gardens.

Route 7B • Enna to Palazzolo Acreide

Route 7B continues south of Enna on the SS561, through **Pergusa**, where there is an oval-shaped lake. The lake is associated with the legend of Persephone's abduction by Hades to the underworld, although nowadays, it is best known for the autodrome which encircles it. The route continues south of Pergusa for 9km (6 miles) before turning right onto the SS117. After a further 8km (5 miles) visitors can make the 12km (7 mile) excursion to the picturesque site of ancient *Morgantina*. To reach the site, take the turning on the left to **Aidone**. At the outskirts of this small, agricultural town, turn right and follow the road to Catania, and at 4km (2 miles) take the roughly-surfaced road on the left which is signposted to Morgantina Scavi. The last 500m (547yd) to the site is extremely bumpy, and visitors may wish to use the parking area, which is on the right, and proceed on foot.

π   Part of the attraction of *Morgantina* is its delightful rural setting in the heart of the Erei hills, where the silence is only broken by the occasional tinkling of a sheep's bell or the braying of a donkey. Indeed, it is hard to imagine that in the fourth century BC *Morgantina* was a bustling and prosperous city, under the protection of Syracuse. The ruins are nonetheless evocative and the site has a distinct character. From the site entrance, the footpath leads past the foundations of a 100m (328ft) long stoa, or walkway, on the left, to the centre of the excavations. To the right, there is an angular flight of steps, which date from the late-fourth century BC, and although there is no other known structure in the ancient Greek world that resembles it, it is thought that it probably served as a meeting place for the worship of underground divinities. The footpath traces the top of the steps, to the theatre, which is contained within a well-preserved wall. A faint inscription, carved on the fifth row of seating, says that the theatre was dedicated to Dionysius in the third century BC. The cavea, which could hold 5,000 spectators, looks out across the hills, although only the central three sections of seating now remain.

The route continues along the SS117 for a further 3km (2 miles) to the town of **Piazza Armerina**. This busy town has attractive old streets, lined with *palazzi* and crumbling churches, although the main attraction is the mosaics at Villa Romana del Casale, 5km (3 miles) away. Follow through the outskirts of Piazza Armerina, taking care not to miss the abrupt right fork at the Hotel Villa Romana. The road winds along the Nociara valley for 4km (2 miles), before reaching a turning on the left. After a further 1km (½ miles) the road ends at a carpark, from where steps lead to the ticket office.

π   The villa was built in the third century, probably as a hunting lodge for Maximian, who was co-emperor with Diocletian, from AD286 to 305. It covers an area of 3,500sq m (37,670sq ft), most of which is paved with mosaics, thought to be the work of master craftsmen from North Africa. They rate amongst the finest Roman mosaics yet to be discovered anywhere in the world, as well as being the most extensive and best-preserved.

From the ticket office, follow the footpath down to the villa, which is entered via an adjoining baths complex. The first octagonal room is the frigidarium. This adjoins the atrium, which has a fountain at its centre and is surrounded by columns. The formal entrance hall, on the left, has a fragment of mosaic showing an attendant holding an olive branch in the traditional greeting. Beyond is the peristyle, the large central courtyard, around which the villa is built.

The itinerary starts at the northern side of the villa where there is a *palestra*, or games area. This long room has an apse at either end, and is paved with the remains of a mosaic that depicts a chariot race. The walkway proceeds along the northern side of the peristyle where there are a series of rooms, most of which have mosaic floors with geometric designs. The largest room has a mosaic that depicts hunting scenes, with some of the hunters gathered around a brazier grilling meat. The room next to it also has a mosaic showing fishermen casting their nets from boats.

Along the north-eastern side of the peristyle is the most impressive mosaic in the villa. It vividly depicts a hunting scene and fills a 60m (197ft) long corridor. The scene is probably set in Africa where Maximian was one of the Imperial Tetrarchy, and the animals: lions, tigers, ostriches and elephants included; would probably have been

The richly-carved Baroque portal of the Annunziata church, Palazzolo Acreide

used in Roman circuses. The hunters are equipped with round shields, spears and arrows, while at the head of the hunt, on the far right, is Maximian himself, wearing a cloak and a fez-shaped hat. His attendant, Herculiani, stands behind and is distinguished by an ivy motif on his epaulet.

Steps lead up from the corridor to the Sala delle 10 Ragazze, which is on the right. The mosaic in this room is the most famous in the villa for it shows ten girls sporting the Roman version of a bikini. The girls are partaking in an athletics contest, the winner of which has a crown of laurels on her head. The footpath continues outside the villa to the private apartments along the eastern end. The first room on the right, has a mosaic of Ariadne holding a lyre, seated on the back of a sea creature. Next to it are a suite of rooms featuring children: the first shows a chariot race, where small chariots are pulled by birds; the second has children fishing from small boats. A third room has children hunting and gathering fruit from pomegranate and citrus trees.

The footpath continues around the outside of the villa to the basilica which has a large apse at one end and an adjoining chamber which has a mosaic depicting the sacrifice of a ram. In the last room on the itinerary, a pair of lovers are the centrepiece of a geometric patterned floor. From here, the footpath heads along the northern side of the villa, through a grove of bay trees, back to the carpark.

Return to Piazza Armerina and follow signs to Gela on the SS117. After 15km (9 miles), take the sharp left turn, signposted to Caltagirone. The SS124 proceeds through a tranquil landscape which is neatly-carpeted with cactus plantations and fields of melons and grain. At **San Michele di Ganzaria**, which lies at an altitude of 490m (1,607ft), there are views, on a clear day, of Mount Etna. The peak of Etna can also be seen from **Caltagirone**, a further 14km (9 miles) to the south-east. This seventeenth-century town is well-known for its majolica pottery, and colourful tiles decorate many of the buildings. Those interested in ceramics should head for Piazza Umberto I, which is the main square in the upper part of the town. To the north, the church of Santa Maria del Monte, lies at the top of La Scala, a flight of 142 steps, each of which is tiled. To the south of Piazza Umberto I, the Museo Civico has a modest assortment of contemporary ceramics, but to see a more comprehensive collection head for the Museo della Ceramica in the lower part of the town. The museum is set in the public gardens and is approached by the *teatrino*, a monumental staircase, decorated with majolica tiles which date from 1792. The museum documents the history of pottery-making in Sicily, from Neolithic times to the present day. It also houses a good collection of china figures, dressed in traditional Sicilian costume, dating from the eighteenth and nineteenth centuries.

Grammichele, 11km (7 miles) east of Caltagirone, is a hexagonal shaped town with an attractive circular piazza at its centre. It dates from the seventeenth century, although the symmetry of its original plan is marred by its modern day outskirts.

The route continues to follow the SS124 which winds back and forth over the railway, passing through extensive forests of eucalyptus trees. **Vizzini**, 16km (10 miles) south-east of Grammichele, is perched on a ridge, encircled by thick forests. There is a fine panorama to be had from the town and its attractive streets are lined with gracious *palazzi*.

The SS124 continues to wind along the foothills of the rocky Iblei mountains, passing through **Buccheri**, which has a lonely position high on a ridge. From here, follow signs to Siracusa and continue for 16km (10 miles) to **Palazzolo Acreide**. This small Baroque town has a fine position on a high ridge and many attractive, eighteenth-century churches. The large church of San Paolo dominates Piazza Roma, while the Annunziata, 300m (328yd) to its east has a richly-carved Baroque portal with spiralling columns on either side. The main street, Vittorio Emanuele, is lined with elegant *palazzi*, but the town's main tourist attraction, is the site of ancient *Akrai*, which lies 1km (½ mile) to the south-west of the centre and is rather haphazardly signposted as *teatro Greco*.

The theatre is a short walk from the site entrance and is one of the best-preserved edifices at *Akrai*. It dates from the city's heyday in the third century BC, and held 600 spectators. The original paving covers the stage floor and the nine segments dividing the cavea are clearly visible. Behind the theatre, to the right, there are the remains of a *bouleuterion*, a meeting place for the local council. A rectangular wall encloses a semi-circle of seating, which would originally have been roofed over. Behind the theatre to the left are the Intagliata and Intagliatella, which are stone quarries dating from the fourth and third centuries BC. The quarry walls are covered with niches and recesses, and in the Intagliatella, which is the narrower and deeper of the two, there is an impressive carved relief, some 2m (7ft) long, of sacrificial and banqueting scenes.

Route 7C • Palazzolo Acreide to Siracusa

Route 7C heads east of Palazzolo Acreide on the SS267 to Siracusa, down a wide, stony valley. At the spa town, **Canicattini Bagni**, the sea comes into sight, and after a further 10km (6 miles), **Siracusa** itself is visible with the ruined castle, Castello Eurialo, in the hills to the left. Follow signs to *centro storico*, the historic centre, which sits on a

small island, known as **Ortigia**. The main parking area is on Piazza della Posta, which is on the edge of the island, between the two bridges that link Ortigia to the mainland. The main sights are all within reasonable walking distance of the piazza; the island being no more than 1,000m (3,280ft) long and 500m (1,640ft) wide.

Ortigia was the site of the original settlement of Siracusa, which was founded by Greek colonists from Corinth, in 734BC. The Tempio di Apollo (Temple of Apollo), a relic from this early era, lies a short distance east of Piazza della Posta, and is a good starting point from which to make a tour of Ortigia. A couple of columns remain standing while the wall at the southern side was built in Byzantine times, when the temple served as a church.

From the temple, follow the wide shopping street, Corso Matteoti to Piazza Archimede, which is named after the great mathematician, who was born in Siracusa in 287BC. A narrow street leads from the north-east corner of the piazza to Palazzo Montalto, which was built in 1397, and has a fine façade with mullioned windows. Return to Piazza Archimede and continue south along Via Roma for 150m (164yd) before turning right. The street proceeds along the side of the *duomo* to the narrow and elongated, Piazza del Duomo. The piazza is neatly lined with oleander trees and smart cafés, while at the northern end is the elegant, white stone façade of Palazzo Beneventano, which dates from 1788. The façade of the *duomo*, which lies along the eastern side of the piazza, dates from the same era and is also white stone. The cathedral interior is fascinating as it is built around the Greek temple that was erected here in 530BC. The fluted columns that once surrounded the temple are now embedded in the walls, while the original arcades, built of finely cut stone blocks, divide the three aisles. The font, in the first chapel on the right, also dates from ancient Greek times, although the seven small bronze lions on which it rests are thirteenth century. The chapel to the left of the main apse is constructed around a part of the former cella, or inner sanctuary. The white marble statue of the *Madonna della Neve* in the apse is by the sixteenth-century sculptor, A. Gagini. The rest of the decoration of the cathedral dates from the seventeenth and eighteenth centuries, including the Baroque high altar and the choir stalls. The open beam ceiling, which is attractively decorated with simply carved rosettes, was added in 1518.

Back on Piazza del Duomo, those interested in ancient coins, may wish to visit the **Museo Archeologico Nazionale**, which is opposite the *duomo*. The museum contains the Galleria Numismatica, which has the most comprehensive collection of ancient Syracusan coins in

(Opposite) Siracusa

existence. Leave Piazza del Duomo from the southern end and follow Via Picherale for 150m (164yd) to the Fontana Aretusa which is built over a natural spring. There is a legend behind this spring which recounts that the water nymph, Arethusa, sought refuge here, having been hotly pursued by the river god, Alpheus, all the way from the Greek Pellopenese. Today, it is a popular meeting place, at the end of the busy promenade, Foro Italico, from where there are fine views across the Bay of Syracuse. At the centre of the fountain grows a patch of papyrus. Siracusa is the only place in Europe where papyrus grows and it is thought that it was probably first brought here from Egypt in the third century BC, as a gift from Ptolemy Philadelphus to Hieron II who ruled the city for fifty-four years. Papyrus paper is still made here and has been painted in the Egyptian style ever since the seventeenth century. There are workshops in the streets surrounding the fountain where the paper can be seen being made, and where visitors may sometimes participate.

Head east of Fontana Aretusa along the narrow street, Via Capodieci, for 150m (164yd) to the thirteenth-century **Palazzo Bellomo**. This simple but attractive building, houses the town's art collection which contains sculpture, dating from the Byzantine through to the Renaissance eras, and paintings ranging from fourteenth-century triptyches, to eighteenth-century oils.

To visit the other places of interest in Siracusa, it is necessary to return to the modern city on the mainland. Bus numbers 4, 5, 12 or 15, can be taken from Largo XXV Luglio, which is near the Temple of Apollo, to Viale Teocrito. Those with their own transport should cross back over Ponte Nuovo and follow Via Umberto I to the public gardens, the Foro Siracusano, which was formerly the site of the ancient agora. Turn right at the gardens, past the Sacrario dei Caduti, a large, concrete war memorial, and after crossing the railway, continue straight ahead, along Corso Gelone. After 1km (½ mile) turn right along Viale Teocrito, then take the second left to the Catacomba di San Giovanni where there is ample parking. Siracusa

is riddled with catacombs, but these are the only ones open to the public. They lie beneath the ruined, seventh-century church of San Giovanni, which was destroyed in the 1693 earthquake. The church, once the city's cathedral, was built at the place where Saint Marcian, the first bishop of Siracusa was flogged to death in AD254. The tomb of Saint Marcian is held in the church crypt, which adjoins the catacombs. The latter are comprised of a main gallery, the *decumanus maximus*, with passages which lead off either side.

From the catacombs, either proceed on foot or by car, to the archaeological museum, which is reached by returning to Viale

Teocrito, turning left, and taking the first left to the museum entrance. The museum is set in the luxuriant gardens of Villa Landolina in a modern building which was opened in 1988. The collection is amongst the most important in Italy and documents the history of Sicily from the upper Paleolithic era to Byzantine times. One of the most famous of the museum's exhibits is placed in the entrance hall. It is the Venere Anadiomene, a Roman copy, made in the second century BC, of a Hellenistic statue. Of the original Hellenistic sculptures, the most outstanding are those of *kouroi*, (athletic youths), which date from 500BC. The *Mother Goddess*, from *Megara Hyblaea* ,is also notable and depicts suckling twins. The collection of Greek ceramics is outstanding, as are the terracotta votive statues.

Those interested in the history of papyrus, may wish to visit the Museo Papiro, which is on the left, a short distance beyond the archaeological museum.

Demonstrations of paper-making can be seen here and the papyrus paper is for sale. Otherwise, return back along Viale Teocrito and keep straight ahead, along Viale Augusto to the archaeological park. There are parking spaces at the site entrance, on the left, from where a footpath, lined with souvenir stalls, leads to the entrance gates, past San Nicolo. This small, eleventh-century church has been well-restored and now contains a tourist information office. From the entrance gate, proceed downhill past the amphitheatre on the left. The amphitheatre dates from the third century and was built for circus games. It is one of the largest of its kind in existence, only slightly smaller than that of Verona. Next on the left, is the Ara di Leone II, a monumental altar which is 200m (656ft) long, and over 20m (65ft) wide. It was erected in the late-third century BC, under Hieron II, who wanted the altar to be larger than any other in *Magna Graecia*. Only the rock-hewn base remains today, as the stone was plundered by the Spanish, in order to fortify the city. The size however is impressive and it is not hard to believe the historian Diodorus' account that 450 bulls could be sacrificed here at one time.

The ticket office is on the right at the foot of the white stone quarries, the Latomie. Take the right fork from the ticket office to the only part of the quarry which is open to the public, the great cavern, known as Dionysius' Ear. It was Caravaggio who first alluded to the ear-shape opening to the quarry, when he visited it in 1608. It is also said to have functioned as an 'ear', for due to the excellent acoustics, Dionysius was able to overhear the conversations of prisoners who were kept captive here. Inside, the walls are smoothly chiselled and taper to a point, 23m (75ft) from the ground. It is little more than 10m (33ft) at its widest point, but extends back in a swirling shape, some

65m (213ft). To enable visitors to test the acoustics, jew's harps are sold at souvenir stalls. Someone twanging inside can be clearly heard outside.

Back outside the cave, to the right, the opening can be seen to the Grotta dei Cordari. This spacious cavern, now flooded with water, was also formed by quarrying, but was used in later years as a ropemakers' workshop. Grooves can be seen in the rock where the ropes were stretched and a rock-hewn pillar supports the roof.

Return to the ticket office and take the left fork to the ancient Greek theatre. The theatre is cut out of the natural rock, which, although pitted and worn with time, is still a startling white colour. It was started in the fifth century BC, but under Hieron II, two centuries later, the seating capacity was enlarged to hold 15,000 spectators. Today, it ranks amongst the largest, as well as the best-preserved, theatres in the ancient world and has 49 of the original 52 rows of seating still intact, as well as a covered gangway. Around the top of the theatre are a series of grottoes, the central one of which holds a fountain. The water gushes from the rock into a stone-hewn basin and was once adorned with statues, which are now in the archaeological museum. To the left of the fountain, a roadway is carved into the rock and is lined with tombs and niches along either side. Via dei Sepolcri, as it is known, is 150m (492ft) long and served as a burial place in late Roman times, but is now closed to the public.

Route 7D • Siracusa to Messina

Route 7D heads 8km (5 miles) due west of Siracusa on the SP49 to Castello Eurialo, which was built to defend the city, from the Carthaginians, in 401BC. There are signposts from the centre of Siracusa, although they are rather haphazard once out of the city, and visitors should fork left when in doubt. The road passes through the remnants of the walls, which were built at the same time as the castle, before heading up to **Belvedere**. At the edge of this small village, take the first turning on the right and proceed to the parking area at the castle entrance.

The first of three defensive trenches is just inside the entrance gates, while the second and third trenches lie a short distance beyond. The third trench can be entered by steps down on the right. It is hewn from the natural rock and has a gallery with regularly-spaced openings, and carved steps and tunnels, giving access to the second trench. At one end, are piers which are all that remain of the drawbridge to the keep. The keep walls are defended by five large towers, each of which would have had a catapult. Inside the keep walls there is a large, flattened area, strewn with rocks and stones, at the far side of which is a gate.

From Castello Eurialo, continue through Belvedere and turn right onto the Siracusa road. After 5km (3 miles) the road meets the SS114, whereupon visitors should turn left and follow the coast. The Bay of Augusta, once the tranquil setting of ancient Greek *Megara Hyblaea*, is now a centre of petro-chemical industry, employing 10 per cent of Sicily's total population. **Augusta**, itself is also industrialised although the old town is pleasantly clustered on an island joined by a causeway, and has a castle, built by Frederick II in 1232. The route, however, continues for a further 35km (22 miles) north, on the SS114 to **Catania**, the home of the musician Bellini. Until the motorway is completed, it is necessary to pass through the city to reach the A18. Piles of lava line parts of the road, and are a chilling reminder of the 2km (1 mile) wide, lava flow that erupted from Mount Etna and quite

The defensive trenches of Castello Eurialo, Belvedere

recently flowed through the city. Those who wish to make the excursion to Mount Etna, should fork right at **San Gregorio**, just before reaching the A18 toll booth. The road winds up through **Nicolosi** and eventually, after 35km (22 miles), ends at a parking area, from where a cable car operates. A minibus makes the final ascent, from where it is compulsory to tour the crater with an official guide. It should be remembered that Mount Etna is still dangerous. It has erupted eight times over the last thirty years, the most recent being in 1985, and in 1979 nine tourists were killed by surprise explosions. However, the smouldering crater with its lunar landscapes is a unique sight. The temperature around the crater is quite warm, and in places it is hot enough underfoot to melt plastic-soled shoes.

The route continues north of Catania along the A18, past the large spa resort of **Acireale**. There have been baths here since Roman times and the waters are renowned for their high sulphur content. The town is well-endowed with Baroque architecture, including the *duomo* which has a fine Baroque portal and a lavishly frescoed interior.

Taormina, the most popular resort in Sicily, is 36km (22 miles) north of Acireale. Leave the motorway at the Taormina Sud exit and follow the coast, through **Giardini Naxos**, where there are the scant remains of ancient Greek *Naxos*, and an archaeological museum. **Taormina** looms on a cliff top, a short distance beyond Giardini Naxos, above a narrow headland where beaches fill two small bays. From here the road hairpins up Monte Tauro to the edge of Taormina. Parking is difficult and the narrow streets in the centre are to be avoided. The best solution is probably to use the carpark at the *funivia* station, which is at the north-eastern side of the town. From here, visitors can proceed on foot up to the main town gate, Porta Messina.

Piazza Vittorio Emanuele, the central square, is less than 100m (110yd) south of Porta Messina. The small square is overshadowed by the bulky walls of Palazzo Corvaia. This fine building was constructed in the early fifteenth century on the foundations of an Arabic fort that stood here in the eleventh century. The walls, which are patterned with black lava and white pumice stone, are topped by fishtail battlements. On the south side there is a long inscription. The main portal, a Gothic arch, leads through to a charming inner courtyard which has an open staircase in one corner and mullioned windows all round. The interior is only open when an exhibition is in progress.

From Palazzo Corvaia, head alongside the tiny park at the centre of Piazza Vittorio Emanuele, to Via Teatro Greco, which leads to the Greek theatre. From the ticket office, which is on the left, follow the steps up to the brick walls, enclosing the theatre. The walls were added in Roman times in the first century, but the theatre was originally built by the ancient Greeks in the third century BC. The sheer drop from the middle row of seating to the stage floor, is where the Romans disposed of the lower seats, in order to enlarge the orchestra, and make an animal pit. The stage buildings still stand in reasonable condition with a colonnaded wall along the back and deep arches at either end. The cavea is clad in plastic seating, as from July to September it is the venue of the arts festival, Taormina Arte.

Return to Piazza Vittorio Emanuele and follow Corso Umberto, which heads from the west corner of the square. This is the main shopping street, and it is lined with smart boutiques, ice-cream parlours and souvenir shops. On Piazza 9 Aprile, 400m (437yd) along the street, there is a panoramic terrace, perched on the cliff edge, with fine views out to sea. The fifteenth-century church, Sant'Agostino, fills the eastern side of the piazza, while on the northern side of the square, a fine stairway leads to the façade of San Giuseppe, which dates from the seventeenth century. Directly overhead, towering on the rocky summit of Monte Tauro, are the ruins of a castle.

Continue along Corso Umberto, from the western end of Piazza 9 Aprile, through the arch of the twelfth-century clock tower. The street proceeds for a further 250m (273yd) to the *duomo* which has crenellated walls and a simple thirteenth-century façade with a neo-Classical portal. The façade overlooks an attractive flag-stoned piazza, at the centre of which there is a seventeenth-century fountain, topped by a centauress, the symbol of Taormina. The interior of the *duomo* has three aisles, divided by monolithic columns, with sixteenth-century polyptyches in the chapels along either side. To the right of the main altar there is a fine, alabaster statue of the *Madonna* which dates from the 1400s.

From Taormina, follow signs back to the A18, which continues northwards high above the rocky coastline. After **Forza d'Agro**, which is positioned on a steep spur, the landscape becomes flatter and there is a chain of modern resorts as far as Messina. Keep following the motorway to the Boccetta exit, at the northern end of Messina from where there are signs to the *traghetti*, ferry port. Viale Boccetta leads steeply down to the water's edge, where visitors should either turn right for the state-run ferry company, or left for Caronte, the private ferry company. Those with return tickets should have them stamped at the ticket booth before embarking.

Additional Information

Places to Visit

Acireale
Thermal Establishment
Terme di Santa Venere
Via delle Terme
☎ (095) 601508
Open: all year round

Agrigento
Western Arcaeological Zone
Valle dei Templi
☎ (0922) 29008
Open: 9am-1 hour before sunset.

Museo Archeologico Nazionale
Corso da San Nicolo
☎ (0922) 29008
Open: Tuesday to Sunday 9am-2pm.

Casa di Pirandello
Frazione Vilaseta
☎ (0922) 590111
Open: winter, daily 9am-1pm, 3-5pm. Summer, daily 9am-1pm, 3-7pm.

Aidone
Scavi di Morgantina (Archaeological Site)
Open: winter, daily 9am-4pm. Summer, daily 9am-6pm.

Belvedere
Castello Eurialo
☎ (0931) 711773
Open: daily summer 9am-4pm. Winter 9am-7pm.

Caltagirone
Museo Civico
☎ (0933) 31590
Open: Monday, Tuesday, Saturday 9.30am-1.30pm. Wednesday,
Friday 4-7pm. Sunday, 10am-12noon.

Museo della Ceramica
☎ (0933) 21680
Open: Tuesday to Sunday 9am-2pm.

Enna
Castello Lombardia
Open: daily, 9am-1pm, 3-7pm.

Museo Alessi
Via Roma
☎ (0935) 24072
Open: Tuesday to Sunday 9am-1pm, 4-7pm.

Museo Archeologico Varisano
Piazza Mazzini
☎ (0935) 24720
Open: Monday to Saturday 9am-1.30pm, 3.30-6.30pm. Sunday and holidays 9am-1pm, 3.30-6.30pm.

Eraclea Minoa
Zona Archeologica & Antiquarium
Frazione Eraclea Minoa
☎ (0922) 847182
Open: Zona Archeologica, daily 9am-1 hour before sunset.
Antiquarium, Monday to Saturday 9am-3pm. Sunday and holidays 9am-1pm.

Palazzolo Acreide
Akrai Zona Archeologica
Open: Tuesday to Sunday 9am-1 hour before sunset.

Piazza Armerina
Villa Romana del Casale
5km (3 miles) south-west of Piazza Armerina
☎ (0935) 680036
Open: daily 9am-1 hour before sunset

Sciacca
Thermal Establishment
Nuove Terme
Via Agatocle
☎ (0925) 21620
Open: April to November.

Thermal Establishment
Lipari e Alicudi
Sciacca a Mare
☎ (0925) 93000
Open: March to October.

Siracusa
Duomo
☎ (0931) 65328
Open: Monday to Saturday 8am-12.45pm, 4.30-7pm. Sunday and holidays 8am-12.30pm, 4.30-7pm.

Museo Bellomo
Via Capodieci 14
☎ (0931) 65343
Open: Tuesday to Saturday 9am-2pm. Sunday and holidays 9am-1pm.

Museo Papiro Fabrica del Papiro
(Paper-making workshop)
Fonte Aretusa
☎ (0931) 703572

Catacomba di San Giovanni
☎ (0931) 67955
Open: daily except Wednesday Guided tours (obligatory), winter, 10am, 11am, 12noon. Summer, 10am, 11am, 12noon, 4pm, 5pm, 6pm.

Museo Archeologico Regionale Paolo Orsi
Villa Landolina
Viale Teocrito 66
☎ (0931) 464023
Open: Tuesday to Saturday 9am-1pm. Sunday and holidays 9am-12.30pm.

Parco Archeologico
☎ (0931) 66206
Open: daily 9am-5.30pm.

Anfiteatro Romano (Roman Amphitheatre)
Open: winter 9am-3pm. Summer 9am-6pm.

Taormina
Teatro Greco
☎ (0942) 23220
Open: daily 9am-1 hour before sunset.

Cattedrale
☎ (0942) 23123
Open: daily 10am-12noon, 4-6pm.

Useful Information

Acireale
Events and Festivals
August to September, every Tuesday, Opera dei Pupi (Traditional Sicilian Puppet Performances).

Tourist Information Centres
Azienda Autonoma Turismo
Corso Umberto 179
☎ (095) 604521

Azienda Autonoma delle Terme
Via Terme 61
☎ (095) 606120

Agrigento
Events and Festivals
1st-2nd Sunday February, Sagra del Mandorlo in Fiore (Festival at Temple of Concordia, with international folk-dancing, flag-throwing, and traditional costume).

1st Sunday July, Festa di San Calogero (Feast of St Calogero).

Tourist Information Centres
Azienda Autonoma Soggiorno e
    Turismo
Via Empedocle 73
☎ (0922) 20391

Ufficio Informazioni Assistenze
    Turisti
Piazzale Aldo Moro 5
☎ (0922) 20454

Azienda Provinciale Incremento
    Turistico
Viale della Vittoria 255
☎ (0922) 26922

Emergencies
Carabinieri (Military Police)
Piazzale Aldo Moro
☎ (0922) 506322

Polizia Stradale (Traffic Police)
Via Crispi
☎ (0922) 26777

Ospedale Civile San Giovanni di
    Dio (Hospital)
Via Giovanni XXII
☎ (0922) 20755

Automobile Club d'Italia
Via Cimarra
☎ (0922) 604284

Caltagirone
Tourist Information Centres
Pro Loco
Palazzo della Corte Capitaniale
☎ (0933) 22539

Azienda Autonoma di Turismo
Volta Libertini 3
☎ (0933) 54610

Enna
Events and Festivals
2 July, Festa della Madonna
(Feast of the Madonna, fireworks
and apple biscuits).

July August, Estate Ennese
(Season of concerts and plays in
Castello Lombardia).

Tourist Information Centres
Azienda Autonoma di Soggiorno e
    Turismo
Piazza Colaianni 6
☎ (0935) 26119

Azienda Autonoma Provinciale per
    l'Incremento Turistico
Piazza Garibaldi
☎ (0935) 24007

Emergencies
Vigili Urbani (Municipal Police)
☎ (0935) 40321

Polizia Stradale (Traffic Police)
☎ (0935) 29850

Ospedale Civile Umberto I
(Hospital)
☎ (0935) 45245

Automobile Club d'Italia
Via Roma 200
☎ (0935) 26299

Palazzolo Acreide
Events and Festivals
29 June, Sagra di San Paolo
(Festival of St Paul)

Piazza Armerina
Events and Festivals
13-14 August, Palio dei Normani
(Re-enactment of the Norman
Conquest of the town, and
procession with statue of Madonna
dell Vittorie).

Tourist Information Centre
Azienda Autonoma di Soggiorno e
    Turismo
Via Cavour 15
☎ (0935) 680201

Sciacca
Tourist Information Centres
Azienda Autonoma di Soggiorno e
    Turismo
Corso Vittorio Emanuele 84
☎ (0925) 22744

Azienda Autonoma delle Terme
Via Figuli 1
☎ (0925) 23405

Azienda Autonoma Terme
Via Agotocle 2
☎ (0925) 27522

Emergencies
Polizia Municipale (Municipal
    Police)
☎ (0925) 28957

Polizia Stradale (Traffic Police)
☎ (0925) 21000

Ospedale Civile Riuniti (Hospital)
☎ (0925) 21241

Siracusa
Events and Festivals
13 December, Festa di Santa Lucia
(Feast of St Lucia).

Tourist Information Centres
Azienda Provinciale Turismo
Via Sebastiano 43
☎ (0931) 67607

Azienda Provinciale Turismo
San Nicolo
Zona Archaeologica
☎ (0931) 60510

Azienda Autonoma Turismo
Via Maestranza 33
☎ (0931) 65201

Transport
Ferrovie dello Stato (Railway)
Piazza della Stazione
☎ (0931) 66640

Agenzia Servizi Marittimi (Ferry)
Viale Mazzini 4/5
☎ (0931) 66956

Emergencies
Polizia (Police)
Via San Sebastiano
☎ (0931) 21122

Carabinieri (Military Police)
Viale Tica 147
☎ (0931) 441344

Ospedale Provinciale (Hospital)
Via Testaferrata
☎ (0931) 724111

Automobile Club d'Italia
Foro Siracusana 27
☎ (0931) 66656

Taormina
Events and Festivals
May, Raduno del Costume e del
Carretto Siciliano (Parade of Sicilian
costume and folk dancing).

Tourist Information Centre
Azienda Autonoma di Soggiorno e
    Turismo
Palazzo Corvaia
☎ (0942) 23243

Transport
Ferrovia (Railway)
☎ (0942) 51026

Emergencies
Polizia Municipale (Municipal
Police)
☎ (0942) 23850

Polizia Stradale (Traffic Police)
☎ (0942) 51308

Pronto Soccorso (First Aid Service)
☎ (0942) 53745

Guardia Medica Turistica (Medical
    Officer for Tourists)
☎ (0942) 625419

8

IONIAN COAST

Chapter 8 explores the Ionian Coast, which runs along the under side of Italy's boot to the instep, and offers the visitor ample opportunity for swimming and sunbathing. The route also ventures into the green heart of Calabria, the Sila mountains, where there is plenty of scope for hiking and a great variety of scenery. On the whole, the peninsula is exposed and isolated, both up in the mountains or down on the coast. In summer the landscape is baked under a hot and unrelenting sun, while in winter snow lays thick on the rugged mountain tops, cutting off many areas altogether. The rather barren land yields olives, figs, and citrus fruits, including bergamot and *cedri*, a type of lime, but the local diet, especially in the more remote mountain regions, can be fairly restricted. Olive oil features in most dishes, and is used to preserve out-of-season vegetables such as aubergines, peppers, courgettes and artichokes. Anchovies, small tuna and cod which are grilled with oil and lemon are available on the coast, and are often accompanied by unleavened bread, which is similar to the Greek Pitta.

The geography of this peninsula, however, not only shapes the landscape and the local cuisine. It has also provided, over the millennia, a natural landing stage for invaders and migrants from the south. The earliest known were the Ancient Greeks who, in the eighth century BC, sailed across the Ionian Sea from northern Achaea and the southern Spartan lands of Laconica, with the principal aim to establish trading colonies. The relics of their cities remain dotted along the coast, and local museums have excellent collections of Greek and Hellenistic pottery and bronze.

The next invaders to leave their mark came with the expansion of the Byzantine Empire in the ninth century, which brought the entire peninsula within its boundaries under the name of the Capatanate.

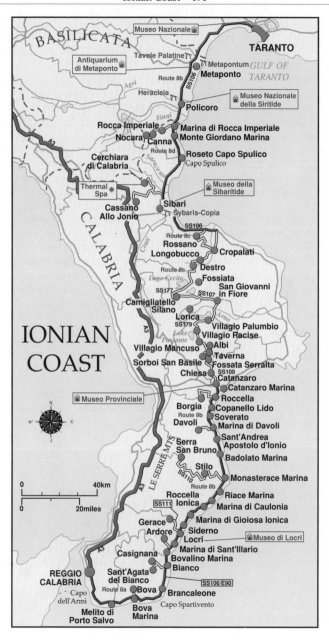

BASILICATA

Museo Nazionale 🏛

TARANTO

Tavole Palatine

Antiquarium
di Metaponto

Metapontum 🏛

GULF OF
TARANTO

Metaponto

Route 8b

Agri

Heraclea

Museo Nazionale
della Siritide 🏛

Policoro

Sinni

Rocca Imperiale

Marina di Rocca Imperiale

Nocara

Canna

Monte Giordano Marina

Route 8d

Cerchiara
di Calabria

Saraceno

Roseto Capo Spulico

Capo Spulico

Thermal
Spa ✳

Museo della
Sibaritide 🏛

Cassano
Allo Jonio

Sibari

Sybaris-Copia

CALABRIA

SS106

Route 8c

Rossano

Longobucco

Crati

Cropalati

Destro

Route 8c

Fossiata

Lago Cecita

San Giovanni
in Fiore

SS177

SS107

Camigliatello
Silano

A3

Lorica

SS179

Arno

Villagio Palumbio

Villagio Racise

Lake
Passante

Albi

IONIAN

COAST

Villagio Mancuso

Taverna

Sorboi San Basile

Fossata Serralta

Chiesa

SS109

Catanzaro

Museo Provinciale 🏛

Catanzaro Marina

Roccella

Borgia

Copanello Lido

Route 8b

Soverato

Davoli

Marina di Davoli

Sant'Andrea

Serra
San Bruno

Apostolo d'Ionio

Badolato Marina

Stilo

SS110

Monasterace Marina

LE SERRE MTS

Route 8b

Roccella
Ionica

Riace Marina

SS111

Marina di Caulonia

Gerace

Marina di Gioiosa Ionica

Ardore

Siderno

Locri

Museo di Locri 🏛

A3

Casignana

Marina di Sant'Illario

Bovalino Marina

REGGIO
CALABRIA

Sant'Agata
del Bianco

Bianco

SS106/E90

Capo
dell'Armi

Route 8a

Bova

Brancaleone

Bova
Marina

Capo Spartivento

Melito di
Porto Salvo

0   40km

0   20miles

N
W   E
S

Cross-shaped churches, battered frescoes, and ruined castles are testimony to their rule, and much the same can be said for the Normans, who arrived in 1071, and Frederick II who closely followed them.

The lack of picturesque ports and harbours along the Ionian Coast could be blamed on the Saracens who constantly threatened it from their secure base on Sicily. The hills inland offered protection to the local inhabitants, and from the Byzantine era onwards towns and villages were rarely built on the coast. Monastic orders such as Carthusians, Cluniacs and Cistercians also sought shelter inland, and many of their fine monasteries can still be seen in the remote mountain areas. The development all along the coast is, therefore, all comparatively recent, many of the resorts being offshoots of inland towns in the guise of an affiliated marina. Few have any real character, although they offer good resort facilities, and at the end of a day on one of the Ionian's many long, sandy beaches, it is always possible to retreat to a historic spot inland.

The route ends at the large port of Taranto. From here visitors can either tour the heel of Italy, Puglia, in chapter 9, or return northwards, through the Murge, to the Adriatic coast, following the routes in chapter 10.

Route 8A • Reggio Calabria to Gerace

Route 8A heads south of Reggio Calabria on the SS106 Ionico, through the city's interminable suburbs, which extend along the coast as far as Capo dell'Armi. This rocky cape offers a last glimpse across the Straits to Sicily, before the coast rounds the tip of Italy's toe. The road follows the coast, parallel with the railway line, along the lowlands of the Aspromonte hills. The land is predominantly dry and barren, although the climate, which is mild all year round, is ideally suited to the bergamot that is cultivated here. Fig and olive trees thrive too, as do cacti, particularly the prickly pear which grow up to 5m (16ft) high, and form a dense wall of racket-shaped leaves.

After rounding Capo dell'Armi the road passes an oil refinery and the town just beyond. **Melito di Porto Salvo**, has considerable industrial outskirts. Despite this it has an interesting history, for it was here on 18 August 1860, that Garibaldi first stepped foot onto mainland Italy in his campaign of independence, having already announced himself dictator of Sicily. By 7 September, faced with only very feeble resistance, he had travelled as far as Naples, where he received a rapturous welcome. The town is also of interest for its production of bergamot essence, as well as smokers' pipes, and can lay claim to being positioned on the most southerly point of mainland Italy.

The SS106 continues past Melito di Porto Salvo, by-passing the centre. The next two villages **Condofuri Marina** and **Bova Marina** have merged into a large resort with popular beaches. However, the small village of **Bova**, which lies in the hills, 14km (9 miles) inland from its marina, is quite untouched. Its small houses are pictur-esquely clustered around the head of a fortified rock, from where there is a magnificent panorama of the coast. After Bova Marina, the SS106 climbs along cliffs, past a defense tower. The landscape beyond is empty, and quite beautiful in its barren loneliness. Ahead, jutting out into the sea, is Capo Spartivento, a severe, limestone capeland with a lighthouse marking the most south-easterly point of Italy, which in Roman times was known as *Heracleum Promontorium*.

After passing the cape, the SS106 turns northwards to the Brancaleone, an area where Jasmine is widely cultivated. The town of **Brancaleone** has a long, sandy beach which extends to the north and is backed by gentle hills and pine forests. The road continues alongside the beach, to **Feruzzano**, where the small headland is topped by a round tower. The coast continues north to **Bianco**, which as the town's name suggests has a centuries-old tradition in the making of white wines, amongst which are the well-reputed dessert wines, Greco di Bianco and Mantonico di Bianco. It is well worth stopping by in the town to buy some of the local wine as very little is distributed outside the region. A pleasant, 8km (5 mile) excursion can also be made, to the vineyards in the hills behind Bianco. The unspoilt hamlets of **Sant'Agata del Bianco**, **Caraffa del Bianco**, and **Casignana** all produce wine and some of their inhabitants still wear traditional costume.

The SS106 continues along the coast north of Greco, past more vineyards, where grapes have probably been grown since ancient Greek times, to **Bovalino**. This large, unwieldy town has a busy marina, but those that do not need to stop here can by-pass it by continuing along the SS106. The flat coastal area north of Bovalino is covered by olive groves, and peppered with resorts, including **Ardore** and **Marina di Sant'Ilario**. The next point of interest is reached just after crossing the River Portigliola, which is just to the north of Marina di Sant'Ilario. Here the road passes by the ancient Greek site of **Locri Epizefri**, and at the roadside, on the left, is a museum, the Museo di Locri. It houses some of the locally excavated finds, including Hellenistic pottery and votive statues dating from the sixth century BC, which were found in tombs. The site was established by Greek colonists, between 710 and 683BC, and is one of the oldest *Magna Graecian* cities in Southern Italy. The ruins are spread over a vast area, and parts, such as the Centocamere, are still under excavation. However, there are some ruins to walk around, just behind the museum. A section of the city wall, which was once 7½km (5 miles) long leads from the back of the museum, between an avenue of ancient olive trees, to the scant remains of the Temple of Zeus Marasa. The temple was built in the fifth century BC in the Ionian order. Today, amongst the odd blocks of stone, the foundations of the cella (inner sanctuary) are just discernible, while a solitary column base is all that remains of the temple's portico. To visit the ancient theatre, follow the road alongside the ruins and turn left after 1km (½ mile) into a large parking area. The theatre, on the right, stands above an olive grove, and in typical Greek style is set into the hillside. Only the contour, worn in the earth, of the cavea remains, but the lower wall around the stage floor is still standing. The other ruins, lower down the hillside, are the remnants of a Doric temple.

The terracotta-tiled rooftops of Stilo, surrounding the dome of San Domenico

The SS106 continues along the coast, past the large modern day town of **Locri** from where visitors are well recommended to make the 10km (6 mile) excursion inland, to **Gerace**, on the SS111. The road winds up through pretty countryside, dotted with olive groves, and becomes very narrow as it passes between the houses of **Borgo Maggiore Vasai**. Shortly after this follow the signs to *centro storico monumentale*. The old centre of Gerace is on the crest of a hill, at an altitude of 500m (1,640ft). Turn off the road, which continues up around the town walls on tall piers, and park on Piazzale Santa Maria Egizicca, which is on the left, just outside the Porta del Borgetto gate.

Continue on foot, up through the Porta del Borgetto, which dates from the twelfth century, past the small, dishevelled Baroque church of San Martino. The street continues uphill, with a fine panorama to the coast from the left side, to a second gate, Porta del Sole o delle Bombarde, which is thirteenth century. Shortly after the gate, Via Sant'Anna, branches left to the church of the ex-convent of Sant'Anna, which also has a crumbling, Baroque façade, but originally dates from the fourteenth century. Return to the main street, and continue uphill to Piazza del Tocco, which is the town's central square. This sun-bleached piazza is surrounded by simple houses, characterised by their stout, French windows and wrought-iron balconies, and sleepy cafés. From the top end of the piazza follow Via Zaleuco, a picturesque, cobbled street, up to the apse of the *cattedrale*. The entrance leads into the crypt, which is filled with antique columns, originating from *Locri*, and has a high vaulted ceiling. From the right transept of the crypt, a stone staircase leads up into the main body of the cathedral.

The cathedral was consecrated in the early days of the Norman Conquest of Southern Italy, in 1045, under Robert Guiscard, who went on to control Calabria, Puglia and Sicily. In 1222, Frederick II, known to his contemporaries as *(Stupor Mundi)* — Wonder of the World — in keeping with his reputation, had the building enlarged, so that today, it is the largest cathedral in Calabria. Built on a Latin-cross ground plan, the central aisle is typically Norman, having a very high clerestory and an open timbered roof. The clerestory walls are supported by elegant, lancet arches, which spring from an assortment of ancient granite and marble columns taken from Locri. The deep apse, holds a decorative altar, which was added in the eighteenth century, when the cathedral was restored. The Cappella del Sacramento, to the right of the main altar, is also a later addition.

The street continues to wind uphill, beyond the cathedral, to the ruins of the Norman-built castle. Its position atop a rocky summit affords a fine panorama to the coast as well as across the hills behind.

On the way back down through the town, there are numerous attractive churches to look out for. The most important of these can be reached by turning left at the apse of the cathedral along Via Caduti Sul Lavoro. This narrow street leads to Largo delle Tre Chiese. Here, there is a charming eleventh-century church, San Giovanello, on the right which has a distinctly Byzantine-style, tiled dome. A little beyond San Giovanello is the church of San Francesco which was built in 1252. Its portal, set into a side wall, is attractively carved with geometric motifs, reminiscent of Norman as well as Islamic architecture. For those that wish to see the house where Edward Lear stayed in August 1847, return to Piazza del Tocco and follow the street from the right side. By continuing down this street it is possible to rejoin the carpark on Piazzale Santa Maria Egizicca, via a fine belvedere that looks out from the town walls to the coast.

Route 8B • Gerace to Catanzaro

Route 8B continues along the coast, passing through a series of busy resorts, including **Siderno** and **Marina di Gioiosa Ionica**, which stretch alongside vast expanses of flat beach. The resort of **Roccella Ionica** has a difference in that it surrounds a bare rocky headland, perched on the top of which, is a ruined medieval castle. The landscape beyond Roccella Ionica also offers something quite different, for here there is an appealing tranquility, with nothing to break the view except age-old olive groves which are dotted about chalky-white, eroded hillocks. After passing through the resort, **Marina di Caulonia**, the road crosses over the Allaro river, which in ancient times was known as the *Sagras*. It was in the flood plain of this river, that, in the fifth century BC, a memorable battle was staged between the ancient Greek colonists of Crotone and Locri Epizefri. The Locreans, with an army of 10,000, defeated the Crotoneans whose army of 130,000 greatly outnumbered them.

The SS106 continues along the coast, through Riace Marina, to **Monasterace Marina** from where an excursion of 15km (9 miles) can be made to one of Calabria's most celebrated, Byzantine churches, the Cattolica, in **Stilo**. The turning is signed on the left to Serra San Bruno on the SS110. The road passes through orchards of citrus and peach, before joining the wide gravel bed of the Stilaro river. The road then starts to climb, following the river valley, towards Monte Consolino, the cliff-faced mountain on which Stilo is perched. As the road approaches the town, the dome of the ruined convent, San Domenico, comes into view across the valley on the right, while the monastery of San Giovanni, with its twin belfries, is to the left. Perched high above the town, on the tip of the crag are the rambling ruins of a Norman fortress. Below the fortress, tucked neatly onto a small ledge, is the little church, Cattolica. There is a fine panorama as the road climbs the final stretch up into the village, past the four-teenth-century bell tower, Torre de Guardia, on the left, and into the main piazza.

The piazza, overlooked by the crumbling, Baroque façade of San Biagio, has a rather neglected air. At its centre is a statue of Stilo's unfortunate son, Tomasso Campanella. Born in 1568, Campanella grew up under the Spanish domination of Southern Italy, in the suffocating atmosphere of the Counter-Reformation, which saw Italian intellectual freedom at a very low ebb. As a philosopher and astrologer, Campanella, was continuously prosecuted by the Span-ish Inquisition for his beliefs and spent twenty-seven years of his life languishing in prison. One of the more concrete of his offences was to lead the Calabrian revolt of 1599. The uprising was, however, quickly quashed and the revolution that Campanella had hoped for, was not seen until long after his death, in 1647.

The main street, leading through the town from the piazza, is named after the thwarted hero, Via Campanella. It leads through the old town walls onto the little square, Piazza Vittorio Emanuele, and continues round to the *duomo*. This Gothic structure, built in the thirteenth and fourteenth centuries, has a plain façade with an attrac-tively carved portal. From here, a fascinating warren of steep alleys and steps, extend right the way round the valley, to the convent of San Domenico, and the derelict town gate next to it, Porta Stefanina.

The Cattolica, can also be reached by a picturesque walk up through the town, although it is a fairly steep hike, and those who prefer to drive can take the main road up. Visitors on foot should follow Via Salerno, which winds and twists between the pretty, flower-bedecked houses, up the hill. Near the top, a plaque marks the house where Tomasso Campanella lived. Turn right at the top of the hill and follow the road to the parking area, at the far end of which a gate leads through to Cattolica. The footpath from the gate leads along a terrace, lined with Century Plants, to the neat brick façade of the church which is wedged against the cliff face.

The Cattolica was built in the tenth century, a period when the Byzantine Empire was extending its boundaries, more than ever before, and Calabria was under Byzantine control. The architecture is similar to that found in churches throughout provincial Greece, having five domes arranged like the five on a dice, along the equal arms of the Greek cross. It also bears a resemblance to the churches of Armenia and Georgia, as the domes rest on distinctively high drums. The interior, which only measures 6m (20ft) by 6m (20ft), holds four centrally placed, antique columns of attractive grey marble. The first column on the left stands on an inverted ancient capital, symbolising the defeat of Paganism, while the column on the right is inscribed with a simple Greek cross. The Greek inscription next to the cross reads 'God is the Lord who appeared to us'. The frescoes have mostly been lost, but traces remain in places; the best preserved are those on the left wall.

To the north of Stilo, there extends a dramatic range of granite mountains, known as Le Serre. The scenery is amongst the most spectacular in Southern Italy, but those who wish to make the excursion into these mountains, should allow at least an hour for the 22km (14 mile) climb to the Passo di Pietra Spada (1,335m/4,379ft). From the pass, it is a further 12km (7 miles) to **Serra San Bruno**, a remote mountain village, containing numerous Baroque churches with façades carved from the local granite stone. The village was founded in the eleventh century by the initiator of the Carthusian Order, St Bruno, for the families of the nearby Carthusian monastery. Carthusian monks still live at the monastery, following vows of silence and solitude, although the buildings seen today are reconstructions of the original Gothic ones that were destroyed in the earthquake of 1783.

From Stilo, the route returns to the coast and continues north of **Monasterace Marina**, on the SS106 (E90). The landscape is exposed and treeless, with the bare, rocky foothills of the Serre mountains stretching inland, and the Ionian Sea gently lapping at long and desolate, sandy beaches. In the shelter of the hills there are many attractive towns and villages, although their corresponding marinas lack character. **Badolato Marina** is one such example, although there are all the facilities of a beach resort on offer. Just to its north there is a wide belt of olive groves and citrus orchards that reach down to the water's edge, set above which is **Sant'Andrea Apostolo d'Ionio**. It enjoys a fine view and makes a pleasant 5km (3 miles) excursion from the road. **Davoli**, further along the coast, also makes a pleasant inland excursion, the old town being 11km (7 miles) from its marina.

The SS106 (E90) continues to the large town of **Soverato** where there is a wide, sand beach, which is well-protected and suitable for young children. The town centre is frantically busy and holds nothing of particular interest. Those passing by on 15 August, however, may wish to stay to see the impressive display of fireworks which is held at sea. To by-pass the town, simply continue along the SS106 (E90) which passes through a series of tunnels. To the north of Soverato, the coastland is hillier and the landscape less arid and rocky. The road climbs up, above the small resort of **Pietra Grande**, and crosses to the rocky headland of Stalleti, which was guarded in ancient times by the Torre di Palombar. A tunnel leads through to the north side of the headland, where **Copanello Lido** fills a sheltered bay and is a pleasant spot for bathing. For the next 7km (4 miles) the road passes through extensive groves of olives, before reaching the town of **Rocella**. On entering the town, take the abrupt left turn, signposted to Borgia, to visit the remains of the pretty church of Santa Maria della Roccella. Dating from the eleventh century, it was built under the Cluniac Order, that had drifted with the tide of Normans and Crusaders, from France. The church stands on a latin cross ground plan and has a single nave which terminates in three rounded apses that are reminiscent of Byzantine architecture as well as Norman.

The SS106 (E90) continues for a further 2km (1 mile) to **Catanzaro Marina**, which lies at the narrowest point of the Calabrian peninsular. Its fast expanding belt of industry and suburbs, stretch nearly all the way to the city of **Catanzaro**, which lies 14km (9 miles) inland. The city has a dominant location, high on a ridge with deep gorges falling away at either side. The Byzantines, who founded the city in the tenth century, undoubtedly saw the distinct advantage of such an easily defended site. However, as the modern day capital of Calabria, it is plainly unsuited to the mass of traffic that grinds through its streets and its aspect is marred by the concrete apartment blocks that sprout from the steep hill sides. Little remains of the Byzantine city apart from the labyrinthine network of streets, today choked by chronic traffic and parked cars. Those who do not wish to get involved, can simply by-pass the city by taking the *tangenziale*, (ring road), which forks off left at Le Croci, and join the route again at the north side of the city, by following signs to Sila.

Visitors, however, who do wish to visit Catanzaro should fork right at Le Croci and follow the road steeply uphill. There is no solution to parking, the best that can be hoped for is to find a space at the side of the road near the Villa Comunale, which is at the eastern edge of the city and is one of the main touristic attractions. Also known as Villa Trieste, the villa has a fine public gardens, which contains dozens of busts of illustrious Calabrians, and offers fine views of the coast. At the western edge of the park, next to the main entrance, is the Museo Provinciale. The museum houses a collection of local archaeological finds, dating from prehistoric to Byzantine times, as well as paintings that date from the sixteenth century to the present day. A number of art works can also be seen in the church of San Domenico which lies roughly 300m (328yd) west of the park. It contains a fine statue of the *Redeemer*, which dates from the fifteenth century, and various Madonnas, amongst the best of which are: the *Madonna della Purita*, dated 1613; the *Madonna della Rosario* which is in the left transept and is the work of a Flemish painter; and the *Madonna della Vittoria*, housed in the fourth chapel in the left aisle, which dates from the sixteenth century.

The *duomo*, a short distance to the north of San Domenico, was completely rebuilt after World War II and the only other church of historical interest is the Osservanza, which lies at the north edge of the city. It was built in the fifteenth century, although has been reconstructed on numerous occasions since, and contains a fine marble statue of the *Madonna* by A. Gagini, which was carved in 1504.

Route 8C • Catanzaro to Rossano

The route continues by heading north of Catanzaro through the Sila mountains. This great massif is formed of three distinct parts: Sila Greca in the north, Sila Grande at the centre, and Sila Piccola in the south. Together they cover a total area of 3,300sq km (1,269sq miles), and average between 1,300m (4,264ft) and 1,400m (4,592ft) in height. The Parco Nazionale della Calabria, which was established in 1968, protects large areas of both the Sila Grande and the Sila Piccola, providing a refuge for endangered species such as wolves, deer and black squirrels. In most parts the mountains are richly forested with chestnut, beech and oak, and at altitudes of over 1,000m (3,280ft) a native pine, *pino loricano*, which grows more than 40m (131ft) tall, can be seen. In the spring, the forests and glades are carpeted with wild violets, narcissi, orchids and other flora. In June and July wild strawberries grow in the pine forests and in Autumn, funghi are in abundance. The Sila is also known for its excellent cheeses, which are rated amongst the best in Italy. Of the great selection that is produced, some of the names worth looking out for while travelling through the region are: *butirro, burrino, tumu, rinusu*, and *impanata*, all of which are made from cow's milk. Those visiting in winter should be warned that due to their high altitude, the mountains are snow-covered and the roads are often icy and may be blocked either by snow or by landslides.

The SS19bis winds up above Catanzaro, to the village of **Chiesa**, which as its name suggests, has a large, white Baroque church, at which visitors should fork left. After a highly panoramic 3km (2 mile) drive, with views across a liberal scattering of hill towns to the coast, there is another fork. Here visitors who do not wish to visit the mountain town of Taverna, which involves a considerable amount of climbing up and down, can fork left and follow the scenic itinerary, marked by signs to Sila Laghi, which takes in lake Passante. However, those with an interest in art should most definitely not forfeit a visit to Taverna, which is reached by forking right and following the SS109bis.

The road winds down through the bleak villages of Fossato Serralta and Pentone, to Sorbo San Basile, from where **Taverna** can be seen on the far side of the valley. The SS109bis crosses down to the valley floor, before climbing up the other side to Taverna's outskirts. Fork left at the edge of the town and follow Via Mattia Preti to the town centre where there is a small piazza with a magnificent open vista along one side looking across the valley. Along the east end of the piazza is the seventeenth-century church of San Domenico, the town's greatest asset. It contains an outstanding collection of paintings by the painter Mattia Preti, who was born in Taverna in 1613. Known as 'Il Cavaliere Calabrese', Preti lived for most of his life in Malta, but his paintings show the influence of M. Caravaggio who was known to Preti through the Neapolitan school. To get inside the church it is necessary to locate the key. Go to the Palazzo Municipale, next door to the church, and ask at the Ufficio Anagrafe, on the first floor.

Hung in their original setting, rather than in the anonymous surroundings of a gallery, the paintings hang in graceful harmony with the rich stucco and gilt decoration of the church interior. In the right aisle, the first altar holds *The Martyrdom of St Peter*; the second altar, *St Francis de Paola*; the third altar *St Sebastian*, who is Taverna's patron saint; and the fifth altar the *Infant Christ*. The main apse holds *Christ in Majesty* as well as attractive, carved choir stalls. In the left aisle, at the first altar is the *Madonna of the Rosary*; while the third altar holds one of the painters' greatest works, the *Crucifixion*; the fourth altar holds a *Madonna with Saints*; and another outstanding work is hung at the fifth altar, depicting *John the Baptist*. The sacristy, to the left of the main apse, is also finely decorated with stucco ornamentation, like the icing on a wedding cake, and also frescoes by the Neapolitan school dating from the seventeenth and eighteenth centuries. Preti also endowed both the churches of Santa Barbara and San Martino with his paintings, but after San Domenico, neither are as impressive.

Leave Taverna by heading left of San Domenico, past the church of San Giovanni, and follow signs to Albi. The road winds tortuously up and down, but with good views, to the olive-covered slopes that surround **Albi**. The centre of the village is off right, but the route continues into the Sila Piccola, where the scenery becomes increasingly panoramic and the rocky hills are covered by pine and Mediterranean broom. A steep hill with a 12 per cent gradient leads up into the Parco Nazionale della Calabria. The road continues gradually upwards onto a high rolling plateau, which is thickly-forested

Longobucco

and rich in flora. **Villagio Mancuso**, at an altitude of 1,289m (4,228ft), is 17km (11 miles) north of Taverna, and is the main centre of the Sila Piccola National Park. It has neatly painted wooden chalets, several restaurants, and on a clear day both the Ionian and Tyrrhenian coasts can be seen. During September, a Calabrian Folk Festival takes place, and on 1 October there is a mushroom fair, the Sagra del Fungha.

Another popular resort, **Villagio Racise**, lies 4km (2 miles) further north along the SS179dir. It was built in the 1930s, but being at a lower altitude, it does not offer the same panorama. The SS179dir continues to head gently downwards, offering a brief glimpse of Lake Passante to the left. The road on the left, which leads to the lake, is also where the alternative Sila route emerges. The SS179dir continues north, through one of the loveliest parts of the park, where forests of pine and beech are interspersed with grassy pastures and gentle hills. Those that wish to venture into the heart of the Sila Piccola National Park can make a 15km (9 mile) excursion, by turning off right, to **Buturo**, which is a picturesque village. The route, however, continues downhill for a further 5km (3 miles) to a junction at which visitors should turn right, following the SS179 to Lago Ampollino. The road winds along the south shore of the Ampollino lake, which is just over 9km (6 miles) long. The lake is artificial and was formed by damming the Ampollino river, but has been attractively landscaped and has grassy banks and pines lining its banks. Midway along the lake, the road passes through the small resort of **Villagio Palumbio** where a cluster of chalets look out across the water. Fork left, after Villagio Palumbio, and follow the road along the eastern end of the lake, passing over the River Ampollino and the dam. The road then leaves the lake and winds steeply down through forests to the wide valley of the River Arvo which is quarried for its dark, granite stone. High on a spur at the far side of the valley is **San Giovanni in Fiore**. A series of hairpin bends lead up to the drab outskirts of the town, the centre of which is unfortunately no more cheerful. However, the town is of interest as it is the centre for craft weaving. A technique, known as *spugna*, is used to make thick bed and floor coverings with coarsely embroidered patterns, and occasionally, it is also possible to find knotted carpets, made in a tradition that has been handed down by the small Armenian community that settled here. Also of interest is the recently-restored, Cistercian abbey, Badia Fiorense, which is to be found in the lower part of the town. It was founded in 1189, under Abbot Gioacchino da Fiore, and is typical, in the austere simplicity of its architecture, of the early Cistercian period. A simple Gothic portal, dating from the thirteenth century, leads into a spacious interior, comprised of a vast, single nave. The high, open-timbered ceiling rests on plain stone walls, but the main apse has a pretty rose window. The decorative, high altar dates from the Baroque era, as do the choir stalls behind. The sacristy, to the right of the apse, contains a collection of photos and drawings, documenting the development of the Cistercian church.

Leave San Giovanni in Fiore by heading up to the top end of the town, where the main highway, SS107, is joined. The road passes over a high, undulating plateau, before following the Garga river valley down through the centre of the Sila lake region, where fresh trout are a speciality. Lake Arvo lies 12km (7 miles) south of the SS107 and makes a pleasant excursion. The lake is artificial, but is attractively surrounded by pine forests, and has a dramatic setting at the foot of the tallest peak in the Sila massif, Monte Botte Donato, which has a height of 1,928m (6,324ft). **Lorica** is the main resort on the lake shore, and is a popular base from which to go skiing in the winter.

The route continues west along the SS107, past the small lake of Ariamacina, to **Camigliatello Silano**, which lies in a valley, at an altitude of 1,275m (4,182ft). This busy resort is the main centre of tourism in the Sila Grande, and has facilities for both winter and summer sports, as well as a good selection of accommodation. Turn right at Camigliatello Silano, following signs to Rossano on the SS177. The road winds over gentle hills to Lake Cecita and then closely follows its southern shore. Well-stocked with trout, the lake is edged by gentle wooded hills and is over 14km (9 miles) from end to end. There are facilities for horseriding around the lake, while the road to **Fossiata**, from the eastern end of the lake, is recommended for cyclists. Fossiata, 8km (5 miles) east of the lake, lies inside the Grande Sila National Park, where roe and fallow deer are protected and Silan flora grows in a neat Alpine gardens.

The SS177 winds high above the eastern end of the lake before turning right, and passing through the chalet resort, **Cava di Molis**. After a further 3km (2 miles) another right turn, signposted to Longobucco, winds steeply up on a series of hairpin bends along the northern edge of the Sila Grande National Park. The road passes through beautiful forests of the tall lorican pines to a grassy pasture at the top. From the summit, which is 1,651m (5,415ft) high, a further series of hairpin bends winds down the other side. The views are spectacular and before long the picturesque rooftops of **Longobucco** come into sight.

This small town covers a lonely ridge, high above a valley, at the foot of the Sila Greca mountains. The Sila Greca are named after the large communities of Greek Orthodox Albanians that have inhabited the area since the Turkish invasions of their homeland in the fifteenth century. The textiles that are woven in Longobucco today, probably hark back to Albanian origins, or possibly even further back in time to the Byzantines. The streets of the town are fascinating to wander around, while the Baroque parish church with its medieval *campanile*, contains a notable wooden sculptural group, dating from the fifteenth century.

The SS177 winds steeply down into the Trionto river gorge below Longobucco. The road twists and turns precariously along one side of the gorge, but the scenery is excellent. After passing through **Destro** the valley widens into an alluvial flood plain, with olive groves dotted along either side. A short distance further, perched on a smooth rock above the boulder-strewn alluvial bed, is **Cropalati**. Known in Byzantine times as *Kouropalates*, this lovely old village has a large Baroque church containing numerous eighteenth-century paintings, and many picturesque streets to wander around.

From here visitors can either continue directly to the coast, or turn left and continue on the SS177, through the foothills of the Sila Greca to **Rossano**. This large town preserves some of the best relics of Byzantine Calabria. The Museo Diocesano, which is next door to the town's Baroque cathedral, houses the Codex Purpurus, a unique Greek manuscript that dates from the sixth century, containing beautiful miniatures depicting evangelical scenes. The church of San Marco, on a hill top to the south-east of the town, also dates from the Byzantine era. It is similar to the Cattolica, with its five domes, and contains fragments of frescoes dating from the eleventh century.

Route 8C • Rossano to Taranto

From Rossano, a winding road leads down from the hills, for 8km (5 miles) to the coast. The route then continues northwards along the SS106 coastal road. The landscape is flat, densely populated, and cultivated with groves of citrus fruits and giant olive trees. The first to inhabit this fertile plain were the ancient Greek colonists of *Magna Graecia* and it was here that the Achaen colony of *Sybaris* was founded in 720BC. They prospered in their trade with the Etruscans, and lived in the lap of luxury. So famed was their way of life that the term 'sybaritic' has survived to this day. However, all good things come to an end, and in 510BC their Greek neighbours, the Crotonians, flooded the Crati river and obliterated the city. The survivors of the flood were to build a new city, *Thurri*, the remains of which can still be seen. It was built with the financial assistance of Athens and was to become a centre of Athenian culture, as well as home to the great historian, Herodotus (480-425BC). In 290BC, it was Romanised and its name was changed to *Copiae*. The site, now known as **Sybaris-Copia**, lies on the left of the SS106, immediately after crossing the Crati river. The entrance is marked by signs to *parco archeologico*. The neat grid lay-out of the city's streets is discernible, while archaeological finds from the site can be seen in the Museo della Sibaritide. The museum is reached by continuing along the SS106 for a further 3km (2 miles) before taking the left turn to modern day **Sibari**. After the second railway crossing, turn left and continue for 50m (55yd) to the museum entrance which is also on the left. The collection is modestly displayed in four simple rooms and comprises ceramics, bronzes and funeral objects.

For those that wish to bathe in the same thermal waters as the ancient Sibarites did, a 15km (9 mile) excursion can be made, inland from Sibari, to the Terme Sibarite at **Cassano allo Jonio**. The modern establishment now built over the springs is open from May to October. The waters are at a constant temperature of 25°C (77°F) and along with the therapeutic application of mud, are said to cure rheumatism, skin complaints, respiratory problems and gynaeco-logical disorders.

Continuing north for a further 6km (4 miles) along the SS106, another inland excursion can be made to the hill-town, **Cerchiara di Calabria**. Just visible from the road, the town lies 18km (11 miles) away, above the steep valley of the Caldanelle river. The valley is dotted with thermal springs, and grottoes oozing with thermal mud. One such grotto was dedicated by the ancient Greeks to the Eusiadi nymphs. Today, the dark mud is available at the local thermal spa which opens from June to September. Visitors lounge around a large outdoor thermal pool, baking their mud-covered bodies in the sun — a treatment said to cure all skin complaints.

The SS106 continues north, crossing the wide, alluvial delta of the River Saraceno, before climbing along the foothills at the southern end of the Taranto gulf. These lovely hills are covered in olive groves and afford fine views of the sea. The road passes through a series of short tunnels and crosses over several wide, alluvial river beds, to the promontory, Capo Spulico, which is guarded by a ruined defense tower. After crossing the River Ferro to the northern side of the cape, the road passes by a fine medieval castle, which dates from the thirteenth century and has been well-restored, complete with its crenellations and inner keep. Opposite the castle, to the left of the road, is the popular resort of **Roseto Capo Spulico** which has traces of its medieval walls.

The road continues along the hills, above pebble beaches, crossing the wide, gravel bed of the River Cardona, to **Monte Giordano Marina**. After a further 7km (4 miles), at the southern end of a sweeping, gravel bay, is **Marina di Rocca Imperiale**, from where a delightful, 4km (2 mile) excursion can be made inland, to the town of **Rocca Imperiale**. The road follows the River Canna and then climbs a series of hairpins to the base of the hill on which the village is neatly stacked. There is a carpark on the left at the edge of the village from where visitors can proceed on foot to the *cattedrale* which marks the town's centre. The finest feature of this motley cathedral is its pretty *campanile*. It sits, stout and square, on the right corner of the façade, and has two layers of large twin openings. The interior of the *cattedrale* dates from the eighteenth century and has a number of altars decorated with ceramic statues. Any of the town's attractive alleys, lined with whitewashed houses, leads eventually up to the ruined castle that crowns the top of the hill. The castle was built by Frederick II in the thirteenth century, although the tall residential buildings inside the crenellated walls were added in the fifteenth and seventeenth centuries. The monument is badly in need of restoration and it is not possible to get inside the walls, so visitors must content themselves with the fine view of the coast.

Those with time may wish to make the scenic drive further up the Canna river valley. The wide river bed is lined with oleander and shrubs, while in the hills above are the remote and unspoilt villages of Canna and Nocara. To continue along the route, return to the SS106 and cross the fertile flood plain of the Sinni river. The Sinni lies just inside the region of Basilicata, which has no more than 30km (19 miles) of coastline on this side of the peninsula. Citrus, peach and olive groves abound, and there are two ancient *Magna Graecian* sites. The first, *Heracleia*, is reached after crossing the Sinni, at the modern day town of **Policoro**. Follow signs through the town to the *museo* which is on Via Colombo. In ancient times the flat plain between the Sinni and the Agri rivers was known as the *Siritide*. The museum, the Museo Nazionale della Siritide, contains a wealth of archaeological finds discovered within this area. The exhibits are well displayed and arranged in chronological order around six spacious rooms. Amongst the finest pieces in the collection are the Hellenistic vases, some of which are signed works by the Greek artist, Policoro. The scant remains of *Herecleia* itself are reached by continuing beyond the museum and turning right, past a free-standing, ancient tomb. From the carpark, steps lead up to the main excavation area, where the foundations and low walls of houses and streets have been uncovered. The ruins date from the fifth century BC, when the *Thurri*, descendants of the *Sybarites*, founded a colony here with the *Taras*, the inhabitants of present day Taranto.

The second ancient site in this part of Basilicata is *Metapontum*.

Follow the SS106 for a further 20km (12 miles) north, and turn right to the present day village of **Metaponto**. Follow signs to the *zona archeologica*, an extensive area, set amidst flat fields of corn and vineyards, to the north of the village. *Metapontum* was founded in the eighth century BC by Achaen colonists and grew to be one of the most important cities of *Magna Graecia*. The site, which occupies a vast grassy area, is well-cared for, but most of the remains are rather scant. Those short of time, should drive along the south-east side of the site, past the ruins of three temples, where the ground is littered with fragments of fluted columns, dating from the sixth and fifth centuries BC, to the theatre where the lower range of seating has been restored.

The most impressive of all the remains of *Metapontum*, however, is the temple of Tavole Palatine, which lies outside the archaeological zone, on the SS106, 2km (1 mile) north of the intersection with the SS175, on the left. Park at the Antiquarium di Metaponto and follow the footpath, which is attractively lined with oleander, along the right side of the museum. In an opening at the end of the path stand the bold, fluted columns of the temple. A total of fifteen, out of an original thirty-two are erect, complete with their flat, doric capitals and architrave. The temple was built in the sixth century BC and is thought to have been dedicated to Hera, the Goddess of Women.

The museum, Antiquarium di Metaponto, is also well worth a visit. The exhibits are well displayed and clearly labelled, and include many fine Greek vases, votive statues, funerary jewellery and an Achaen alphabet, all of which were found around the site of *Metapontum* and date from the sixth to the third century BC.

The SS106 continues northwards, along the Taranto gulf, into the region of Puglia. The land is amply irrigated by the numerous wide rivers, such as the Lato, which traverse the plain and empty into the sea, and is covered by large vineyards and cornfields. As the road approaches **Taranto**, which lies 40km (25 miles) from *Metapontum*, the city's massive industrial port comes into view. Taranto has more than its fair share of heavy industry, including Italsider, one of the most important iron works in Europe, and along with La Spezia, is one of Italy's most important naval bases.

It is also a city of great historical importance. Ancient Taranto (*Tarentum*) was founded in 708BC by Greek colonists from Sparta. It became one of Magna Graecia's most important trading colonies, and by the fourth century BC, is said to have had a population of 300,000 who lived inside an impressive city wall, 15km (9 miles) long. With the support of the armies of Pyrrhus, the Greek king of Epirus, the city fought against the Romans, until 272BC when it was defeated. During the Roman era, *Tarentum*, retained a largely Greek population and was granted special privileges due to its great importance as a naval power. The city continued to flourish, and the Augustan poet, Horace (65-8BC), praised its olives, scallops, honey, wool and purple dye, and the Roman elegiac poet, Propertius around (50-16BC), its pine forests. In AD967 the city was sacked by the Saracens, but it grew up again under the Normans and continued to prosper under the Kingdom of Naples.

Today, as with so many of Southern Italy's large cities, crime is rampant. The locals say that the only safe places to park are either near the Capitaneria di Porto, with their permission, or around the walls of the Castello, on Piazza Municipio. Sadly, Taranto's beautiful old quarter, which is idylically isolated on an island, between the two lagoons of Mar Grande and Mar Piccola, is where a lot of the crime takes place. It is not a place to go wandering through the lonely back streets, even though they seem full of crumbling romance, rather, stick to the main sights and watch your bag and camera.

The **Castello**, guarding the south-eastern corner of the island, is a good point from which to start a tour of the city. It was built in 1480 by Ferdinand I of Aragon, who ruled the Kingdom of Naples from 1458 to 1494. Its stout walls are excellently preserved and the building is still used by the navy today, although periodic exhibitions are shown in the Galleria Comunale which is housed in the ground floor. The Citta Vecchia, which was once the site of ancient *Tarentum's* acropolis, extends to the north-west of the castle. The two principal monuments to be visited here can both be reached by following Corso Vittorio Emanuele II along the sea edge. After 500m (547yd), turn right, past the Capitaneria di Porto, to the *duomo*. The building was erected in the tenth and eleventh centuries, and dedicated to San Cataldo, St Cathal of Munster, who stayed in Taranto on his return from a pilgrimage in the seventh century. The fine cupola, supported on a high, decorated drum is reminiscent of the Byzantine era, while the façade is distinctly Baroque and dates from 1713. The interior is divided into three aisles by attractive columns, each of which is capped by an ancient capital, either Roman or Byzantine. Patches of the original black and white mosaic remain on the floor, while the tall ceiling, over the central aisle, is richly coffered in the seventeenth-century Baroque style. The Cappella di San Cataldo, to the right of the main apse, is also Baroque. The walls are inlaid with exquisite marbles and are pierced by niches holding statues, although that of San Cataldo has been stolen. The altar is also finely decorated with coloured marbles, and in the semi-dome above there are rich frescoes.

Return to Corso Vittorio Emanuele II and continue for a further

250m (273yd) to the north-western corner of the island, from where signs point right to **San Domenico Maggiore**. A grand, Baroque staircase leads up to the church façade, which dates from 1302. The finely carved portal is covered by a baldachin, while the wall above holds a pretty rose window. The interior comprises a single nave with plain white walls and an open timber ceiling. A triumphal arch divides the presbytery which is covered by a dome and has an ornate, Baroque altar. To the left of the high altar a glass coffin holds the relics of an esteemed Domenican.

Returning to the Castello, head from its north side to the swing bridge, Ponte Girevole. In the Mar Piccolo and the Mar Grande, which stretch either side of the bridge, *cozze*, mussels, and *ostriche*, oysters, are cultivated, although they have to sit in a purifying plant before they are edible. At the other side of the bridge is the new city, the Citta Nuova. The main piazza, a short walk away has the best museum of antiquities in Southern Italy, after that of Naples. To reach the museum, simply continue straight ahead (avoid the underpasses which are filthy) to the palm trees which fill the Villa Garibaldi gardens at the centre of the piazza. The **Taranto Museo Nazionale**, is on the left, in the north-east corner of this piazza.

The museum's outstanding collection of Tarentine antiquities is arranged on the first floor around fifteen spacious rooms. The exhibits range from the Greco-Roman to the Byzantine era and include ceramics, carvings and jewellery. An explicit guide is provided for each room, but it is in Italian only. As a rough outline: Room 1 contains Greek statues dating from the fifth and fourth centuries BC, carved from a fine white marble that was quarried from the Greek island of Paro.

Room 2 holds further marble statues, but from a later period. They date from the Hellenistic era to that of Imperial Rome. They are mostly works of minor importance, many were funerary ornaments and were modelled on ancient Greek copies. The fragments of black and white mosaics, in the same room, date from the second and first centuries BC.

Room 3 contains an impressive collection of sculpted heads, originating from Roman *Tarentum*. To the right of the entrance is the head of Augustus, which is dated, two years after the great emperor's death, 12BC. The room also contains two interesting sections of mosaics that date from the fourth and fifth centuries AD.

Room 4 holds the finest of the tombs that were excavated at *Tarentum's* necropolis. In the centre of the room there are two archaic sarcophagi, beautifully painted, and thought to date from the fifth century BC. The first, is the best preserved, and is complete with three of the original four amphoras, decorated with black figures on a red ground, that stand at the corners of the sarcophagus. The tomb belonged to an aristocrat who was evidently a dedicated athlete. The numerous stone fragments mounted on the walls of this room are funerary monuments and originate from the Hellenistic city.

Room 5 contains an unequalled collection of ceramics, all originating from the necropolis, and dating from the time of the city's foundation in the eighth century BC, to the mid-sixth century BC. Amongst the most valuable pieces are the Corinthian vases, which together form the largest collection of their type in the world.

Room 6 contains further ceramics excavated from the necropolis, but dating from the seventh and sixth centuries BC, the Ancient Greek period, known as the Archaic.

Room 7 has still further ceramics, with striking black figures set on a red ground, but many of the pieces, termed Attic, are believed to have been imported from Athens.

Room 8 also contains Attic ceramics but here a turning point is seen in the glazing techniques. In 530BC, Athens led the way in a new style, where instead of the figures being black on a red ground, they were made red on a black ground. This enabled a greater degree of detail to be achieved by using fine black lines on the red figures.

Rooms 9 and 10 hold ceramics that were produced locally throughout Puglia, dating from the fourth to the first century BC. Of particular interest are the large Gnathian vases in the corner of the room which date from the end of the fourth century BC.

Room 11 holds a collection of jewellery and statuettes made of precious metals. The exhibits are arranged chronologically and span the centuries from the sixth century BC to the Byzantine epoque which lasted from the ninth to the eleventh century.

Rooms 12 to 15 surround an inner cloister and contain Greek statuettes and small figurines, originating from the Taranto Gulf. The second floor contains relics of prehistoric Taranto, while the ground floor is reserved for exhibitions.

Additional Information

Places to Visit

Cassano allo Jonio
Thermal Establishment
Terme Sibarite
Via Terme 2
☎ (0981) 71376
Open: May to October.

Catanzaro
Museo Provinciale
Villa Trieste
☎ (0961) 25434
Open: Thursday and Friday 10am-12noon.

Locri

Museo di Locri
Via Nazionale
☎ (0964) 390023/20844
Open: winter, Monday-Saturday
9am-1pm, 3.30-4.30pm, Sunday &
holidays 9am-1pm. Summer, Monday-Saturday 9am-1pm, 4.30-7.30pm,
Sunday & holidays 9am-1pm.

Scavi di Locri
Via Nazionale
Contrada Marasa
Open: 9am-1 hour before sunset.

Metaponto

Antiquarium di Metaponto
Open: winter, Tuesday to Sunday
9am-12noon, 2-5pm. Summer,
Tuesday to Sunday 9am-1pm, 3.30-6.30pm.

Policoro

Museo Nazionale della Siritide
Via Colombo
☎ (0835) 972154
Open: winter daily 9am-1pm.
Summer daily 9am-1pm, 3.30-4pm.

Rossano

Museo Diocesano
Palazzo Arcivescovile
Open: Winter, Monday to Saturday
10.30am-12noon, 4-6pm. Sunday
and holidays 9am-12noon.
Summer, Monday to Saturday
10.30am-12noon, 5-7pm. Sundays
and holidays 9am-12noon.

Sibari

Museo della Sibaritide
Via Taranto
☎ (0981) 74077
Open: winter, Monday to Saturday
9am-2pm, Sunday and holidays
9am-1pm. Summer, Monday to
Saturday 9am-2pm, 5-7pm, Sunday
and holidays 9am-1pm.

Stilo

Cattolica (custodian)
Via Salerno 16
☎ (0964) 71341
Open: daily 8am-sunset

Taranto

Museo Nazionale
Piazza Archita
☎ (099) 432112
Open: Monday to Saturday 9am-2pm, Sunday and holidays 9am-1pm.

Useful Information

Camigliatello Silano

Tourist Information Centre
Pro Loco
Centro Assistenza Comunita
Montana Silana
☎ (0984) 578091

Cantanzaro

Tourist Information Centre
Ente Provinciale per il Turismo
Galleria Mancuso
☎ (0961) 29823

Ufficio Informazione Turistiche
Piazza Prefettura
☎ (0961) 45530

Parco Nazionale Sila Piccola
Ufficio Amministrazione
Via Cortese
☎ (0961) 21731

Transport
Ferrovie dello Stato (Railway)
☎ (0961) 31514

Emergencies
Polizia Urbana (Town Police)
☎ (0961) 21014

Vigili Urbani (Municipal Police)
☎ (0961) 31039

Ospedale (Hospital)
☎ (0961) 883111

Pronto Soccorso (First Aid Service)
☎ (0961) 45025

Guardia Medica (Medical Officer)
☎ (0961) 745833

Automobile Club Italiano
Viale dei Normanni 99
☎ (0961) 754131

Gerace
Tourist Information Centre
Ufficio Turistico
Municipio
☎ (0964) 356003

Locri
Tourist Information Centres
Ente Provinciale per il Turismo
Via Matteotti angolo Via Fiume
☎ (0964) 29600

Pro Loco
Via Matteotti 57
☎ (0964) 29393

Transport
Ferrovie dello Stato (Railway)
☎ (0964) 29677

Emergencies
Polizia (Police)
☎ (0964) 38144

Polizia Stradale (Traffic Police)
☎ (0964) 381035

Pronto Soccorso (First Aid Service)
☎ (0964) 21753

Guardia Medica (Medical Officer)
☎ (0964) 21755

Rossano
Tourist Information Centre
Pro Loco

Piazza Matteoti 2
☎ (0983) 32137

Soverato
Festivals and Events
Third Sunday of September, Sagra
della Melanzana (Aubergine Fair).

Tourist Information Centre
Azienda Autonoma di Soggiorno e
    Turismo
Via San Giovanni Bosco 1
☎ (0967) 21465/25432

Taranto
Events and Festivals
4-5 September, Sagra del Pesce e
della Cozza Tarantina (Festival of
Fish and Tarantine Mussels,
procession at sea in honour of the
Madonna Stell Maris, patron of
fishermen).

8-10 May, Sagra di San Cataldo
(Festival of city's patron saint,
procession at sea).

Tourist Information Centre
Ente Provinciale per il Turismo
Corso Umberto 115
☎ (099) 432392

Transport
Ferrovie dello Stato (Railway)
☎ (099) 4711801

Emergencies
Polizia (Police)
☎ (099) 26305

Polizia Municipale (Municipal
    Police)
☎ (099) 3204/339866

Polizia Stradale (Traffic Police)
☎ (099) 352115

Ospedale SS Annunziata (Hospital)
☎ (099) 422155

9

SALENTINE PENINSULA

Chapter 9 tours the Salentine peninsula, the heel of Italy's boot, which thrusts out between the Adriatic and Ionian Seas. The entire peninsula lies within the region of Puglia. It is mostly flat, with hills no higher than 200m (656ft), and has the richest agricultural land in Southern Italy. This may seem surprising since the region is devoid of rivers and has a very low rainfall, but the peninsula has been supplied with water carried by aqueducts since Roman times. The driest part of the peninsula is the limestone plateau, which snakes all the way down the heel, known as the Murge. However, vines and olives thrive on its dry, chalky soils, and Puglia produces a great quantity of wine, although at present only 2 per cent of it has achieved DOC classification, as well as supplying a lot of Europe's olive oil.

Wine and olives form an important part in the Puglian diet, along with fresh herbs, wild onions, known as *lampascioni*, and ricotta cheeses. Fish is more widely eaten than meat, as both the Ionian and Adriatic seas yield a plentiful selection, including mackerel, anchovy and sea bass, as well as sea urchins, octopus, squid, lobster, mussels and prawns. The Spanish domination of Southern Italy has left its mark on the cuisine, with dishes such as Tiella which is made up of layer upon layer of rice, vegetables, potatoes, cheese and meat or seafood. Capriata is more typical of rural Puglia and consists of broad beans, chicory and *lampascioni*, made into a puree.

The touristic attractions of the Salentine peninsula are various, and include its many fine Baroque towns, ancient Messapian sites, idyllic sandy beaches, picturesque villages and cool, dark caves. The peninsula also has the pervasive character of the Mediterranean, and as the perennial gateway to the Orient, it is spiced with a hint of the East. Amongst the first to land on Puglia's shores from the East were

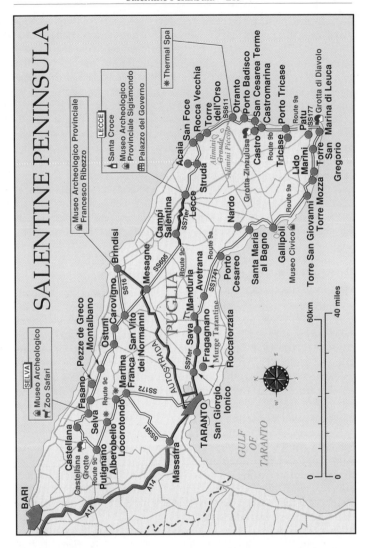

the Ancient Greek colonists, whose trading posts were kept active throughout the Roman period. The Byzantines, also from the East, endowed the peninsula with churches and castles, but during medieval times the tide changed as Puglia became a major point of departure for the Crusaders. At the same time, their eastern enemies, the Saracens, periodically came and devastated parts of Puglia, and it was during this period that the numerous defense towers that punctuate the coastline were erected. Further fortifications were also erected by the Normans and the Aragonese, when their turn came. Perhaps the best-known feature, however, of the Puglian peninsula is the *trulli*, the small, circular houses with conical roofs, which are found in a region of about 100sq km (38sq miles) at the top end of the heel.

With such a wealth of attractive features, tourism in Puglia is well-developed, particularly along the coasts where the beaches are well-frequented by Italians during August. There is a good range of accommodation throughout the region and a wide range of sports facilities, including horse-riding, cycling and watersports. The route makes a circular tour of the peninsula and ends at Martina Franca, from where visitors should join chapter 10, which heads northwards to the Adriatic coast. Those that wish to travel west to Calabria can join chapter 8 at Taranto and follow the itinerary in the reverse order.

Route 9A • Taranto to Porto Badisco

Leave Taranto by the motorway, which is signposted to Brindisi. Follow the northern shore of Mar Piccolo for 2km (1 mile), and then turn off the motorway, and cross over the lagoon, from where there are good views of old Taranto. Continue, following signs to Lecce on the SS7ter Murge Tarantine, through the industrial town of **San Giorgio Ionico**. The SS7ter continues over the undulating slopes of the Murge Tarantine, the limestone plateau that backs Taranto, passing **Roccaforzata**, where there is a low fortress at the brow of the hill. A little further on the SS7ter climbs high enough to be able to see the coast, which is dotted with defense towers.

The next town along the SS7ter, **Fragagnano**, has a high-domed, Baroque church, surrounded by flat-roofed buildings, which are typical of the region. The same type of architecture is to be found at the agricultural market town, **Sava**, which is 7km (4 miles) further east. It is worth stopping here simply to wander about the attractive streets of whitewashed houses, that are focused around a prettily-decorated, medieval bell tower.

The SS7ter continues for a further 7km (4 miles) to another attractive, agricultural town, **Manduria**, which gives its name to the heady, local wine, Primitivo di Manduria. The town is built on the impressive remains of an ancient city, founded by colonists from Illyria, in what was Yugoslavia. The best ruins lie just outside the town. To reach them, continue on the SS7ter, to the northern side of Manduria, and take the right turn, signposted *zona archeologica*.

There are good remains of the megalithic city walls, which, built between the fifth and third centuries BC, successfully kept out the Greeks, and also of the necropolis which extends some distance along the road. Many of the graves are cut out of the natural rock and in places the ground resembles a honeycomb. During the excavation of the site the necropolis yielded much of the Gnathian ceramic ware that is now held in the Taranto museum.

From the *zona archeologica* follow the small road that leads past the austere, Capucin church of San Pietro Mandurio. Take the first left after the church to see the Fonte Pliniano, the site of an ancient spring. It is named after Pliny the Elder, who documented it in his voluminous work, the *Natural History*.

Continue along the road to the town centre of Manduria where there are many attractive buildings, their simple whitewashed exteriors a striking contrast to the darkness of the local stone. Piazza Garibaldi, the town's hub, is surrounded by eighteenth-century architecture, including the Palazzo Imperiale which was built in 1719 on the foundations of a Messapian bastion. The *duomo* is older, although, with the exception of the Romanesque *campanile*, it was remodelled during the Renaissance. The façade has three portals, with carved reliefs above the central one, that depict the *Annunciation* and *Trinity with Angels*. The interior, comprised of three aisles, has a Renaissance font and there are twelve statues of saints, dating from the seventeenth century, in the apse.

Leave Manduria on the SS174 via Salentina, which is signposted to Avetrana. A small idiosyncracy of the road system around here is that the signs are sometimes coloured orange, rather than the blue, black or white used throughout the rest of Italy. The road passes through extensive vineyards, where the Primitivo grape grows on stocky, unsupported vines. **Avetrana**, 10km (6 miles) south-east of Manduria, is a pleasant town, but holds nothing of particular interest. The SS174 passes through its centre and then gradually heads towards the coast. After 17km (11 miles), after passing through groves of giant olives, turn off the SS174 to the coastal resort of **Porto Cesareo**. This once sleepy fishing village is now a popular holiday destination. Festooned with bourgainvillea and other Mediterranean flora, the village has lovely views across to the offshore islets of Conigli. The fishing harbour at the centre of the resort, is guarded by a tower and is overlooked by a good selection of fish restaurants. The resort also has a long, sandy beach, suitable for children, and a busy marina.

Continue south along the coast, following signs to Gallipoli. There is little to spoil the view along this idyllic stretch of the coast. Private villas are secluded in lush, walled gardens and only the occasional defense tower dents the horizon. A small holiday resort has grown up around Torre Isidoro, which lies at one end of a long, white sandy beach, but further development is restricted, as there are plans afoot to make this beautiful area a Natural Park. **Santa Maria al Bagno**, in keeping with the natural beauty, is dotted with attractive villas. From here, an excursion of 7km (4 miles) can be made inland to the wine-making town of **Nardo**. The town contains much fine Baroque architecture, particularly around its central square, Piazza Salandra. It also has an attractive Romanesque *duomo* which contains a thirteenth-century, Spanish crucifix.

The route, however, continues along the coast, south of Santa Maria al Bagno, along a rocky ledge towards the promontory of **Gallipoli**. Old Gallipoli lies in blissful isolation on the tip of this headland, quite oblivious to the new city and the industrial outskirts that have mushroomed inland. Follow the road, through the modern developments, to the bridge that leads across the water to the old town. Before the bridge, to the left, there is a carpark, at the north end of which stands Gallipoli's most ancient relic, the Fontana Ellenistica. This beautiful monument is the only significant part of Greek *Kallipolis*, which was founded in 450BC, to have survived. The fountain was reconstructed in 1560 using the ancient bas-reliefs, on the front side, which depict the metamorphosis of three nymphs who are shown both recumbent and then standing. The top is crowned by a fancy pediment and a richly carved frieze.

From the fountain, head towards the seventeenth-century bridge which crosses over to the old city on seven low arches. On the other side of the bridge, to the left, is a squat fortress. It is quadrilateral in shape, and has four towers, the largest of which projects over the water. The Byzantines were the first to build this fortress, but the successive rulers of Southern Italy, namely the Angevins in the fourteenth century and the Aragonese in the sixteenth century, also added their touches.

Follow the picturesque shopping street, Via Antonietta de Pace, from the west side of the fortress to the *cattedrale*. The exuberant façade, that was begun in 1630 but not finished until 1696, is richly decorated with carvings, statues and pillars. Continue along Via Antonietta de Pace for 150m (164yd) to the Museo Civico on the right. Housed in a fine *palazzo*, the museum collection is fairly modest and consists mainly of ceramics, and other locally excavated finds.

Via Antonietta de Pace continues to the sea walls where the Baroque façade of San Francesco is worn quite smooth by the wind and salt. Riviera Sauro can be followed right the way along the sea-

The ancient Fontana Ellenistica, Gallipoli

facing walls. At the southern end of Riviera Sauro, the pretty blue and white façade of San Domenico, looks out across a wide bastion built into the walls. At the northern end of the riviera is Chiesa di Purita, which has an ornate, stucco interior. A short distance further north of Chiesa di Purita is the fishing harbour where mussels and fish are brought in daily. From here, it is possible to continue along the water's edge, past the port, back to the bridge at the town entrance, where visitors may wish to sample Gallipoli's fresh sea food in one of the numerous restaurants that are clustered around here.

Leave Gallipoli, following the coastal road along the broad sandy bay which lies to the south of the town. There are numerous holiday resorts along this coastal stretch, which is known as the Costa Brada. At **Torre San Giovanni**, which is 24km (15 miles) south of Gallipoli, the road heads inland slightly, creating a pleasant strip of sandy beach, which is accessible from the road by numerous tracksd. The track from **Mare Pineta** is one of the easier points of access and has a small park with picnicing and washing facilities, beneath the pine trees at the back of the beach.

The road continues south, past the ruins of several defense towers, and through the small resorts of Torre Mozza and Lido Marini, both of which have box-like houses and sandy beaches. **Marina de Pescoluse**, a somewhat larger resort, surrounding a well-restored tower, also has a good, sandy beach. From here onwards the coast becomes increasingly rocky and at **Torre San Giorgio**, an excursion can be made inland to **Patu**. The main attraction of this hill village is the Centopietra, an ancient monument, thought to be of Messapian origin, built of fine ashlar stone. The route, however, continues along the jagged, limestone coastline to the southernmost tip of the Salentine peninsula.

The Grotta di Diavolo, which is passed on the outskirts of **Marina di Leuca**, is just one of a number of cave complexes in the locality, many of which were inhabited by early man. Boat excursions to the caves can be made from Marina di Leuca. This smart resort with its luxuriant palm trees and elaborate villas, has a simple stone church with a rose window, and a popular marina. Follow the road up above the marina to the *santuario* and lighthouse that mark the land's end. Known to the Romans as *Salentinum Promontorium*, in ancient times there was a temple to Minerva here. The temple foundations now support the sanctuary, Santa Maria Finibus Terrae, which was built in 1720. Its neo-Classical façade looks onto a square, Piazza Giovanni. On the tip of the headland, beyond the square, is a large, white lighthouse, 47m (154ft) tall. Nearby, a column marks the terminus of the great Apulian aqueduct. On rare occasions, when there is excess water, it is allowed to escape and cascades into the sea from here. Most of Puglia is supplied with water by this aqueduct, which with a channel, 2,700km (1,674 miles) long, rates amongst the longest in the world.

From the sanctuary, follow the SS173 delle Terme Salentine, northwards along the Adriatic coast. The road offers magnificent views as it climbs up and down, along the rocky shore, where cacti sprout profusely amongst the dry stone walls and the olive trees. There is hardly a building in sight, until **Tricase**, which is reached after 20km (12 miles). Tricase's picturesque marina is overlooked by a neat, converted castle. There is another castle, dating from the sixteenth century in the town itself which lies 4km (2 miles) inland.

The SS173 continues to wind along the coast, through **Marina d'Andrano**, and then down to **Castro Marina**. This handsome resort is dotted with small, white houses, like neat sugar cubes, and has a lively marina which is surrounded by fish restaurants. Above the marina, in the upper town of **Castro**, is a fine castle, that was built in 1572 on the foundations of an earlier Byzantine, and then Norman fortress. In ancient times there were Roman fortifications here. Just to the north of Castro, are the most famous caves on the Puglian coast, Grotta Zinzulusa. To visit the caves, turn off right and follow the road down to the carpark, where there is a popular restaurant and swimming pool. From the ticket office, which is just beyond the restaurant, steps lead down into a deep rocky inlet. A footpath leads along a ledge into the inlet, from where the caves extend back to a distance of 140m (459ft). There are two lakes in the caves, one of which is salty, while the other one contains fresh water. The unique species of crustacea that have been found to inhabit the caves are too small to be visible to the eye, but there are some interesting rock formations and a great many stalactites and stalagmites, which in the local dialect are *zinzuli*. As with many of the caves along the Puglian coast, evidence of early man has been found. Some of the traces discovered by excavators have been carbon-dated to around 10,000BC. In the Grotta Romanelli, which can be visited by a thirty-minute boat trip from Zinzulusa, fragments of cave paintings have also been found, the earliest yet documented in Italy.

The SS173 climbs along cliff edges, past the ruined tower of Torre Miggiano, which stands on a bare rocky promontory, to the bulging headland of **San Cesarea Terme**. This well-developed resort, lies at the foot of the cliffs, and has three major spa establishments, supplied by the nearby natural springs. The spas, open from March to November, offer treatments for arthritis, rheumatism, respiratory ailments, metabolic disorders and skin complaints. The waters, rich in sulphur, iodine and lithium, are not drunk, but are bathed in, inhaled or applied in mud packs. The resort also has a smart marina, to the north of which are numerous big hotels.

The SS173 continues north, along the scenic, rugged coastline, past the ruins of a tower, before heading down to **Porto Badisco**, a deep, rocky creek. It is said to be here that Aeneas first stepped foot onto Italy's shores, on the long and eventful search for his homeland. In the rocks to the north is a complex of caves, the Grotta dei Cervi, where traces of prehistoric murals have been discovered, depicting hunting scenes.

Route 9B • Porto Badisco to Lecce

From the deep creek of Porto Badisco, the road climbs up onto the flat, wide top of the Otranto cape. This windswept platform is quite desolate, apart from a ruined defense tower and the occasional shepherds' croft where *pecorino*, sheep's cheese, is sold to passers by. There is also a communications centre here and a military base. The road follows along the edge of the cape, to its long tapered tip above the sea, and then heads down to **Otranto**. Take the left fork at the outskirts of the town and follow signs to *centro storico*. There is ample parking along the sea front, although the town centre itself is pedestrianised.

Otranto is located at the easternmost point of Italy. Its history is closely tied up with Asia Minor, and perhaps more than anywhere else in Italy, the town has the feeling of being on the edge of the Orient. Its port has seen ships roll in from Asia Minor since the early trading days of the Greek colony, *Hydruntum*, but the town reached its zenith in the ninth century under the Byzantine Empire when it was the closest port in Italy to Constantinople. Terra d'Otranto, as the region was then known, became one of the most important Byzantine territories in Italy. It was also amongst one of the last Byzantine strongholds to fall to the Normans, although even under their rule it continued to trade with the East. In 1480 disaster struck the town in the form of invading Turks. All but 800 of the inhabitants were slaughtered in the attack, the survivors, offered mercy on the condition that they converted to Islam, refused. The entire population was therefore wiped out. So amazed were the executioners at the strength of the Otrantans Christian faith, that they converted to Christianity themselves, and promptly lost their own heads. Otranto was never really to recover from the massacre, and certainly its subsequent inhabitants have never forgotten it.

Fishing boats at Otranto

The town is built around two deep bays. The westernmost bay holds a port, from where ferries embark for Corfu and Igoumenitsa. The town is centred around the eastern bay. There is a lively covered market, shady public gardens with a small children's playground, and many cafés and restaurants. Pistacchios, hazelnuts and sunflower seeds, brought in with the ferries from Greece, are sold from barrows, while flat-weaves from Albania, which lies just 100km (62 miles) across the water, are sold in the shops.

To visit the historic centre, head through the gate, Porta Alfonsina (1483), which is opposite the public gardens, and follow the main shopping street, Via Duomo. The street heads up to the *duomo's* side entrance. Its portal, which is carved with papal busts, leads into the crypt. The crypt is the oldest part of the building and dates from the eleventh century. The remains of Byzantine frescoes can be seen on the walls, while its five aisles are divided by a forest of columns. There are forty-two in all, each one different, topped by a mixed selection of capitals, either antique, Byzantine or Romanesque. At the back of the crypt, on the left, steps lead up to the cathedral's interior.

The floor of the vast interior is covered by one of the most exceptional works of art in Southern Italy, a magnificent mosaic that was created from 1163 to 1166. It depicts an extraordinary vision of the universe, where world politics, economy and religion are encompassed in a beautiful pictorial tale. It is to be read from top to bottom, starting with the months of the year, and following down through the branches of the massive tree of life that fills the central aisle. Each branch of the tree holds a rich scenario, ranging from biblical to mythical subjects, and including Nordic, Breton and Oriental legend. The roots of the tree are supported on the backs of two elephants, who stand amidst a kingdom of animals. Since 1986, it has been under restoration, but a good deal is open to public view.

The ceiling of the cathedral is richly coffered and beautifully decorated with paintings, and dates from 1696. The columns, which divide the interior into three aisles are antique and have exquisitely carved capitals. In the right aisle, the Cappella dei Martiri, is dedicated to those massacred by the Turks. A glass cabinet above the altar holds the skulls and bones of 560 of the victims.

Continue uphill to the façade of the cathedral which faces onto a small piazza. The façade holds a large rose window, which dates from the fifteenth century, and has an imposing Renaissance portal that was added in 1514. The cathedral's unusual, wide belfry is to the left of the façade, and is quite a prominent landmark on the town's skyline. Continue up through Otranto's tidy streets, to the little

Byzantine church of San Pietro. It sits at the top of some steps on a small square, Piazza del Popolo. Dating from the tenth century, it is typical of the Byzantine era, in being built on a Greek cross plan. The interior is richly decorated with the remains of frescoes, some of which date from Byzantine times and have Greek inscriptions.

Also of interest in the town, is the well-preserved fortress that looks over the port. It was built under the Neapolitan House of Aragon, who built Otranto up again following the massacre, between 1485 and 1498, and was further strengthened in the sixteenth century. It stands on a quadrilateral ground-plan, and is bounded by strong bastions on all sides.

Leave Otranto on the SS611 di Otranto, following signs to San Cataldo and Laghi Alimini. The latter are a pair of lakes which are passed to the left, a short distance north of Otranto. The first, Alimini Piccolo is surrounded by pine forests, while the second, Alimini Grande, lies in open countryside and has a tourist village nearby with facilities for horse-riding. The SS611 continues north of the lakes to the town of **Torre dell'Orso** which is named after its robust tower. It is worth passing through the attractive town centre, which lies alongside a popular beach, particularly as the by-pass road is rather complicated. A further 2km (1 mile) north of Torre dell'Orso, is **Rocca Vecchia**. This charming resort stands on the site of a Messapian settlement. Remains of the megalithic walls are still standing in places and the necropolis has yielded a good deal of ceramic ware, dating from the fourth and third centuries BC, as well as earlier Messapian earthenware, which is now exhibited in the Lecce museum.

At **San Foce** turn left and follow the road inland towards Lecce. The road, lined with dry stone walls, passes through a vast expanse of olive groves. After 15km (9 miles) a short excursion can be made to the *citta fortificata*, **Acaia**. The road passes through **Struda** which resembles something of a dusty, Spanish peasant town, to the Aragonese walls that surround Acaia. Started in 1506 and completed in 1535, this now forlorn, fortified village, captures the essence of the Renaissance under the Spanish rule of Southern Italy. A grand, stone-carved gateway, studded with coats of arms, leads through the walls to a desolate piazza, Largo Castello, which is quite bare apart from a few lonely palm trees. To the left, a drawbridge crosses a moat to the castle's overgrown entrance, which is locked by a rusted padlock. However, this does not prevent the visitor from admiring the finely fortified walls which are a good example of Renaissance military architecture.

Return to the main road, and continue for a further 9½km (6 miles) to the delightful, Baroque city, **Lecce**, which is the capital of the Salentine peninsula. The road enters the city at its southern side, where the Museo Provinciale is located. Visitors can look for a parking space in one of the wide streets around here, and start a tour of the city at the museum.

Housed in a modern building, the museum is designed around a circular ramp. Take the ramp up to the first floor where the best of the museum's collection is displayed. This mainly comprises Apulian red and black ceramics, dating from the fifth century BC. Of particular note are the beautifully decorated Attic vases, the Gnathian ware with their fluted surfaces and geometric designs, and the simple Messapian earthenware. There is also a collection of local pitcher handles which show the ancient imprint of the Salentine ceramicists. Hellenistic figurines, terracotta statuettes and many Messapian and Roman inscription stones are also good features of the collection. On the ground floor there are further antiquities, arranged topo-

Renaissance gateway, Acaia

(opposite) The Roman amphitheatre, Lecce

graphically. There are also the painted panels from an iconostasis and altar of a local church, San Niccolo dei Greci. Those with time, can take the elevator up to the *pinacoteca* on the second floor, which houses Byzantine icons, Venetian triptychs dating from the four-teenth century, and a collection of large seventeenth-triptyches and eighteenth-century oil paintings, as well as china and glass dating from the same era.

The museum is a ten-minute walk from the city centre. Follow Viale Francesco Lo Re along the right side of the museum, for 350m (383yd), to Piazza Roma. Turn left, passing through the eighteenth-century gate, Porta Biagio, onto Via dei Perroni. This narrow street, lined with fine *palazzi*, leads past the decorative façade of San Matteo. Built between 1667 and 1670, the church has a curved front and an elliptical interior. Continue north, along Via d'Aragona, for a further 100m (110yd) to the seventeenth-century church of Santa Chiara. Follow the alley along the left side of the church to see the Teatro

Romano. This small theatre is simple, but well-preserved, and is complete with twelve rows of its seating as well as the original stone paved stage floor.

Return to Santa Chiara, and continue north along Via Augusto Imperiale. After 150m (164yd), Piazza Sant'Oronzo, the historic centre of the city, opens out to the right. At the southern end of this spacious square lie the remains of a Roman amphitheatre. It dates from the first century BC and has twelve rows of its original seating. During the summer, the amphitheatre hosts a season of drama and theatrical performances. Perched at the north edge of the arena is the Palazzo del Sedile. Built in 1592, its façade has a large pointed arch, while the interior contains the tourist office and a small exhibition space. The piazza takes its name from the column which stands in front of the Palazzo del Sedile. It is one of a pair that originally stood at the end of the great Roman road, the Appian Way, which was extended in 244BC, from Campania to Brindisi. The Roman column is topped by a statue of St Orontius (Sant'Oronzo), Bishop of Lecce, who was martyred during Nero's persecutions in the first century.

Leave Piazza Sant'Oronzo from its northern side, and continue for 120m (131yd) to Lecce's Baroque jewel, Santa Croce. Started in 1548 and completed in 1646, this formidable church is the finest example of Lecce's distinctive Baroque style. Leccese Baroque is exemplified by exuberant, decorative carvings, chiselled from the soft local stone. The effect is that of a thickly embroidered cloth, dripping with heavy garlands and clumps of globular foliage. However, although the local stone is soft to carve, over time the surface naturally becomes hardened and so resistant to erosion. The façade of Santa Croce, therefore, is as crisply incised as the day it was created, and is shown to advantage, having recently been cleaned. The lower façade, pierced by three portals, is decorated with Corinthian columns which have clusters of figures decorating their capitals. The upper façade is the work of the main exponent of the Leccese Baroque, Giuseppe Zimbalo. It has a richly-encrusted balcony, supported on thirteen caryatids, and a large rose window that is festooned with garlands and rosettes.

The interior, lit by the large rose window of the façade, stands on a Latin-cross ground plan and has a cupola over the crossing. It has three aisles, divided by columns which are topped with elaborate capitals bearing faces. The dark wood coffered ceiling is studded with gilt rosettes, while lavishly carved altars line the side aisles. The high altar, which is contained in a deep presbytery, is contrastingly simple. The altar to its left is more elaborate and is the work of F.A. Zimbalo and dates from 1614. The reliefs, composed around twelve panels, depict the *Life of San Francesco di Paola*.

To the left of Santa Croce's façade is the Palazzo del Governo. It was designed by G. Zimbalo with the help of his pupil G. Cino who was to carry the Leccese Baroque on into the eighteenth century, and has a spacious inner courtyard. To visit the interior, apply to the Ufficio della Provincia, at the times indicated in the Additional Information section at the end of this chapter.

Head west of Santa Croce to Piazza Castro Mediano in which the severe façade of Gesu stands. Built in 1579, the church has a highly decorative interior, in keeping with the style of Lecce's Baroque. Next door, housed in the vaults of the Tribunale, those interested in the region's wines, can visit the Enoteca di Terra d'Otranto. All seven of the Salentine peninsula's DOC regions are represented here, and there is a very good selection of wines to choose from. Continuing south, along Via Rubicini, the newly-cleaned façade of the eighteenth-century Municipio is passed to the left. After the Municipio, take Via Vittorio Emanuele, which forks off right. The street is lined with smart shops and elegant houses with stone balconies, and after 100m (110yd) Sant'Irene is passed to the right. This small church was built for the Theatine Order between 1591 and 1639, and contains numerous elaborately carved altars in the style of Zimbalo.

Continue along Via Vittorio Emanuele for a further 120m (131yd) before turning right to Piazza del Duomo. This beautiful square is surrounded by Baroque architecture, including the *duomo*, which was designed by G. Zimbalo in 1559, although it was not finished until 1570. The *duomo's* ponderous *campanile* is 68m (223ft) tall and stands to the left of a flight of steps that ascend to the cathedral's façade. Above the portal, a statue of St Orontius, looks down from a triumphal arch. The interior of the *duomo*, which stands on a Latin-cross plan, is divided by columns into three aisles, and has a beautiful coffered ceiling with painted panels depicting the *Life of St Orontius*.

To the left of the *duomo* is the Palazzo Vescovile. Built in 1632, it has a fine loggia, and from its inner courtyard there is another entrance to the *duomo*. The Seminario fills the right side of the Piazza del Duomo and is built to a design by Zimbalo's prodigy, G. Cino, in 1709. Its inner courtyard is edged by lemon trees and arcades, and has an ornately carved well at the centre.

Route 9C • Lecce to Martina Franca

Route 9C heads north-west of Lecce, on the SS7ter, which is signposted to Taranto. The road crosses a vast, red-earthed plain, covered in vineyards, to one of the many wine-making towns in this area, **Campi Salentina**. Those passing through this region in the second half of September will see the Salentine grape harvest, which is often celebrated with small, local fairs. Shortly after Campi Salentina, turn right and follow the SS605 for 22km (14 miles). The road passes through further vineyards, and olive groves too, to **Mesagne**, which was originally an ancient Messapian settlement, called *Messapia*. Today, this large market town is guarded by a well-restored castle that was built by the Orsini family in 1430, but later modified in the seventeenth and eighteenth centuries. The town also has a number of attractive churches, including the Chiesa Matrice, which dates from the seventeenth century. The Baroque Palazzo del Comune, which also dates from the seventeenth century, was once a Celestine convent, and now houses a small museum of archaeological finds. The town's weekly market, held every Wednesday, is well worth visiting if convenient as it has a wide range of fresh local produce.

Those that wish to make the excursion to **Brindisi**, should head north-east along the SS7. This large, industrial city, 14km (9 miles) from Mesagne, is mainly visited for its museum, the Museo Archeologico Provinciale Francesco Ribezzo. The museum contains a good collection of antique finds from local excavations, including Puglian ceramics, inscription stones, statuettes and Roman mosaics. Otherwise, the city holds little of interest for the tourist, except as a point of embarkation for Greece. Visitors to Brindisi should also be warned that crime is rife in the city, and the theft of cars is commonplace.

The route continues north-west, along the SS605, for 14km (9 miles) to **San Vito dei Normanni**. It is well worth passing through the centre of this town as there are several attractive, stone churches, such as Chiesa Santa Rita, and many pleasant shopping streets. Beyond the town, the route joins the SS16, which after 6½km (4 miles) passes **Carovigno**. This charming town, with its neat white houses, covers a gentle mound that was once the site of Messapian *Carbina*. Turn right to visit the town centre, which is enclosed by fragments of megalithic walls, dating from the Messapian era. Of interest is the *cattedrale*, which dates from the fifteenth century, and the impressive castle. Built by the Orsini Duke of Taranto, the castle dates from the fifteenth century, and helped defend the town against Turkish invaders on many occasions. It was later used as a palatial residence and still contains its period furniture.

The SS16 continues for a further 8km (5 miles), through an undulating landscape of almond and fruit orchards, to the large town of **Ostuni**. Its expansive outskirts are unprepossessing, but the *centro* *storico*, which is indicated on the right by yellow signs, is delightful. Head downhill and park at the foot of the old town on Piazza della Liberta. The piazza contains a decorative obelisk, which was erected in 1770, and, including the statue of Sant' Oronzo that stands on top, is 21m (69ft) high. At the opposite end of the piazza, is the imposing Baroque façade of the Biblioteca Comunale, from where Via Cattedrale leads up through the old quarter. The street winds between simple whitewashed houses with neat blue and green shutters, past the small local museum, Museo di Civilta Preclassiche della Murgia, and the eighteenth-century Chiesa delle Monacelle, which has a fine, stone-carved Baroque façade.

Continuing uphill, the narrow flag-stoned street passes beneath

The cathedral at Ostuni

two deep buttresses, which support the side of the *cattedrale*, the façade of which lies on the small piazza at the top of the hill. Built between 1470 and 1495, the façade is typical of the late-Gothic architecture of Spain, having a dainty, bowed top with carved, serrated edges. The central rose window has twenty four, richly carved spokes which radiate from a central sculpted figure. The main portal is attractively carved too, and has a relief in the lunette above the door. The interior of the church retains none of its original features, having been refurbished in the nineteenth century.

From the top end of the piazza, in front of the cathedral, a Baroque arch leads through to the highest part of the town, where there are the ruins of a twelfth-century castle, and views of the sea. From the bottom end of the piazza, follow the alley to the right of the cathedral's façade, along the buttressed walls, to the right transept. Here the cathedral's shiny ceramic dome can be admired, as well as the *campanile* which has the same distinctive, curvilinear top. The end wall of the right transept is also curved and is pierced by a fine rose window, similar to that of the façade.

Ostuni also has a good selection of souvenir shops, restaurants where Puglia's speciality, *orecchiette*, pasta in the shape of 'tiny ears', is served, and prestigious local wines, including Ostuni Bianco, and the light red wine, Ottavianello. Those in Ostuni on a Saturday, will be able to find a good choice of further local fare at the weekly market.

Leave Ostuni from the top of the town, and follow the SS16, which is signposted to Bari. The road, lined with cypress trees, runs parallel with the coast, roughly 5km (3 miles) inland, with occasional glimpses of the sea through the abundant olive groves. Within 10km (6 miles), the first of the region's famous *trulli*, cone-roofed houses, are seen at the roadside. The origin of the *trulli* is uncertain, some say they were tombs built by the ancient Greeks from Mycenaea. Others say they were constructed by Byzantine monks in the eighth century. Another theory is that they were built by the Saracen invaders. Whatever their origin, similar buildings are seen in Malta, Syria and on the Mesopotamian Plain. The oldest *trulli* standing today are dated from the seventeenth century. They are made without mortar, using stones that are picked out of the ploughed earth. All *trulli* are circular in shape and have conical roofs made of small overlapping flat stones, and are seen both singly and in clusters throughout the region. The government, to encourage tourism, subsidises the building of modern day *trulli* as long as they use the same basic design. Most modern *trulli*, however, are constructed with commercially manufactured materials.

The SS16 continues through **Montalbano** where a few *trulli* stand amongst the village houses, and **Pezze di Greco**, to **Fasano**. On the outskirts of this town, signs point right to a Zoo Safari. The safari park contains around six-hundred animals, including lions, giraffes and bears. Beyond the Zoo Safari, it is possible to continue to the Messapian site of *Egnazia*, the ruins of which are just inland from the coast. The route, however, turns left at Fasano's outskirts and climbs steeply up above the town, on the *strada panoramica*, which is signposted to Castellana.

Selva, 6km (4 miles) west of Fasano, is a popular weekend and holiday retreat, and *trulli* holiday homes and *trulli* pizzeria are dotted throughout the area. Four kilometres (2 miles) after Selva, a short excursion can be made to a panoramic viewing point, by taking the right turn, signposted to **Loggia di Pilato**. The view looks across gentle hills, scattered with *trulli*, to the sea. The road continues for a further 13km (8 miles) over the hills, which are covered in olive groves, dry stone walls and picturesque clusters of *trulli* farm houses, to **Castellana**. Follow signs through Castellana, which has a pleasant old centre, to the caves, **Castellana Grotte**, which lie 2km (1 mile) south-west of the town. The road ends at a large carpark next to the cave entrance, which is surrounded by souvenir shops and restaurants. The caves, which are amongst the most spectacular in Southern Italy, can only be visited by guided tour. There are two possible itineraries: the 1km (½ mile) tour takes one hour and visits the Caverna del Precipizio; the 3km (2 mile) tour takes two hours and includes the famous Caverna Bianca which is 70m (300ft) below ground and takes its name from its glistening, white calcite crystals.

Leave Castellana Grotte on the SS172 dei Trulli which passes through the official *territorio dei trulli*. At **Putignano** which has a fine historic centre, turn left and follow the SS172 to **Alberobello**. This small town is the touristic centre of the *trulli* region. Follow *zona monumentale* signs, downhill to Largo Martellota, where there is a fee-paying carpark. Head from the south side of the carpark to the main concentration of *trulli* which cover the hill slope above. The narrow streets are lined with neat, whitewashed *trulli*, each one immaculately restored, and some with traditional symbols painted on their roofs. Most roofs, rather incongruously, also have television aerials and modern chimneys. The people who live here are nearly all involved with tourism in some way, whether they are sitting outside their homes crocheting shawls, or selling ornamental ceramic *trulli* from one of the many souvenir shops. A number of *trulli* contain restaurants and some people have opened the interior of their homes to the public.

Traditional **trulli** *houses, Alberobello*

At the top of the new town, which lies on the north side of the carpark, it is possible to visit the tallest *trulli* in Alberobello, known as Trullo Soverano. To get there, follow the steps up past the tourist office to the church of Santa Luca. Cross over Piazza Popolo, which extends in front of Santa Luca, to the left corner, and follow Corso Vittorio Emanuele. This street leads past a large church, along the left side of its walls, to the Trullo Soverano. Built on two storeys, the *trullo* is well preserved. The interior, open as a museum, contains a large room on the ground floor and two smaller ones upstairs which are covered by a low curved ceiling.

Leave Alberobello by following signs to Locorotondo on the SS172. The road undulates gently through a picturesque landscape where olive groves and white *trulli* contrast with the vibrant rust colour of the earth. **Locorotondo**, 9km (6 miles) east of Alberobello, commands the surrounding countryside from the top of a small, conical hill. After crossing the railway, follow signs up the hill to *centro storico*. There are fee-paying parking spaces at the top of the hill along Via Nardelli, which rings the old town and is within easy walking distance of the centre. Locorotondo, as its name suggests, is circular in plan and neatly caps the hilltop, which is 430m (1,410ft) high, and overlooks the Itria valley. The best place from which to admire the Itria valley, which is full of *trulli*, is the Villa Comunale, the public gardens at the entrance to the town. From the gardens, proceed through the gate, Porta Napoli, to the main square, Piazza Vittorio Emanuele II, which is surrounded by smart white-painted houses. Leave the piazza from its north corner and follow Via Antonio Bruno. Continue north-east, along the tidy, flag-stoned alleys, to Piazza G.A. Fra Rodio which holds the town's principal church, San Giorgio Martire. Built of stone, it has a tall, neo-Classical façade and a high dome, topped by a lantern. The vast interior contains attractive, fifteenth- and sixteenth-century bas-reliefs, depicting scenes from the New and Old Testaments, in the Santissimo Sacramento chapel on the left.

Back on Piazza G.A. Fra Rodio, follow Via Gianone, to the left of the church façade. At the end of the street, take the steps down to Via Cavour, and turn right to the small, late-Gothic church, Madonna della Greca. Its simple façade holds a pretty rose window and has statues at each corner. The church is kept locked, but the key is held at the general stores opposite. The interior is attractively decorated with clean, white stone. Its rib-vaulted ceiling is supported on clusters of stone columns that have crisply carved capitals. Statues, dating from the fifteenth century, decorate niches, while the remnants of a fresco, depicting the Madonna della Greca, can be seen to the left, and fragments of bas-reliefs, to the right of the entrance.

Head back up the steps and spend some time wandering about the narrow streets in the town, where flowers spill out, over attractive stone porches and exterior staircases, and cascade down white-washed walls. Those interested in wine, should not miss Locorotondo's well-esteemed DOC white wine, which is rated amongst the best of its type in Puglia. Locorotondo also has its own distinctive cuisine. *Orechiette*, Puglia's ear-shaped pasta, are made with wholewheat flour and served with a variety of vegetables as well as fresh ricotta and basil.

Leave Locorotondo by following signs to Martina Franca on the SS172. The road follows the famous Itria valley which is richly cultivated with orchards and vineyards and is dotted with pictur-esque *trulli* farms. Many of the grapes around here are the variety known as Uva Regina, which are amongst Italy's most popular table grapes and are widely exported throughout Europe too. **Martina Franca**, 6km (4 miles) south of Locorotondo, is a large city with extensive outskirts and a quantity of severe, eighteenth-century Baroque architecture. A tree-lined road leads to the main city gate, Porta Sant'Antonio. The gate dates from the eighteenth century and is surmounted by a statue of St Martin who is the city's patron saint. Park inside the gate and explore the rest of the city on foot. The centre is around Piazza XX Settembre in which stands the church of Sant'Antonio and the Villa Comunale public gardens. The city's best Baroque architecture, however, is on Piazza Roma, where the impos-ing Baroque façade of Palazzo Martucci can be seen and also the beautiful Palazzo Ducale, which houses the *municipio*. Built in 1668, Palazzo Ducale stands on the site of a former Orsini castle, and has a rich façade with a decorative balcony, attributed to the creator of the Baroque, G. Bernini. The main shopping street, Corso Vittorio Emanuele, leads to the church of San Martino which is dedicated to the city's patron saint. The church was started in 1747 and completed in 1775, and has a fine relief above the main portal depicting *St Martin and the Beggar*. To the left of the church stands Palazzo della Corte (1763) and the clock tower next to it, Torre dell'Orlogio, which was erected in 1734.

A panoramic road follows the city walls, which has a total of twelve towers, of antique origin, and four city gates. The views from the west walls are particularly good of the Itria valley.

From Martina Franca, visitors should take the SS581 to Massafra, which is the starting point for chapter 10. It is an enjoyable drive, over gentle hills dotted with olive groves and dry stone walls, of just under 30km (19 miles).

Additional Information

Places to Visit

Brindisi
*Museo Archeologico Provinciale
    Francesco Ribezzo*
Piazza Duomo
☎ (0831) 23418
Open: winter, Monday-Friday 9am-1.30pm. Summer, Monday-Friday 9am-1.30pm, Saturday 9am-12noon.

Castellana
Grotte di Castellana
Open: winter, daily, guided tour (long), every hour 9am-12noon, 2-5pm. Summer, daily, guided tour (long), every hour 8.30am-12.15pm, 2.30-6pm. Daily guided tour (short) 11am, 1, 4, 7pm.

Castro
Grotta Zinzulusa
☎ (0836) 97326
Open: daily winter 10am-1pm, 2-6pm, daily summer 10am-6pm.

Fasano
Museo Archeologico
Scavi di Egnazia
☎ (080) 729056

Zoo Safari
☎ (080) 713055
Open: daily 9am-1hr before sunset.

Gallipoli
Museo Civico
108 Via Antonietta de Pace
Open: winter, daily 4-6pm.
Summer, daily 9am-1pm, 5-7pm.

Lecce
*Museo Archeologico Provinciale
    Sigismondo Castromediano*
Viale Gallipoli
☎ (0832) 27415

Open: Monday to Friday 9am-1.30pm, 2.30-7.30pm. Sunday and holidays 9.30am-1.30pm.

Palazzo del Governo
Via Umberto
Open: Monday and Friday 9am-12noon, Wednesday 4-6pm.

Mesagne
Museo Civico 'U. Granafei'
Palazzo del Comune
Open: Weekdays 9am-1pm.

Ostuni
*Museo di Civilta Pre classiche della
    Murgia*
Chiesa delle Monacelle
Via Cattedrale
☎ (0831) 336383
Open: by appointment only.

San Cesarea Terme
Thermal Establishment
Stabilimenti Gattulla e Sulfurea
Via Roma 32
☎ (0836) 944070

Thermal Establishment
Stabilimento Palazzo
Via Roma 223
☎ (0836) 944007

Useful information

San Cesarea Terme
Tourist Information Centre
Azienda Autonoma di Cura
Soggiorno e Turismo
Via Roma 209
☎ (0836) 944043

Alberobello
Tourist Information Centre
Pro Loco
Piazza del Popolo 52
☎ (080) 721916

Transport
Ferrovie del Sud Est (Railway)
☎ (080) 9323308

Emergencies
Polizia Municipale (Municipal
    Police)
☎ (080) 725340

Pronto Soccorso (First Aid Service)
☎ (080) 721022

Guardia Medica (Medical Officer)
☎ (080) 721112

Brindisi
Events and Festival
July, Sagra dei Pittori.
(Festival of Painters and Artists).

Tourist Information Centres
Ente Provinciale per il Turismo
Via Cristoforo Colombo 88
☎ (0831) 521944

Uffici Informazioni
Via Regina Margherita
☎ (0831) 21944

Azienda Autonoma di Soggiorno e
    Turismo
Via Rubini 19
☎ (0831) 21091

Transport
Stazione Ferroviaria (Railway)
Piazza Crispi
☎ (0831) 21975

Emergencies
Polizia (Police)
Via Provinciale San Vito
☎ (0831) 21013

Pronto Soccorso (First Aid Service)
☎ (0831) 21410

Automobile Club d'Italia
Via Aldo Moro 61
☎ (0831) 83053/86462

Carovigno
Events and Festivals
Week after Easter, La Nzegna
(Traditional flag-throwing contest).

Tourist Information Centre
Associazione Turistica Pro Loco
Castello

Transport
Stazione Ferroviaria (Railway)
Carovigno Scalo
☎ (0831) 968084

Emergencies
Polizia Urbana (Town Police)
Via Verdi 1
☎ (0831) 991014

Guardia Medica (Medical Officer)
Via Adua
☎ (0831) 991020

Castellana
Events and Festivals
June, Incontri di Alternativa
    Musicale alle Grotte
(Alternative music performances
held at the caves).

8 September, Sagra delle Specialita
    Locale
(Fair of local specialities).

Last week September, Sagra del
    Pollo (Chicken Fair).

Tourist Information Centre
Pro Loco
Piazza Garibaldi 5
☎ (080) 735191

Transport
Ferrovie del Sud Est (Railway)
☎ (080) 8961884

Emergencies
Polizia Municipale (Municipal
    Police)
☎ (080) 8965014

Polizia Stradale (Traffic Police)
☎ (080) 8965215

Pronto Soccorso (First Aid Service)
☎ (080) 8965122

Guardia Medica (Medical Officer)
☎ (080) 8966456

Castro
Grotta Zinzulusa
☎ (0836) 97326
Open: daily winter 10am-1pm, 2-6pm, daily summer 10am-6pm.

Fasano
Events and Festivals
24-26 February, Carnevale
(Carnival and masked ball).

18-21 June, Festa della Madonna
    del Pozzo
(Festival of the Madonna of the
Well, fireworks/music).

Tourist Information Centre
Azienda Autonoma di Cura
    Soggiorno e Turismo
Piazza Ciaia 9
☎ (080) 713086

Transport
Stazione Ferroviaria (Railway)
☎ (080) 713025

Emergencies
Polizia Stradale (Traffic Police)
Via Morchiaturo
☎ (080) 713215

Polizia Urbana (Town Police)
Piazza Ciaia
☎ (080) 714254

Pronto Soccorso (First Aid Service)
Ospedale
Via Nazionale dei Trulli
☎ (080) 713033

Gallipoli
Events and Festivals
14 July, La Cuccagna (Greasy pole
contest, held on a barge at sea).

Tourist Information Centre
Pro Loco
Corso Roma
☎ (0833) 476290

Transport
Ferrovia Informazione (Railway)
☎ (0833) 476214

Emergencies
Polizia (Police)
☎ (0833) 476113

Polizia Municipale (Municipal
    Police)
☎ (0833) 476105

Pronto Soccorso (First Aid Service)
☎ (0833) 471191

Guardia Medica (Medical Officer)
☎ (0833) 476250

Lecce
Events and Festivals
24-26 August, Festa di Sant'Oronzo
(Festival in honour of the patron
saint and animal fair).

July, Spettacoli Classici
(Classical productions held in the
amphitheatre).

August, Festival Musicale
    Internazionale
(International Music Festival).

December, Fiera dei Pupi
(Doll Fair).

Tourist Information Centres
Ente Provinciale per il Turismo
Via F. Rubichi
☎ (0832) 24443

Azienda Autonoma di Soggiorno e
Turismo
Via Zanardelli 66
☎ (0832) 56461

Ufficio Informazioni Turistiche
Piazza Sant'Oronzo
Il Sedile
☎ (0832) 24443

Transport
Ferrovie dello Stato (Railway)
Piazzale Ferrovia
☎ (0832) 21016/21015

Ferrovie Sud Est (South East
Railway)
Piazzale Ferrovia
☎ (0832) 41931

Emergencies
Vigili Urbani (Municipal Police)
Viale Brindisi
☎ (0832) 21014

Polizia Stradale (Traffic Police)
Via Adua
☎ (0832) 21215

Ospedale Generale Regionale 'Vito
Fazzi' (Hospital)
Via San Cesario
☎ (0832) 6851

Automobile Club d'Italia
Via G. Candido 2
☎ (0832) 40441

Locorotondo
Events and Festivals
16 August, Sagra di San Rocco
(Festival of patron saint, San Rocco,
firework display).

Tourist Information Centre
Pro Loco
Piazza Vittorio Emanuele II 1
☎ (080) 711088

Transport
Stazione Ferroviaria (Railway)
Ferrovie Sud Est
☎ (080) 9311360

Emergencies
Vigili Urbani (Municipal Police)
Piazza Aldo Moro
☎ (080) 9311090

Pronto Soccorso (First Aid Service)
Ospedale Montanaro
Piazza Marconi
☎ (080) 93118111

Martina Franca
Events and Festivals
July, Concorso Ippico Nazionale
(National horse race).

July-August, Festival della Valle
d'Itria
(Festival of the Valley of Itria).

Tourist Information Centre
Azienda Autonoma Soggiorno e
Turismo
Piazza Roma 35
Martina Franca
☎ (080) 705702

Transport
Ferrovie del Sud Est (Railway)
☎ (080) 8808151

Emergencies
Polizia (Police)
☎ (080) 902110

Pronto Soccorso (First Aid Service)
☎ (080) 701717

Guardia Medica (Medical Officer)
☎ (080) 705592

Ostuni
Events and Festivals
22 April, La Palomma
(Local traditional festival)

15 August, Sagra dei Vecchi Tempi (Festival of Old Times).

26 August, Cavalcata di Sant'Oronzo
(Procession in honour of the local patron saint, Sant'Oronzo, celebrating the end of the plague in 1657).

Tourist Information Centre
Azienda Autonoma di Soggiorno e Turismo
Via Dottore Vittorio Continelli 45
☎ (0831) 303775

Transport
Stazione Ferroviaria (Railway)
Via Stazione
☎ (0831) 333936

Emergencies
Polizia Urbana (Town Police)
Piazza Liberta
☎ (0831) 331994

Ospedale (Hospital)
Via Villafranca
☎ (0831) 972590

Otranto
Events and Festivals
August, Mostra di Artigianato (Crafts, Exhibition, held in the castle).

Tourist Information Centre
Azienda Autonoma di Soggiorno e Turismo
Via Rondachi 8
☎ (0836) 81436

Emergencies
Carabinieri (Military Police)
☎ (0836) 81010

Guardia Medica (Medical Officer)
☎ (0836) 81676

Ostuni
Museo di Civilta Pre classiche della Murgia
Chiesa delle Monacelle
Via Cattedrale
☎ (0831) 336383
Open: by appointment only.

San Cesarea Terme
Tourist Information Centre
Azienda Autonoma di Cura Soggiorno e Turismo
Via Roma 209
☎ (0836) 944043

San Vito dei Normanni
Events and Festivals
13 May, Bentornata Primavera (Spring Festival).

July-August, Estate Sanvitese (Summer Festival).

Tourist Information Centre
Associazione Turistica Pro Loco
Via Cairoli 1
☎ (0831) 962377

Emergencies
Polizia (Police)
Piazza Carducci 12
☎ (0831) 961014

Guardia Medica (Medical Officer)
☎ (0831) 391837

10

MURGE AND THE ADRIATIC COAST

Chapter 10 heads north across the Murge, Puglia's expansive limestone plateau, to the Adriatic Coast. This north-western part of the plateau is carved by a series of thirty or more dramatic canyons, known as *gravine*, which, in the Middle Ages provided a place of refuge from the Saracen raiders. Canyon walls are peppered with hidey-holes, hewn dwellings, and even simple churches, some of which are complete with their Byzantine frescoes. Generally, the frescoes are in poor condition, being neglected and little-visited, however, those equipped with a torch, and with a little perseverance, will be rewarded by the many delightful sights that are tucked away in overgrown canyons and gorges.

After crossing the Murge, the route follows the Adriatic Coast in a north-westerly direction, through an area known as the Terra di Bari. The area, which stretches west of Bari along the coast, is well endowed with Norman cathedrals and impressive castles built under Emperor Frederick II in the thirteenth century. Unfortunately, however, the area also has its fair share of crime. This is particularly dominant in the string of cities that line the coast from Bari to Barletta, and the visitor should take great care when stopping at these places as to where they leave their car, and always keep a watch on their personal belongings.

North of Barletta, it is as though an invisible line were crossed and crime is no longer a concern. The Tavoliere, the vast plain to the north-west of Barletta is an intense area of agriculture, while the Gargano peninsula, the spur of Italy's boot, is well-developed with tourism. The Gargano, mainly attracts tourism by the rugged beauty of its coasts and its enticing coves and beaches. However, it also has a very scenic interior, most of which is either richly-forested or covered in olive groves.

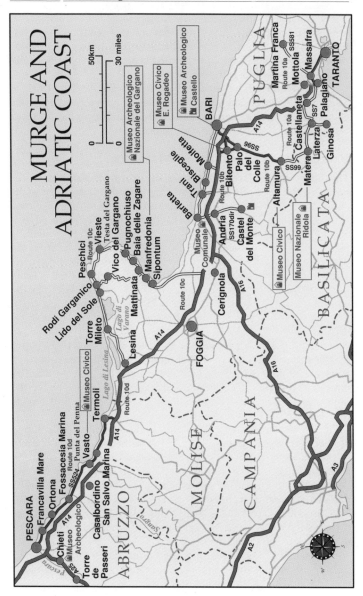

MURGE AND ADRIATIC COAST

50km

30 miles

PUGLIA

BASILICATA

CAMPANIA

MOLISE

ABRUZZO

TARANTO

Massafra
Mottola SS581
Martina Franca
Route 10a
Palagiano
Castellaneta
SS7
Ginosa
Laterza
Route 10a
SS99
Matera
Route 10b
Altamura
Museo Nazionale Ridola
Museo Civico
Palo del Colle
Bitonto
Route 10b
96SS
A14
BARI
Museo Archeologico E. Rogadeo
Museo Civico Castello
Museo Archeologico Nazionale del Gargano

Molfetta
Bisceglie
Trani
Barletta
Museo Comunale
Andria
SS170dir
Castel del Monte
Cerignola
A16
Route 10c

FOGGIA
A14
A16

Manfredonia
Sipontum
Baia delle Zagare
Pugnochiuso
Vico del Gargano
Vieste
Testa del Gargano
Peschici
Route 10c
Mattinata

Rodi Garganico
Lido del Sole
Lago di Varano
Torre Mileto
Lesina
Lago di Lesina
Route 10d

Termoli
Museo Civico
Vasto
Route 10d
Punta del Penna
SS524
Fossacesia Marina
Ortona
Francavilla Mare
PESCARA
Chieti
Museo Archeologico
A14
A25
Torre de Passeri
Casalbordino
San Salvo Marina
Pescara

A3

A2

The coastland, along which the route proceeds northwards, beyond the Gargano, is contrastingly flat and monotonous. There are, however, some attractive seaside towns to visit, and a vast selection of resorts with well-kept, but crowded beaches, and good facilities for leisure and sports activities.

The route finishes by heading inland from the Adriatic Coast to Torre de Passeri, from where visitors can either proceed along chapter 2 to Rome, or head south through the interior of the Abruzzo, by following chapter 3 in the reverse order.

Route 10A • Massafra to Matera

The SS581 from Martina Franca approaches **Massafra** from the north. At the edge of the town, take the turning on the right to the Santuario della Madonna della Scala and Laura Bizantina. The road heads down for 1km (½ mile) to a car park which lies at the edge of a deep ravine. The ravine, filled by a tangle of undergrowth, is peppered with caves and laura, hermits' cells, that date from the early Byzantine era when a community of Basilian monks lived here. The community originated from Asia Minor, where St Basil was the Bishop of *Caesareia*, present day Kayseri in Central Turkey. Like the rock-hewn churches of Cappadocia, in Turkey, those of Massafra are decorated with warm-coloured frescoes, typified by their loose brushwork.

From the carpark, descend the monumental staircase to the eighteenth-century Santuario della Madonna della Scala, which sits on a ledge above the ravine floor, on the site of the Basilian church. The interior dates from 1731, although the section of fresco above the high altar is Byzantine. It dates from the twelfth century and depicts the *Madonna and Child* above two kneeling deer.

Further Byzantine frescoes can be seen in the Cripta della Buona Nuova. The entrance to the crypt is opposite the façade of the church, in the corner beneath the monumental staircase. Hewn from the rock, the interior has a simple altar, above which there is a niche decorated with a fresco of the *Madonna della Buona Nuova*. The fresco dates from the thirteenth century, as do the other fragments that are still discernible around the walls. Those on the left are the best-preserved. A rock-carved passage also leads from the left of the crypt to the back of the sanctuary.

For those that wish to explore the ravine, steps continue down from the sanctuary to the bottom. Otherwise return to the carpark and continue along the road to Massafra.

Massafra is well-endowed with Byzantine frescoes, and for those interested, there are more to be seen just before the bridge which crosses the ravine at the northern end of the town. Take the first right, before the bridge, and park at the apartment blocks, 100m (110yd) along, on the left. Ask at the ground floor apartment, on the left, for the key to the Cappella della Candelora. The key unlocks a gate, which is behind the apartment blocks, at the top of a flight of rock hewn steps. The steps lead down the side of the ravine, to a chapel which is carved into the cliff-face. Three arches, supported on two pillars, span the façade, while the interior, which is 8½m (28ft) wide and 6m (20ft) long, has three shallow aisles. The walls of the interior are lined with niches, each of which contains the remains of frescoes, dating from the thirteenth and fourteenth centuries. The *Presentation in the Temple* is particularly well-preserved, as is the portrait of *Simeone* to its right. At either side of the central niche there are inscriptions in Latin and Greek, there are also Greek crosses incised in the stone at either side of the church's entrance.

Return to the main road and proceed across the bridge, Ponte Nuovo, from where the arches of the Cappella della Candelora can be seen. To visit another chapel, on the opposite side of the ravine, take the first right after the bridge. After a short distance turn right again and follow signs to San Marco. The key is held at 159 Via Fratelli Bandiera, which is to the left of the entrance gate. Stone steps lead down to a terrace where the little church of San Marco is carved into the rock face. The church is neglected and badly littered, and visitors should take a torch as it is very dark. A fresco of *San Marco* can be seen on the right, and although the other walls are plain, they are attractively carved from the natural rock.

Return to the main road, and follow signs right to *centro*. At the bottom of the hill turn right again and cross over Ponte Vecchio to the old town, which is known as Terra. Park on Piazza Garibaldi, the square on the other side of the bridge, and explore the rest of the town on foot. From the left side of the piazza a narrow road winds down to the Castello Medioevale. Built in the fifteenth century, the castle is now under restoration, but its fine walls and octagonal bastion can nonetheless still be admired. Return to Piazza Garibaldi and head from its right side into the warren of streets that lead through the old quarter. Of particular interest is the twelfth-century church of Sant'Antonio Abate, which has a Byzantine crypt, although the key is held at the *municipio*. The high leaded dome seen above the rooftops belongs to the more modern church of San Lorenzo.

Leave Massafra by following signs to the A14 in the direction of Bari. The road winds down to the plain below the town, from where visitors should turn right onto the SS7. Heading in the direction of

Matera

Bari, the road passes beneath Massafra's castle and the mouth of the ravine. After 3km (2 miles) there is a junction, from where the SS7 diverges off westwards, in the direction of Matera. The hill town of Mottola is passed to the right, while Palagiano lies to the left. The SS7 by-passes Palagiano and continues for 6km (4 miles), to the edge of another ravine. From here an excursion can be made to **Palagianello** which is built on the brink of the ravine, 3km (2 miles) from the road, on the right. Like Massafra, the ravine contains rock-hewn churches some of which are decorated with frescoes dating from the twelfth century up until the fourteenth. San Nicolo and San Girolamo are the two most important churches here.

The SS7 continues across the ravine, which is riddled with caves, before climbing uphill to **Castellaneta**. This large town is well worth a brief visit, as although it is encircled by unpleasant suburbs, it has an attractive centre. The *cattedrale* is at the focus of the old town, which was begun in the thirteenth century, but did not receive its

Santa Chiara, Matera

façade until 1771. The *campanile*, has not been altered and is crowned by a pointed cupola. Via Seminario leads behind the cathedral to the Episcopio, the Bishop's Palace, which contains a famous polyptych by G. da Santacroce (1531). Visitors may also be interested to know that Castellanata was the birthplace of Rudolph Valentino, whose home can be seen at number 114 Via Roma.

The SS7 continues across rolling countryside to the modern, agricultural town of **Laterza**. The Gravina di Laterza, a deep ravine, which lies along the eastern side of the town is amongst the most spectacular in the region and is filled with rock dwellings and churches. Further troglodyte caves can also be seen at **Ginosa** which is 7km (4 miles) south of Laterza. There are three ravines surrounding this ancient town, each of which contains frescoed churches dating from the tenth and eleventh centuries.

The route continues west of Laterza, along the SS7 to Matera, across a wide, cultivated plain, which is guarded at the far side by the Torre Spagnola, a square tower built by the Spanish. It stands on a hill, at a height of 407m (1,335ft), to the right of the road. From here the SS7 starts to climb to one of the region's best known canyons, the Gravina di Matera. A panoramic view of the canyon and the *sassi*, the rock-carved dwellings, of **Matera**, can be had by taking the left turn, signposted to Chiesa Rupestre. A narrow road winds up, past several rock-hewn chapels, to a large carpark at the top of the hill, on the edge of the canyon. It is an ideal place from which to hike down to the ravine, and the views across to the town are excellent.

The SS7 crosses the river that runs along the bed of the canyon, before heading up to the centre of Matera. Follow signs through the town's modern outskirts, to *centro* and *sasso*, and look for a parking space on Piazza Vittorio Veneto, the central square. The square is lined with trees and has a small gardens in front of the thirteenth-century church, San Domenico, which stands in the north-east corner. The pretty façade of this church has a characteristic rose window which is held by four primitively carved figures. The small interior was refurbished in the seventeenth century and all its paintings and frescoes have since been removed due to the humidity of the atmosphere. Another thirteenth-century church, San Giovanni Battista, can be seen on Via San Biagio, which passes along the right side of San Domenico. The church is on the right, 150m (164yd) away and has a façade, pierced by a richly-carved portal with two deep, blind arches at either side. The central section is unusually high and is decorated with griffins and lions mounted on columns. The interior has a high central nave, while the side aisles have low rib-vaulted ceilings that are typical of the Gothic era.

Return to Piazza Vittorio Veneto, and head south-east along the main thoroughfare, Via del Corso. Santa Lucia, passed on the right, has a plain façade above a small flight of steps. The interior contains fragments of thirteenth-century frescoes including a portrait of St Michael. The street terminates, after a further 150m (164yd), at Piazza San Francesco, along the left side of which is the church of San Francesco. Its ornate façade, decorated with niches and statues, dates from the seventeenth century and is preceded by a broad flight of steps. The interior comprises a single nave, which is encrusted with white stucco ornamentation, and has chapels along either side. Below the organ, in the main apse there are seven painted panels from a polyptych by the fifteenth-century Venetian artist, B. Vivarini.

Proceed from the southern end of Piazza San Francesco along Via Ridola, past the gruesome façade of Purgatorio, on the right. Dating from the eighteenth century, the façade is carved with skeletons, skulls, macabre symbols, and inscriptions stating the common destiny of all mortal beings. The interior stands on a Greek-cross ground plan and contains numerous Baroque, marble altars and eighteenth-century paintings. A short distance further, also on the right is the seventeenth-century church of Santa Chiara and its adjoining ex-monastery, which now houses the Museo Nazionale Ridola. The museum fills two long halls and consists of two parts: one of prehistoric finds; the other of Greek ceramics, all of which have been found in the local region. The exhibits are well-displayed and clearly labelled.

Continue along Via Ridola for a further 100m (110yd) to the *pinacoteca* which is displayed in a neo-Classical *palazzo*. To the left of the *pinacoteca* there is a panoramic terrace overlooking Matera's famous *sassi*, as well as the cathedral and its bell tower. The canyon along which the *sassi* are carved, has been continuously inhabited from Neolithic times up until the late 1960s when most of the inhabitants were re-housed due to the squalid living conditions. The houses are stacked one above the other in a maze-like tangle. Despite this it is possible to find one's way around without the help of the local guides who are to be found on every street corner, as there are itineraries marked by yellow and black signs. However, the churches are kept locked and to see inside it is necessary to ask a guide who will explain and illuminate the main features of interest. Guides may also show you around the interiors of some of the houses.

Those who prefer to be independent can head down the hill, to the right of the panoramic terrace, and follow the *itinerario turistico* signs through the district known as Sasso Caveoso. One of the main attractions here is the church, Santa Maria Idris, which is hewn from the broad, rocky lump of Monte Errone, on the east side of the valley. Rock carved steps climb up to the façade which, like so many *sassi*, is a superficial cladding, with the greater part of the building carved in the rock behind. Inside, the now dried-up water source that gave the church its name, *idris* meaning 'water' in Greek, can be seen in the rock on the left, while eighteenth-century fresco fragments cover the walls on the right. A dark, rock-carved tunnel which is decorated with the portraits of St Francis, St Nicholas and the Pantokrator, amongst others, leads to a large chapel which is lit by a tiny window in the right wall. In its roughly-hewn apse are the remains of Byzantine frescoes dating from the eleventh century.

Return to the main street and continue past the eighteenth-century church of San Pietro Caveoso which is at the foot of Monte Errone, before turning left and following signs up to the *duomo*. The cathedral juts out on a promontory which divides Sasso Caveoso from a second district, Sasso Barisano. Started in 1230, the cathedral was completed at the end of the thirteenth century, and is typical of the Puglian-Romanesque with its high central nave and low aisles either side. The façade holds a grand rose window which is supported by a statue of St Michael and three angels. In the lunette above the main portal there is a statue of the patron saint, Madonna della Bruna, while the niches at either side hold Santi Eustachio and Teopista. The interior was redecorated in the seventeenth and eighteenth centuries, but the high central nave is lined by the original columns, some of which have ancient capitals that were brought from *Metapontum*. At the first altar in the left aisle there is a venerated Byzantine fresco, dating from the thirteenth century, of the *Madonna della Bruna*. At the end of the left aisle, the Cappella dell'Annunziata, has an arched coffered ceiling decorated with rosettes, which dates from the sixteenth century. The chapel is named after its statue depicting the *Annunciation*. In the presbytery, another chapel on the left, holds sixteenth-century, polychrome sculptures depicting a nativity scene.

Back outside the cathedral, from its left side there is a fine view across the Sasso Barisano district, which is overlooked by the severe seventeenth-century façade of Sant'Agostino. To visit the Sasso Barisano, leave Piazza Duomo from its south side and head along Via Duomo through the arch and follow the *itinerario turistico* signs off right. Those who wish to return to the town centre can continue straight ahead, along Via Duomo, which leads back to Piazza San Francesco. From here Via del Corso heads back to the central square. Those with time may wish to visit the castle, Castello Tramontano, which lies 400m (437yd) south of Piazza Vittorio. Follow Via Lucano to the top of the hill, then turn right through the pleasant gardens that are spread below the castle walls. The castle was started, under a local feudal duke, Carlo Tramontano, in the fifteenth century, but it was never completed, although it has an impressive central tower.

Route 10B • Matera to Barletta

From Matera follow the SS99 to **Altamura** which lies 17km (11 miles) to the north. The town was named after its high surrounding walls, the remnants of which are today mostly lost in the encircling belt of suburbs. The centre of Altamura is nonetheless well-preserved and is worth a visit if only to see its cathedral. The cathedral is positioned on the central square at the highest point of the town. It was founded under Frederick II who passed through here in 1232, but was rebuilt on several occasions, first in 1316 after an earthquake, and then during the Renaissance and Baroque eras. It is constructed from an attractive white stone, and has a fine façade, surmounted by a pair of robust bell towers, that were added in the sixteenth century. The enclosed balcony, between the towers, gives the façade an added sense of height. This was matched, in a fit of Baroque exuberance, by further heightening each tower in 1729. Beneath the balcony, the façade is pierced by a beautiful rose window. It is carved with bold tracery and is typical of the Puglian-Romanesque style. The richly-carved portal is also typical, having a wealth of biblical scenes, including the *History of the Evangelists* in a series of small reliefs and the *Last Supper* above the door. The innermost band of carving is made up of an effusive garland of foliage that sprouts from urns held by women at either door jamb and is rather oriental in character. The coat of arms seen set up high on the left side of the façade belong to Robert of Anjou. The interior, with its tall central nave lit by arched windows is less interesting, apart from the elaborately carved, wooden bishop's throne that dates from the mid-sixteenth century.

The small museum on Via Santeramo, Museo Civico, holds locally excavated finds including ceramics and bronze, dating from the eighth to the fifth centuries BC. There are also some pieces of Peucetian ware, made by the ancient Italic tribe that first inhabited Altamura. Altamura has no other monuments, but it is very pleasant to wander about its old, stone-flagged streets and visit the busy local market in the centre.

From Altamura take the SS96 Barese to Bitonto. The road traverses a gently undulating landscape, typical of the Murge plateau region, which is covered with groves of olives. The olive oil produced in this region is considered to be amongst the best in Southern Italy. Turn left, 30km (19 miles) north of Altamura, to **Palo del Colle**. It is worth passing through the centre of this town, following the signs to *centro storico*, to see its attractive, late-Romanesque church. It has a slender *campanile* built of a snowy-white stone which is pierced by rows of mullioned windows. The simple façade in true Puglian-Romanesque style has a rose window and an elaborately-carved portal.

Continue through Palo del Colle, heading north for a further 6km (4 miles) to **Bitonto**. The city is quite large, and like so many places in this region, suffers from a considerable amount of crime, although its *centro storico* is well-preserved and contains one of the most important Romanesque cathedrals in Puglia. As car theft is one of the favourite pastimes of younger criminals, it is best to park right outside the cathedral rather than in the carpark near the large, cylindrical tower on Piazza Cavour. Locals do not recommend wandering around the picturesque streets of the *centro storico* due to pickpockets and thieves, so it is best to restrict a visit to the *cattedrale* itself. The façade, which faces onto the piazza, has all the typical features that distinguish the Puglian-Romanesque. It is divided into three sections, the central one being the tallest, and has a traditional rose window and a richly-carved portal. It was started in 1175, but not completed until the beginning of the thirteenth century. Inside the *cattedrale* is an ambo decorated with a relief of Frederick II and his family, by Maestro Nicolo (1229), and a pulpit, reconstructed from the fragments of an ancient altar, in 1240.

Back outside the cathedral, walk around the piazza along its right flank, from where the fine arcading on its upper walls can be seen. Also on the piazza, behind an obelisk is the noble façade of the Episcopio, the Bishop's Palace. A narrow street leads behind the Episcopio to the Museo Civico E. Rogadeo which houses a small collection of local archaeological finds.

An excursion of 16km (10 miles) can be made east of Bitonto to **Bari**. Visitors should be warned, however, that the crime problem in Bitonto is a microcosm of that in Bari, and those that wish to visit the city should be particularly alert to theft. This is unfortunate for Bari, the capital city of Puglia, is of great historical significance, and has a lot to offer visitors. The city has always been one of the more important sea-trading ports and has traded across the Eastern Mediterranean since the ancient Illyrians first founded a colony here. The Greeks, Romans and Byzantines expanded ancient *Barium*, which reached its zenith in the medieval era, first under the Normans and then under Frederick II. It was during this period that Bari's finest monuments were erected.

To visit historic Bari, follow signs through the city's vast outskirts to the *citta vecchia*, which lies on a promontory at the eastern end of the port. Head straight for the *cattedrale*, which is at the centre of the old quarter and is Bari's most important monument. It dates from the twelfth century, and is built in the Puglian-Romanesque style with a tripartite façade, fine arcading along its side walls and rose windows carved in the transepts as well as on the front. The interior is richly decorated with marble, and the finely paved floor dates from the fourteenth century. Both the pulpit, on the right of the central nave, and the ciborium at the high altar are reconstructed from the original fragments from the eleventh to thirteenth centuries, while the remnants of frescoes in the left apse date from the thirteenth and fourteenth centuries. The dome, between the two transepts, is 35m (115ft) high, while in the transepts steps lead down to a Baroque crypt, where excavations have uncovered a mosaic pavement that belonged to the basilica that stood here in the eighth century.

Bari's *castello* lies 100m (110yd) west of the cathedral. It was started in 1233 and finished in 1240, under Frederick II, on the foundations of the earlier castles that stood here in Byzantine and Norman times, although it was Isabella of Aragon who had the bastions added in the sixteenth century. Today it is surrounded by a public garden and has a collection of reproduction Romanesque carvings in its central courtyard.

The other monument of major interest in the old quarter of Bari is the church of San Nicola. It lies 200m (218yd) north of the cathedral along Strada dei Carmine. It was built by the Normans in 1087 to house the mortal remains of St Nicholas, which sailors from Bari, in true local style, had stolen from the church in Demre, Turkey, where St Nicholas had been Bishop in the fourth century. However, the church was not dedicated to St Nicholas until 1197, by which time it had already served as a prototype for the numerous Romanesque churches that were built in nearby towns. Its façade is pierced by eight arched windows and has a simple portal, flanked by columns that stand on the backs of bulls. The interior, divided by elegant marble columns into three aisles, contains an outstanding, twelfth-century ciborium at the high altar and a fine Bishop's throne dating from the same period. Both of the side apses hold notable works of art. That on the left contains a *Madonna and Saints* by the Venetian painter B. Vivarini (1476), while that on the right holds a fifteenth-century triptych as well as remnants of fourteenth-century frescoes. The remains of St Nicholas are in the main altar in the crypt, reached by steps down from either transept. Many of the columns in the crypt are topped by ancient Roman capitals.

Bari also has an excellent archaeological museum. It is located in the modern city, just to the north of the railway station. The collection has some of the best ceramics and bronze ware to be found in Puglia, and ranges from the seventh to the third century BC.

After the excursion to Bari the route follows the A14 motorway away from Bitonto in a north-westerly direction. There are several large towns which can be visited as excursions off the motorway, although visitors should again be wary of crime. **Molfetta** has a fine Puglian-Romanesque *duomo* as does the cherry-producing town of **Bisceglie**, further along the coast. Less than 8km (5 miles) further west along the coast is **Trani** which holds the finest of the Puglian-Romanesque cathedrals along this stretch of the Adriatic. It has a lovely position on the water front, pleasantly isolated from the bustle of the town. It was erected during the twelfth and thirteenth centuries, when Trani was at its heyday and rivalled Bari in trade. Frederick II endowed the town with much fine architecture, including a castle which guards the seashore to the west of the cathedral.

The cathedral façade is raised up on the vaults of the crypt and the main portal, which has fine bronze doors cast by Barisano da Trani, is reached by a double staircase. The lower façade either side of the main portal is decorated with blind arcading, while in the upper façade there is a rose window. The interior, has a high, wooden nave and vaulted side aisles, however, it is the crypt which is of most interest. It contains the tomb of San Nicola Pellegrino, for whom the cathedral was built, after the saint was apparently washed up on the shores of Trani on the back of a dolphin. The crypt has a fine, vaulted ceiling supported by twenty-eight columns, each with a carved capital. From the crypt it is also possible to visit the lower church, known as Santa Maria della Scala. It has three aisles divided by Roman columns and remnants of fourteenth- and fifteenth-century frescoes on the walls.

The route continues westwards past **Barletta**, which is a large city with inevitable crime problems. Those prepared to venture in will be rewarded by its interesting *centro storico*. One of the more unusual sights to be seen here is a colossal bronze statue of an emperor, thought to be Valentinian I (AD364-375). It stands over 5m (16ft) tall and was stolen by Venetians from Constantinople. However, instead of ending up in Venice, the boat that was transporting it, ran into trouble and the statue was washed up on the shores of Barletta. Behind the statue rises the basilica, San Sepolcro, while to the east Corso G. Garibaldi, leads past the museum, which has a wide ranging collection of archaeological finds, coins and paintings, as well as a bust of Frederick II, which is said to be the only likeness of the emperor to have survived. The *duomo*, 350m (383yd) north-east

The Murge countryside in springtime

of the museum, was built in 1150 and is another fine example of the Puglian-Romanesque, although it was enlarged in 1305, and again in the fifteenth century. It is interesting to note that Barletta was a point of embarkation for the Crusaders, and the inscription above the left portal lists Richard the Lionheart as one of the cathedral's founders. The ambulatory, which connects the five chapels in the interior, is an unusual feature as it is usually associated with the French-Gothic style and is rarely seen in Italy. Note also the original pulpit and ciborium which date from the thirteenth century.

Route 10C • Barletta to Lesina

Before heading west of Barletta, to the Gargano peninsula, visitors may wish to make an excursion to Frederick II's most famous castle, **Castel del Monte**. To reach the castle, leave the A14 motorway by the Andria exit and head south to **Andria**. An interesting feature of this large city, is its street plan, which is based on a series of concentric circles, although there is little else to deter the visitor here. Continue on for a further 18km (11 miles) south, down the SS170dir, from where the castle is clearly signposted. Resting like a giant crown on a hill top, the castle dominates the Murge for miles around. Its octagonal ground plan is unique and the mathematical perfection of its height and angles is surely a tribute to its founder, Frederick II. This Swabian emperor, who was half-Norman and half-German by birth, was an erudite and dynamic leader. He formulated a regular plan for the great many castles that were built during his reign, mainly characterised by the use of angular towers, and contributed to the design of this castle too, as it reflects his interest in classical ideals and in the architecture of ancient Rome. It is said that it was the favourite of his castles (he had over two hundred), serving him as a hunting lodge, and may have been the place where he wrote his book on falconry. The castle was erected a decade or so before the emperor's death, in about 1240. The walls are girdled by eight identical, octagonal towers, each one being 24m (79ft) high and positioned at equal distances. A Gothic portal leads to an inner courtyard, also octagonal, and is surrounded by eight rooms on two storeys. The rooms are mostly bare of furnishings, but there are fine views across the countryside. Much of the surrounding landscape is cultivated with vineyards. The grapes are used to make one of Puglia's best known DOC wines, named Castel Del Monte, after the castle.

To continue along the route to the Gargano Peninsula follow the A14 motorway as far as the Cerignola Est exit and then take the SS545 to the coast. The road traverses the flat landscape of the Tavoliere, a vast plain that extends around the town of Foggia, just to the south of the Gargano peninsula. It is arable land and the wheat grown here is said to be the best in Italy for making pasta. The local bread is good too, but in terms of landscape the Tavoliere is dull and monotonous.

The coast to the south of the Gargano Peninsula is also flat, and has a series of wide, exposed beaches, lined with camping sites. The peninsula, the spur of Italy's boot, is therefore a dramatic sight. The rugged, limestone mountains rise in a solid mass from the plain and jut out, some 65m (213ft), into the Adriatic Sea. Geologically the mountains are not part of the Appennine chain, but belong to the limestone formations of Dalmatia, and before deposits were carried down by rivers to form the Tavoliere, the peninsula was an island. It is a 230km (142 miles) trip around the peninsula, and plenty of time should be allowed, as the road is bendy, and the scenery some of the most spectacular on the Adriatic.

Manfredonia sits at the foot of the Gargano mountains and is the starting point for a tour of the peninsula. The town is named after Frederick II's heir, Manfred, who founded a port here in 1256. It was built on the site of an ancient settlement, *Sipontum*, the remains of which lie to the south of the town, around the church of Santa Maria di Siponto. It is worth stopping to visit the church, which is passed on the right, on the outskirts of the town. It dates from the eleventh century, although it stands on top of a much earlier church, which dates from the fifth century. Its stout exterior walls, simply decorated with slender blind arcades and rhomboid motifs, are reminiscent of eastern architecture, while the portal, with columns standing on the backs of lions, is more typical of the Puglian-Romanesque. The interior is square with four centrally-placed columns supporting the vaulted ceiling, which focuses on a small cupola at its centre. The plain, stone walls have blind arcading around three sides, with traces of Byzantine mosaics, dating from the fourth century, preserved on the left. The main altar is made up of a Byzantine sarcophagus which is inscribed with Greek crosses. Behind it is a photographic reproduction of the precious, Byzantine *Madonna* that is now in the Manfredonia museum. Steps lead down from the left side of the altar to the crypt with its twelve ancient columns, topped by beautifully-carved capitals. Outside the church, to its left, are the scant remnants of *Sipontum*.

Continue along the coast, by following signs to *lungomare*. The town holds a number of workshops where olive wood is sculpted, but otherwise is of little interest. Most of the town is made up of modern apartment blocks, the old port of Manfred being destroyed by the Turks in 1620. However, Manfred's castle withstood the siege, and has been excellently restored. It is easily accessible and is reached by continuing along the water front to the northern end of the harbour. The massive outer walls were added by Charles I of Anjou, who took the imperial crown after killing Manfred at the Battle of Benevento in 1266. The great spear-headed bastion at the south-western corner of the walls was built in the sixteenth century, but the quadrilateral inner courtyard, which now holds the Museo Archeologico Nazionale del Gargano, dates from the original castle erected by Manfred in 1256. The museum collection is well-displayed in a series of cool, stone rooms that surround the courtyard. Amongst the most interesting of the exhibits, which were all found in local excavations, is a rare collection of inscribed grave stones belonging to the Daunians, an ancient, Iron Age race, who originated from the shores of what was then called Yugoslavia. The slabs of stone are mostly rectangular, measuring between 40-135cm (16-53 inches) high, and 20-60cm (8-24 inches) wide, and are simply carved with symbolic motifs and geometric designs. The museum also holds a collection of Daunian ceramics dating from the sixth century BC, as well as pottery and bronze artefacts made by the Greeks who took over the settlement.

From the castle follow signs to Gargano on the SS89. The road climbs up above the coastline, past Manfredonia's unsightly petrochemical industry, to the bare, rugged rocks that skirt the promontory. After 5km (3 miles) those that wish to make the excursion to **Monte Sant'Angelo** should turn left. The town has an eagle's nest position, at an altitude of 884m (2,900ft) and is reached by an 11km (7 miles), steep and tortuous road. The main attraction of the excursion is the Santuario di San Michele, a holy shrine that was built on the spot where the archangel Michael was said to have appeared to the Bishop of *Sipontum* in AD490. Pilgrims have flocked here ever since, Crusaders included, particularly during the Middle Ages. The entrance to the sanctuary is on the main piazza where there is a fine Gothic portico. The portico was built in 1395 and has two deep arches with carved portals inside. Steps lead down from inside the portals to a bronze door that was cast in Constantinople in 1076 and is covered with biblical scenes. Inside, there is a primitive church, with the grotto where the Archangel made his appearance. It contains an alabaster statue of the Archangel dating from the sixteenth century, while to the left of the main altar is a twelfth-century Bishop's throne.

Back on the piazza, steps lead down, beside the large octagonal belfry, to the Tomba di Rotari. This small, domed building may originally have been built as a baptistery, and is decorated with medieval, carved reliefs. Nearby, the church of Santa Maria Maggiore, is also worth visiting for the rich, carved reliefs that decorate its twelfth-century portal. The interior, divided by fine columns into three aisles, has remnants of frescoes dating from the thirteenth century.

The town's other main monument of interest is its castle which lies 150m (164yd) west of the sanctuary. It was first erected by the Normans, and later enlarged by the Aragonese in 1494. Its robust walls are well-preserved, complete with cylindrical defense towers and a large pentagonal tower, the Torre dei Giganti, on the west side, which dates from the eleventh century.

Visitors may wish to continue inland from Monte Sant'Angelo to the Foresta Umbra, a beautiful area of natural forestation that covers some 11,000 hectares (27,170 acres) of the peninsula. The route, however, continues along the shores of the Gargano promontory on the SS89. After passing through a tunnel, take the right fork through the hill town of **Mattinata**. Turn right again at the centre of Mattinata

The beach at Vieste

and follow signs to Vieste Litoranea. The road heads down to **Porto Mattinata**, where there are campsites along its fine, white-stoned beach, and a picturesque harbour, before climbing up onto a spectacular corniche. Steep, terraced olive groves hang over deep inlets, where sandy coves and dark grottoes can be seen far below. At **Baia delle Zagare** there is a panoramic viewing terrace, from where those keen on hiking can follow the *sentiero pedonale* along the cliff tops to the Torre del Segnale, one of the many defensive towers built by the Aragonese House of Naples to ward off Turkish pirates.

Shortly after Baia delle Zagare the road veers inland, passing through forests of pine, groves of olive and open heaths, which are rich with the pungent scent of Mediterranean maquis. Those that wish to visit the resort of **Pugnochiuso**, where there is a fine, sandy beach, should turn right. Otherwise continue inland to the white-cliffed promontory, Testa del Gargano, which is the easternmost point of the peninsula. The promontory is guarded by a sturdy, square tower which overlooks a sandy bay to its north. Stalls here sell local produce, including bags of olives and olive oil, and excursions can be made from here by boat to the wealth of grottoes that pockmark the limestone headland.

The road continues along the coast, past another defense tower at **Gatarella**. To its north there is a long, sandy beach, filled with neat rows of parasols, from where tiny islets can be seen just offshore. There are fine views of **Vieste** straight ahead, seated atop chalky, white cliffs. After climbing up over a small promontory, the road follows another long, sandy beach, that extends for 2km (1 mile), to the foot of Vieste's cliffs. Lined with hotels and camping sites, most of the beach here is privately owned. At the end of the beach the road passes by a solitary, 20m (66ft) limestone stack, which is known as the Faraglione de Pizzomunno, before climbing up to the town centre. Modern developments have sprung up all around Vieste, but the old centre is well-preserved, and is pleasantly isolated on its cliff-edged spur, which juts out into the sea at the north-easternmost tip of the Gargano. Turn right to visit the centre and head to the summit of the town where there is a fine castle, built by Frederick II. It is typical of the many castles that were constructed during the Emperor's reign, having angular towers at each corner, although it was modified in the sixteenth and eighteenth centuries. Its vantageous position offers a fine panorama along the coast in both directions. Next to the castle is the *cattedrale* which dates from the eighteenth century, but retains the side portal, as well as the carved capitals and columns inside, of the original eleventh-century basilica.

From Vieste visitors can either continue along the splendid

corniche, or take the SS89 inland through the Foresta Umbra, to **Peschici**. This resort has an old centre high on the cliffs as well as a new holiday centre that has grown up around its long, sandy beach. From the harbour, boats can be hired for excursions along the coast to grottoes, while ferries depart for the Tremiti Islands.

The road winds up above Peschici's beach, and follows dramatic clifftops, once guarded by defense towers which now stand in ruins, before descending into another wide, sandy bay. At the far side of the bay, the road climbs once more through pine forests, from where a 9km (6 miles) excursion can be made to the picturesque, hill village of **Vico del Gargano**. The route, however, heads down through the forest to **San Menaio**. This large resort has a vast, sandy beach which extends for 5km (3 miles) to **Rodi Garganico**. This picturesque resort has a lovely position on a gentle headland, surrounded by citrus groves and pines. The sandy beaches, which extend on either side, have shallow gradients and are suitable for children, although in the height of the season they can be quite crowded.

Rodi Garganico is also the closest point from which to make a ferry excursion to the **Tremiti Islands**. During the summer there are daily ferry and hydrofoil services from the harbour. The ferry crossing takes one-and-a-half hours, and the hydrofoil forty-five minutes. The archipelago, which lies just over 20km (12 miles) from the coast, consists of two main islands San Nicola and San Domino, both of which are inhabited, and two smaller islets, Caprara and Pianosa. San Domino, the largest, is 3km (2 miles) long and 2km (1 mile) wide. Its interior rises to a height of 116m (380ft) and is covered in pine trees, while its rocky coastline is peppered with grottoes and has one very crowded, sandy beach.

San Nicola, which is 2km (1 mile) long and 450m (1,746ft) wide is covered in machis and shrub, and rises no higher than 75m (246ft), but has an attractive, historic town with a fifteenth-century castle and a fine abbey. Founded in the eighth century by Benedictine monks, the abbey church seen today dates from 1045. The façade has a Renaissance portal of 1473 and the interior contains a lovely mosaic pavement that dates from 1100. There is a fifteenth-century polyptych at the high altar, and a Byzantine crucifix which dates from the twelfth century.

The waters around all of the islands are lauded for their clarity, and there are many fine spots from which to swim. Legend has it that the Greek mythological leader, Diomedes, is buried here, and that the islands were the boulders thrown by the mighty captain to delineate the boundary of his territory.

From Rodi Garganico, the route continues for a further 4km (2 miles) on the SS89, through abundant groves of olive trees, before turning off right to **Lido del Sole**. This is one of a number of modern, holiday resorts that are built along the flat coastlands, north-west of the Gargano peninsula. The road proceeds through a flat belt of forest, with the Adriatic on one side and the Lago di Varano on the other, which has a small resort at its western end. The road continues through a flat arid landscape, where the fields meet the water's edge, past the fortifications of Torre Mileto, around which there is a second-rate resort. From here, follow signs to San Severo and continue west along the fast main road, the SS16. The road follows the southern shore of Lago di Lesina, before reaching the turn-off to **Lesina** some 19km (12 miles) later. The town, which is best known for its eels, sits on a little spit of land that protrudes into the lake. In autumn and winter it is a popular venue for ornithologists.

Route 10D • Lesina to Chieti

Route 10D continues west along the Adriatic coast on the A14 motorway and crosses briefly into the region of Molise. **Termoli**, 37km (23 miles) west of Lesina, is the only town of any note on the Molise coast. Devastated by earthquakes and destroyed by the Turks in 1566, the town has managed to preserve an attractive, historic centre, which covers a small promontory, projecting into the Adriatic. Parking spaces can be found alongside the sandy beach, which stretches to the north-west of the promontory. From here, proceed on foot to Piazza Castello which lies at an opening in the well-preserved, medieval walls. The piazza is named after the fortress which stands in its western corner. Built under Frederick II in 1247, it now houses a military aeronautical centre and meteorological station. Head north of the fortress along the walls, from where there are fine views out to sea, before turning right to the *cattedrale* which is entangled within a network of picturesque alleyways. The cathedral dates from the twelfth century and is a mixture of Pisan and Puglian-Roman-esque styles. The façade is pierced by a thirteenth-century portal which is flanked by slender blind arcades at either side. The rose window is set unusually high in the upper façade, and is quite small, but attractively carved. The interior is very simple and is mainly of interest for its crypt where the original tenth and eleventh-century mosaics still pave the floor.

From the small piazza in front of the cathedral, head south and stroll through the heart of the old Termoli. There are numerous small restaurants dotted about the streets, many of which serve fish in the traditional Molise manner with plenty of chilli and olive oil. There are also several pizza restaurants, although these will only come to life at night. The narrow streets eventually lead south to the Belvedere Torretta, a fortified gate with a strongly-defended tower from where it is a short walk back to the parking spaces along the beach.

From Termoli, instead of continuing along the A14, follow the SS16, which is a very adequate road and offers fine scenery as it heads west along the coast. After Termoli's beach, the road passes by two defense towers, before climbing up through a gently undulating landscape to the border that divides Molise from the Abruzzo. **San**

San Giovanni, Venere

Salvo Marino, which is just inside the Abruzzo region, is a large and busy resort, and hotels stretch in a continuous chain from here to **Vasto**, which is a further 6km (4 miles) away. The fine, historic town of Vasto is built on a headland, away from the crowded beaches. Handsome, brick buildings line the town's wide, airy streets, which catch the pleasant, sea breezes. The small *duomo*, at the centre of the town, was built in 1293, and has a finely-carved portal and a robust *campanile*. To the east of the *duomo* is the grand Palazzo d'Avalos. It was built in the eighteenth century and now houses the Museo Civico. The museum's collection is quite modest and includes Puglian ceramics found during local excavations and a collection of paintings by the artist, Palizzi, who was born in Vasto in 1818. Vasto is also the home of Brodetto alla Pesce, fish soup, sometimes spiced with a chilli or two.

The route continues along the Adriatic coast on the SS16, gently climbing up to the Punta della Penna. This is the only protusion on the otherwise perfectly straight Abruzzo coastline that runs for some 120km (74 miles) without a break. The slopes to the west of the promontory are cultivated with vines, the grapes producing the local red wine of Casalbordino. The road continues, past a British War Cemetery on the left, before crossing the Sangro river, which is draped with fishermen's nets. Local fish is served in the numerous restaurants in **Fossacesia Marina**, a further 4km (2 miles) west, and the roadsides here are lined with stalls selling fresh mussels.

At the western end of Fossacesia Marina, turn left on the SS524 to make the short excursion to the Cistercian church of San Giovanni in **Venere**. The road winds uphill, a short distance inland, before a turn-off is signposted on the right to the church. There is a carpark just below the church, from where a footpath leads up past two restaurants that have a lovely setting amidst the trees. The church itself also has a delightful position, set above olive groves, with fine views to the coast. It was built in 1165 and has a beautifully-carved portal, Portale della Luna, which dates from this era, piercing the side wall. The interior, built of a warm-coloured stone, is covered by an open-beamed roof. Gracious pointed arches, that spring from square pillars, divide the raised presbytery from the nave. Either side of the presbytery, steps lead down to the crypt which has a stone, vaulted ceiling, supported on ancient columns, originating from a Classical temple to Venus that once stood here. The crypt also has three apses, each of which contains the remnants of frescoes that date from the twelfth to the fourteenth centuries.

Back outside the church, wander around the apse, which is decorated with pretty, blind arcading, to the panoramic balcony on the edge of the hill, from where there are good views to the coast. In the corner to the right of the apse, an opening leads through to the cloisters. Surrounded by a cobbled walkway with mullioned windows that look out across the countryside, the centre of the cloister is filled by a rose garden.

The route continues along the coast on the SS16, for a further 15km (9 miles) to **Ortona**. This quiet town has suffered devastating earthquake damage as well as bombing during World War II, but has a pleasant character nonetheless. Its modern cathedral is testimony to the war damage, and on the piazza opposite its façade, a ceramic memorial has been erected, with a scene depicting the bombing of the church. The main street, which leads beyond the cathedral, is quite lively and is a good place to buy the local wine or have a fish dinner. At the end of the street, stands the Aragonese castle, which is badly ruined, with great fissures in its walls and fallen stone all around. From here the promenade, which runs parallel with the main street, can be followed back to the cathedral. It leads along the cliff tops, past the town's industrial port.

Continue along the SS16, north-west of Ortona, through the resort town of **Francavilla Mare** before turning left and following the SS649 inland for 16km (10 miles) to **Chieti** which lies in the shadow of the Gran Sasso. This prosperous town sits atop a hill, on the site of ancient *Theatre Marrucinorum*, which gave its name to the Theatine Order, founded in Chieti in 1524, by the local Bishop, Paul IV. Parking is somewhat restricted, there being one-hour time limits on most spaces around the town centre. However, aim to park at the northern end of town if possible, near the cathedral square, Piazza Vittorio Emanuele, which is a good starting point for a tour of Chieti. Originally built in the eleventh century, the cathedral has been reconstructed on several occasions, although the last alterations to the *campanile* were made in the fifteenth century. A side portal leads into the crypt, which is the cathedral's oldest and most interesting feature. It has a low, brick-vaulted ceiling, supported by clusters of stumpy columns, and a row of niches along the right side which are decorated with fragments of restored frescoes. Steps lead up from either side of the crypt to the main body of the cathedral which is typically Baroque, with elaborate altars and large paintings.

Head south from Piazza Vittorio Emanuele, along the main street, Corso Maruccino, which is lined with smart shops. After passing the seventeenth-century church of San Domenico on the left, take the first right to the Templi Romani. These scant remains of three Roman temples stand on a small piazza and date from the first century. Return to Corso Maruccino and continue for a further 80m (87.5yd) before turning right along Via Zecca to another remnant of Roman Chieti, its theatre. Hemmed in by the modern day town, the theatre no longer enjoys the fine vista it must once have had across the Appennines, and only a few bricks and stones remain of the original structure. Return to Corso Maruccino and cross over Largo Trento e Trieste to the gates of the Villa Comunale, the public gardens, on the south side. Follow the wide promenade through the gardens, forking left onto Viale R. Paolucci, which leads to the Museo Archeologico Nazionale. The museum is well-appointed in a spacious building, surrounded by peaceful gardens. The collection is arranged on two floors and all of the exhibits are clearly labelled in Italian and English. The rooms on the ground floor contain Roman statues and stone-carved fragments. Amongst the more impressive pieces is the large, seated statue of Heracles in the main hall, and the excellent relief scenes depicting games and gladiators, dating from the first century, in the rooms on the left. On the first floor there is a fascinating collection of exhibits documenting the history of the Abruzzo. There are numerous fine statues, including the Capestrano Warrior, which dates from the sixth century BC. There is also a good selection of ceramic ware and funerary ornaments, that were found in local tombs. Back of the museum there is a panoramic balcony with a spectacular view of the Gran Sasso.

From Chieti visitors should follow the A25 for 20km (12 miles) up the Pescara river valley to **Torre de Passeri** where chapter 5 is joined, at the church of San Clemente a Casauria.

Additional Information

Places to Visit

Altamura
Museo Civico
Via Santeramo angolo Via Genova
Open: Tuesday-Sunday 9am-2pm.

Bari
Castello (Castle)
Open: Tuesday to Saturday 9am-1pm, 4-7pm. Sunday and holidays 9am-1pm.

Museo Archeologico
Open: Monday to Saturday 9am-2pm.

Barletta
Museo Comunale
Via Cavour 8
Open: Tuesday-Sunday 9am-1pm.

Bitonto
Museo Civico E. Rogadeo
Via Rogadeo 52
Open: winter, Monday to Thursday 2-7pm, Friday and Saturday 8.30am-12.30pm. Summer, daily 8.30am-12.30pm.

Castel Del Monte
Castel del Monte (Castle)
Andria

Open: winter, 9am-1pm, summer, 9am-1 hour before sunset.

Chieti
Museo Archeologico Nazionale
Villa Comunale
☎ (0871) 2909
Open: daily 8.30am-1.30pm.

Manfredonia
Museo Archeologico Nazionale del Gargano
Castello Svevo
☎ (0884) 27838
Open: Tuesday to Sunday 9am-1pm, 4-7pm.

Matera
Museo Nazionale Ridola
Via Ridola
☎ (0835) 311239
Open: daily 9am-1pm.

Vasto
Museo Civico
Palazzo d'Avalos
Open: daily 10am-12noon, 6-8pm.

Useful Information

Altamura
Tourist Information Centre
Pro Loco
Piazza Repubblica 11
☎ (080) 843930

Bari
Events anf Festivals
7-8 May, Sagra di San Nicola (Festival of St Nicholas, procession in historic costume).

July-mid August, Festivalcastello (Season of cinema, theatre and concerts in the castle).

September, Fiera del Levante (Mediterranean trade fair).

Tourist Information Centres
Ente Provinciale per il Turismo
Piazza Moro 33A
☎ (080) 5242361/5242359

Azienda Autonoma di Soggiorno e Turismo
Corso Vittorio Emanuele 68
☎ (080) 235186/219951

Transport
Ferrovie dello Stato (Railway)
☎ (080) 5732111

Emergencies
Polizia (Police)
☎ (080) 291111

Polizia Stradale (Traffic Police)
☎ (080) 5044060

Ospedale Regionale Consorziale Policlinico (Hospital)
☎ (080) 370907

Ospedale Regionale di Venere (Hospital)
☎ (080) 350435

Automobile Club d'Italia
Via O. Serena 26
☎ (080) 331354

Barletta
Tourist Information Centre
Azienda Autonoma di Soggiorno e Turismo
Via Gabbiani 4
☎ (0883) 31373

Transport
Ferrovia (Railway)
☎ (0883) 521302

Emergencies
Polizia Municipale (Municipal Police)
☎ (0883) 517655

Polizia Stradale (Traffic Police)
☎ (0883) 31215

Pronto Soccorso (First Aid Service)
☎ (0883) 520221

Guardia Medica (Medical Officer)
☎ (0883) 32796

Bitonto
Tourist Information Centre
Pro Loco
Porta Baresana
☎ (080) 606379

Transport
Ferrovia (Railway)
☎ (080) 611015

Emergencies
Polizia (Police)
☎ (080) 611110

Polizia Municipale (Municipal
  Police)
☎ (080) 611014

Guardia Medica (Medical Officer)
☎ (080) 611311

Castellaneta
Tourist Information Centre
Consorzio Turistico Riva
Occidentale
Piazza Kennedy
☎ (099) 643003

Chieti
Tourist Information Centre
Ente Provinciale per il Turismo
Via B. Spaventa 29
☎ (0871) 65231

Transport
Ferrovie dello Stato (Railway)
☎ (0871) 560811

Emergencies
Polizia (Police)
☎ (0871) 3421

Ospedale Civile (Hospital)
☎ (0871) 347041

Ospedale Civile SS Annunziata
(Hospital)
☎ (0871) 6981

Automobile Club d'Italia
Piazza Garibaldi 3
☎ (0871) 345307

Manfredonia
Events and Festivals
7 February, Sagra di San Lorenzo
(Procession in honour of St
Laurence).

Tourist Information Centre
Ufficio Turistico
Corso Manfredi 26
☎ (0884) 21998

Transport
Ferrovia (Railway)
☎ (0884) 21015

Emergencies
Polizia (Police)
☎ (0884) 21110

Polizia Municipale (Municipal
  Police)
☎ (0884) 21014

Pronto Soccorso (First Aid Service)
☎ (0884) 21410

Guardia Medica (Medical Officer)
☎ (0884) 22488

Massafra
Tourist Information Centre
Pro Loco
Via Garibaldi 3
☎ (099) 8804695

Emergencies
Polizia Municipale (Municipal
  Police)
☎ (099) 681014

Pronto Soccorso (First Aid Service)
☎ (099) 681512

Matera
Events and Festivals
2 July, Sagra di Santa Bruna
(Religious procession in honour of
Santa Bruna).

July, Luglio Materano
(Season of music, ballet and
cinema).

July to August, Rassegna Teatro
Estate (Theatre Season).

Tourist Information Centre
Ente Provinciale per il Turismo
Piazza Vittorio Veneto 19
☎ (0835) 211188

Transport
Ferrovie Calabro Lucane (Railway)
☎ (0835) 382793

Emergencies
Polizia (Police)
☎ (0835) 212222

Polizia Stradale (Traffic Police)
☎ (0835) 211215

Pronto Soccorso (First Aid Service)
☎ (0835) 211410

Rodi Garganico
Tourist Information Centre
Pro Loco
Piazza Garibaldi 4
☎ (0884) 95054

Emergencies
Guardia Medica (Medical Officer)
☎ (0884) 965255

Vasto
Events and Festivals
July to August, Rassegna di Musica
d'Organo
(Season of organ music).

August, Vasto Arte
(National art competition).

Tourist Information Centre
Azienda Autonoma di Soggiorno e
    Turismo
Piazza del Popolo 18
☎ (0873) 2312

Transport
Ferrovie dello Stato (Railway)
☎ (0873) 801935

Emergencies
Vigili Urbani (Municipal Police)
☎ (0873) 2205

Polizia Stradale (Traffic Police)
☎ (0873) 2349

Pronto Soccorso (First Aid Service)
☎ (0873) 2020

Vieste
Tourist Information Centre
Azienda Autonoma di Soggiorno e
    Turismo
Piazza Santa Maria delle Grazie
☎ (0884) 78121

Emergencies
Polizia Municipale (Municipal
    Police)
☎ (0884) 708014

Polizia Stradale (Traffic Police)
☎ (0884) 705222

Guardia Medica (Medical Officer)
☎ (0884) 706530

Southern Italy: Fact File

Accommodation

Hotels are generally classified on a star system, which ranges from one to five. The prices a hotel charges depends on its classification and on the season, the peak season running from 1 July to 1 September. The prices of *alberghi* and *camere* are also determined by the local authorities, and like hotels, should have the tariffs displayed in each room.

Hotel reservations cannot be made through ENIT (Ente Nazionale Italiano per il Turismo) the Italian National Tourist Offices Abroad, although they do hold lists of organisations who can book hotels (normally 4 or 5 star) in all major tourist areas. EPT (Ente Provinciale per il Turismo), APT (Azienda di Promozione Turistica) or AA (Azienda Autonoma di Soggiorno e Turismo), the tourist offices found in most Italian towns, and the Pro Loco offices in smaller centres, hold comprehensive lists of hotels and *pensione*, and some will actually phone and book rooms for visitors. Most of the larger offices will supply accommodation lists on written request.

Camping

Camping is a major part of the Italian tourist industry and tourist offices hold details of the local sites. Federcampeggio, the Italian Camping Federation, publishes two lists of camp sites which cover the whole country. The first of these is a comprehensive list with details of all the country's sites but a price is charged. The second is a more abbreviated list which is issued free. Either list may be obtained from:

Centro Internazionale Prenotazioni
Federcampeggio
Casella Postale 23
50041 Calenzano (FI)
☎ (055) 882391

Youth Hostels

The International Youth Hostel Association has over fifty youth hostels in Italy, full details of which can be found in the International Youth Hostel Federation handbook. They are of a high standard and have good facilities. Many have family rooms but these must be booked in advance. It is important to book in advance for hostels in major centres during busy periods. Reservations are made by placing a 30 per cent deposit. Further information is available from:

Associazione Italiana Alberghi per la Gioventu
44 Via Cavour
00184 Roma ☎ (06) 462342

Student Hostels

Student's hostels are also available in some of Italy's university towns and cities. Applications should be made to the Caso dello Studente. Places with student hostels include: Pescocostanzo, Napoli, Salerno, Sorrento, Bari, Brindisi, Lecce, Scilla, Castroreale and Lipari.

Additional Information

There is an additional information section at the end of each chapter. It is comprised of two parts: Places to Visit and Useful Information. For ease of reference, each part is arranged in alphabetical order. The first part, Places to visit, gives addresses, telephone numbers and opening times of monuments, museums and sites. Where applicable opening times are given for summer which runs from 1 April to 30 September, and winter, which starts on 1 October and ends on 31 March. Separate opening times are also given for Sundays and public holidays. Museum opening times change slightly from year to year but will be substantially as stated.

Information is not given regarding churches and cathedrals, however, they are generally open for times of mass. Many churches also stay open from 7am until about midday when they close for a couple of hours before re-opening until sunset. Visitors should note that when visiting churches and cathedrals, shorts or skimpy clothing are not generally approved of. Visitors should also have 100 or 500 Lire coins to operate lights and phone guides that are provided in churches and cathedrals of major interest. A good torch may also be useful in helping to see frescoes or mosaics that are not illuminated.

The second part of the Additional Information section gives addresses for tourist offices, which are called EPT (Ente Provinciale per il Turismo) if it is a regional office, and AA (Azienda Promozionale per il Turismo), if it is a local tourist office. In small towns the tourist office is sometimes known as Pro Loco. The quality of the service offered by tourist offices is variable, but the vast majority are helpful and speak English.

Other information provided in the Useful Information section includes telephone numbers for police, medical care, transport, and also details of local events and festivals.

Climate

Italy's climate is as varied as its geography. In the winter the mountainous regions of the Abruzzo and the Sila mountains in Calabria have a similar climate to Central Europe. The southern coastal areas, however, enjoy mild, Mediterranean-type winters. The average temperatures for January are: 7°C (44°F) in Rome; 8°C (46°F) in Naples; and 11°C (51°F) in Syracuse. In the summer, the high altitude of the inland mountainous regions offer cooler temperatures than those on the coast. Rainfall is very light throughout the southern region, causing summer droughts for four or five months. The average temperatures for July, the hottest month, are 25°C (77°F) in Rome; 24°C (75°F) in Naples; and 26°C (79°F) in Syracuse.

Credit Cards

All major credit cards (Access, American Express, Visa etc) are taken at most large restaurants, hotels and shops. Eurocheques and traveller's cheques are also usually accepted. The notable exceptions are filling stations, which tend to only accept cash. In the less-frequented parts of Italy it is also useful to have a certain amount of cash on hand as services seen throughout the rest of the country may not exist. Money can be changed at *cambio* offices in major towns, and banks elsewhere. It is normal procedure to show your passport or driving licence, and all receipts should be kept. Banks are normally open between 8.30am and 12.30pm, and for an hour in the afternoon, between 3pm and 4pm, Monday to Fridays only.

Currency Regulations

The Italian monetary unit is the *Lira* (plural *Lire*). No traveller may import or export more than 500,000 Lire in cash, although unlimited amounts of sterling, dollars or traveller's cheques are permitted. It is advisable, however, to check the current situation before leaving.

Customs Regulations

Normal EEC Customs regulations apply. The Italian age limit for the import of duty-free alcohol and tobacco is 17 (this is largely a technicality as supermarket prices in Italy tend to be lower than duty-free prices for alcohol). Normal personal equipment (cameras, jewellery etc) can be taken into the country, but it is advisable to record all serial numbers and keep receipts for valuable items, to prove that they were not purchased in Italy. Any articles purchased in Italy which exceed the custom's allowance set by your country are liable for duty.

No visa is required for stays of less than 3 months for holders of passports issued by the EEC, Britain, Ireland, Canada or the United States, but a valid passport is required.

Electricity

The electricity is 220 volts AC, 50 Hertz (cycles per second). Four different types of plug are commonly used — two with two pins and two with three pins in a line. While a two-pin continental adaptor is recommended, purchasing plugs on arrival is easy and inexpensive.

Embassies and Consulates

Foreign Embassies In Italy
UK
80A Via XX Settembre
00187 Roma
☎ (06) 4755441

USA
119A Via Veneto
00187 Roma
☎ (06) 4674

Maximum and minimum daily temperatures

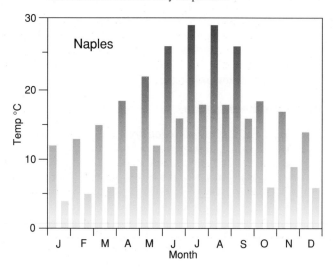

Average monthly rainfall

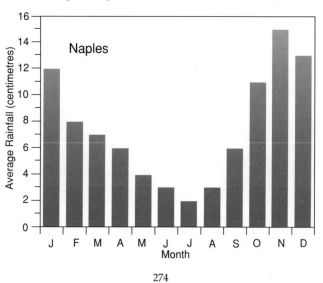

Canada
Via G.B. de Rossi 27
Roma
☎ (06) 445981

Ireland
Largo del Nazoreno 3
Roma
☎ (06) 6782541

Australia
Via Alessandria 215
Roma
☎ (06) 832721

Foreign Consular Offices In Italy
UK
Palazzo Castelbarco
2 Lungarno Corsini
50123 Firenzi (FI)
☎ (055) 212594 or 284133

British Consulate
Via San Lucifero 87
Cagliari
☎ (070) 662750

British Consulate
Via Francesco Crispi 122
Naples
☎ (081) 663511

USA
38 Lungarno Amerigo
   Vespucci
50100 Firenze (FI)
☎ (055) 298276

6 Piazza Portello
16100 Genova (GE)
☎ (010)28274155

32 Piazza Repubblica
20124 Milano (MI)
☎ (02) 6528415

Canada
19 Via Vittor Pisani
20124 Milano (MI)
☎ (02) 652600

Emergency Services

For Fire, Police and Ambulance, ☎ 113.

For immediate attention at airports, main railway stations and hospitals, look for the *pronto soccorso*, first aid service.

The *Carabinieri* are a semi-military police force who take care of civilian disturbances. Their telephone number is posted at the outskirts of every town, the *Vigili Urbani* take care of everyday problems.

Health Care

British and Irish travellers have a right to claim health services in Italy by virtue of EEC regulations. Form E111, available from the Department of Social Security, should be obtained before leaving Britain. Italian health services are administered by USL (Unita Sanitaria Locale). For minor problems it is advisable to use the extensive private sector as the problem may have resolved itself before you manage to see a doctor in the public health service.

American and Canadian tourists will need to check the validity of their personal health insurance to ensure they are adequately covered.

Drugs that are prescribed by a doctor and dispensed at a pharmacy (*farmacia*), are liable for a minimal local tax, which will not be reimbursed. The *farmacia* always has a list of pharmacies open at night and on Sundays.

Those wishing to walk in lonely mountain areas are advised to purchase *siero anti vipera* before beginning their walk. This is a vaccine to be taken after snakebites and is available over the counter in Italian pharmacies.

Holidays and Festivals

Shops, banks, offices, schools and some museums are closed for the national holidays as below.

New Year's Day
Epiphany (6 January)
Easter Monday
Liberation Day (25 April)
Labour Day (1 May)
Republic Day (2 June)
Assumption *Ferragosto* (15 August)
All Saints Day *Ognissanti* (1 November)
Immaculate Conception (8 December)
Christmas Day (25 December)
St Stephen's Day (26 December)

Language

Italian is a straightforward language in which words are written as they are pronounced and each letter has only one sound (except for letters e, o, c and g which have two each).

The basic pronunciation rules are as follows:

c before *e* or *i* is pronounced *ch* (as in cheese) eg *vicino* (near) veecheeno

elsewhere *c* is pronounced as in cat eg *camera* (bedroom)

ch is pronounced *k* eg *perche* (why/because) pairkay

e is pronounced either as in hen or as the a in day eg *ecco* (here) echo or *che* (what) kay

g before *e* and *i* is pronounced *j* eg *Germania* (Germany) jairmarnia

elsewhere *g* is hard eg *grosso* (big)

gl is pronounced *ly* eg *aglio* (garlic) alyoe

gn is pronounced *nye* as at the beginning of new eg *gnomo* (gnome) nye-omo

h is silent eg *ha* (has) a

sc before *e* and *i* is pronounced *sh* eg *fascismo* (fascism) fasheezmoe

elsewhere *sc* is pronounced *sk* eg *tasca* (pocket) taska

z and *zz* are pronounced *ts* or *ds* (*dz*), although this tends to vary according to the local dialect, eg *mezza* (medza)

Useful Phrases

Si — Yes (see)

No — No

Per favore or *Per piacere* — Please

Grazie — Thank you (gratseeay)

Prego — Don't mention it (pray-go)

Va Bene — All right (va bayney)

buongiorno — Good morning (bwon-jorno)

Buona Sera — Good afternoon/Good evening (bwona saira)

Buona Notte — Good night (bwona nottay)

Dov'é — Where is? (doughve)

Quando? — When? (kwandough)

Che Cosa? — What? (kay koza)

Quanto — How much? (kwantoe)

Quanto Costa? — How much does it cost? (kwantoe kosta)

Parla Inglese? — Do you speak English (parla in-glay-say)

Non Capisco — I don't understand (known capee-sko)

Posso Avere — Can I have? (posso av-ay-ray)

Vorrei — I would like (vorray)

Mi Scusi — Excuse me (me skuzee)

aperto — open (a-pair-toe)
chiuso — closed (queue-zoe)
caldo — hot (cal-doe)
freddo — cold (fray-doe)
grande — large (gran-day)
piccolo — small (pronounced as the instrument)
buono — good (bwon-oh)
cattivo — bad (ca-teevoe)
invernale — winter (in-ver-narlay)
estate — summer (e-start-ay)
festivo — holiday (fest-ee-voe)
feriale — working day (fair-ee-arlay)
cambio — currency exchange (cam-bee-oh)

Numbers

zero — 0
uno — 1
due — 2
tre — 3
quattro — 4
cinque — 5
sei — 6
sette — 7
otto — 8
nove — 9
dieci — 10
venti — 20
trenta — 30
quaranta — 40
cinquanta — 50
sessanta — 60
settanta — 70
ottanta — 80
novanta — 90
cento — 100
duecento — 200
mille — 1,000
duemila — 2,000
tremila — 3,000
un milione — 1,000,000
un miliardo — 1,000,000,000
primo — first
secondo — second
terzo — third

In the Hotel

una camera — a room
due, tre camere — two, three rooms
con bagno — with bathroom (cone banyoe)
con doccia — with shower (cone dot-chee-ah)
giorni — days (jor-knee)
una settimana — a week (oona set-tim-arna)
la colazione — breakfast (col-lats-ee-oh-nay)
la cena — evening meal (latchaynah)

Motoring
Accendere i Fari in Galleria — Use Headlights in Tunnel
Tenere la Destra (Sinistra) — Keep Right (Left)
Divieto di Sosta (or Sosta Vietata) — No Parking
Avanti — Walk (at pedestrian crossings)
Entrata — Entrance
Uscita — Exit
Lavori in Corso — Roadworks in Progress
Pericolo — Danger
Rallentare — Slow Down
Polizia Stradale — Highway Police
Senso Unico — One Way Street
Divieto di Sorpasso — No Overtaking
Sosta Autorizzato — Parking Allowed (followed by times)
Vicolo Cieco — No Through Road
Zona Pedonale — Pedestrian Zone
Strada Privata — Private Road
Parcheggio — Carpark
Alt Stazione — Toll booth

In the Restaurant
Il conto — The bill
La lista — The menu
Vino Bianco — White wine
Vino Rosso or *Vino Nero* — Red wine
Vino della casa — House wine, order this by the *litro* or *mezzo litro* (litre or half litre)
Servizio Compreso — Service charge included
Acqua minerale gassata — Fizzy mineral water
Acqua minerale non gassata — Still mineral water

Sightseeing
Duomo/Cattedrale — Cathedral
Chiesa — Church
Campanile — Bell-tower
Chiostro — Cloisters
Cripta — Crypt
Tomba — Tomb
Loggia — Covered gallery, arcade or balcony
Pinacoteca — Picture Gallery
Museo — Museum

Palazzo — Mansion, important building
Centro Storico — Historic Centre
Castello — Castle
Rocca — Fortress

Classical Architectural Terms
Agora — Greek market place (Roman *forum*)
Atrium — courtyard at entrance of a Roman House
Cavea — seating area of a classical theatre
Cella — inner sanctuary in a temple
Impluvium — basin to collect rain water
Nymphaeum — monumental fountain
Peristyle — inner courtyard, surrounded by colonnades
Stylobate — platform on which temple stands

Maps

Both Lascelles and Touring Club Italiano produce good 1:800,000 scale maps of the entire country. Bartholomew's 1:1,000,000 easy fold map is handy for navigating, and the Michelin map of the same scale is clear and reliable. Touring Club Italiano also produce excellent 1:200,000 scale maps of each region. The 1:50,000 scale maps produced by Kompass Carta Turistica show a good amount of detail and are particularly useful for hikers. Most of the local tourist offices in Italy issue free maps of individual provinces, as well as town plans.

Police Registration

All tourists must register with the police within 3 days of entering the country. If you stay at a hotel, campsite etc this will be carried out for you.

Post and Telephone Services

Stamps (*francoboli*) are sold at both post offices and tobacconists. Post offices are normally open from: 8.30am to 1.30pm, Monday to Friday; and 8.30am to 12.30pm on Saturdays. Central post offices in larger towns generally offer postal services up until 7 or 8pm. Tobacconists (*tabaccherie*), recognised by the 'T' sign in front of their shop, are normally open from 8.30am to 1pm, and 3.30 to 8pm, Monday to Saturday.

Public telephones take coins of 100, 200 and 500 Lire, as well as *gettoni* (200 Lire tokens). *Gettoni* are available at tobacconists, bars or news stands, and are sometimes given as change. Some public phones take magnetic phone cards which can be purchased, for 5,000 or 10,000 Lire, at airports, railway stations, public phone offices (SIP) and authorised vendors. Bars often have *telefoni a scatti* which record the number of units for each call; this avoids the need to be continually feeding in small change, but the bar price usually includes a small surcharge. In larger towns, SIP (Societa Italiana Telefoni), the Italian Telephone Company, provide soundproof booths with meters.

Dial codes from Italy are:

Great Britain 0044

Canada 001

USA 001

Remember to leave out the first zero of your home country number — eg to dial the Italian Tourist Office in London (071 4081254) from Italy dial 0044 71 4081254.

Photography

All types of film are readily available in Italy, but prices vary and are generally most expensive in popular tourist centres. In many museums and churches it is forbidden to use tripods or flash so it is well-worth purchasing a 1000 ASA film when planning to visit indoor sights, although in summer any film faster than 200ASA will make outdoor photography difficult.

Travel

By Air

Rome and Naples have the main international airports, but some seasonal flights are handled at Bari, Brindisi, Cagliari, Catania and Palermo. There are also good internal flights. Alitalia, British Airways, Air UK and Aer Lingus are the major airlines flying to Italy from the UK, while Alitalia, KLM or United Airlines handle most flights from the USA. Most airlines offer discounts to students and those under 26. For budget charter flights contact local travel agents.

By Rail

Italy can be reached by rail from all major European cities. It takes about 24 hours from London to Rome. The two main routes are: London Victoria-Paris-Turin-Genoa-Rome and London Victoria-Lille-Basel-Como-Milan-Florence-Rome.

Reduced international tickets, such as Interail cards, are available to those under 26, while in Italy itself a *Carta Verde* can be purchased by young people aged 12 to 26 which gives 30 per cent discount during low season and 20 per cent in high season. Tourists whose normal place of residence is outside Italy may purchase a *biglietto turistico libera circolazione*. This ticket allows unlimited travel on the Italian state rail network, and does not require a supplement for travel on the *Rapido* (see below). Italian National Tourist Offices (see addresses in the Further Information section) will provide details of where tickets may be purchased.

In addition regular reductions are available for day returns (maximum distance 50km/31 miles), and 3 day returns (maximum distance 250km/155 miles). Discounts are also offered to families and to parties of between ten and twenty people. Children under 4, not occupying a seat, travel free, while children under 12 receive a 50 per cent reduction. Those making a round trip of at least 1,000km (620 miles) are also eligible for a special-priced circular ticket. Alternatively, there is a reduced price *chilometrico* ticket, valid for 3,000km (1,860 miles), which can be used by up to five people for a maximum of twenty different journeys over a period of two months.

The Italian rail system is notoriously difficult and prone to strikes, but it is very comprehensive and almost any town can be reached by rail. Visitors are advised to make seat reservations in advance particularly during August.

Italian trains are classified as below:

Super-rapido (Trans Europa Express). Very fast, luxury class only, supplements payable, booking obligatory.

Rapido. Fast inter-city trains. Some are first class only. Supplement charged (about 30 per cent of standard fare, children pay full supplement). On some trains seat booking is obligatory.

Espresso. Long-distance trains between cities, stopping only at major stations.

Diretto. Trains stopping at most reasonable-sized towns.

Look at timetables carefully as there is often little difference between *Espresso* and *Diretto*.

Locale. Stopping at all stations.

By Road
Coaches and Buses

An extensive, long-distance, express coach system operates between cities within Italy, but also offers links to many of the major European cities. The main route from London passes through Dover, Paris, Mont Blanc, Aosta, Turin, Milan, Venice, Bologna, Florence to Rome.

There is also a good network of local bus services and even small villages generally have at least one bus a day to its nearest town. Tickets for buses in towns and cities are sold at main bus stops, tobacconists and news-stands. Some major cities offer a tourist day pass which is valid on all public transport.

Cars
The journey by road from London to Rome is over 1,500km (930 miles). It is best to go over the Alps, as passing through the south of France adds a considerable amount to the journey and the roads are very crowded in summer.

Recommended Routes
1-Boulogne/Calais, Rheims, Lausanne, Great Saint Bernard, Milan, A1 Autostrada.
2-Boulogne, Paris, Bourg en Bresse, Mount Blanc, Milan, A1 Autostrada.
3-Ostende, Munich, Innsbruck, Brenner, Milan, A1 Autostrada.

Fuel
All fuel is comparatively expensive in Italy. Diesel is somewhat cheaper than petrol, and lead-free petrol is offered at a slight discount. Two grades of petrol (gasoline) are available: *Benzina Normale* and *Benzina Super*, and lead free fuel is also widely available. Filling stations usually close for lunch between 12.30pm and 3pm, and many are closed on Sundays. The service stations on motorways, however, are open 24 hours a day.

Driving Restrictions
Nearly all Italian motorways are toll-roads with tickets usually dispensed automatically on entry, and payment made on exit. Speed limits on motorways vary, depending on the day of the week and whether it happens to be an important or popular holiday, and on the size of the car in question. The general limits however are 130kph (80mph) on weekdays and 110kph (68mph) at other times. On country roads the speed limit is 90kph (56mph) and in urban areas 50kph (31mph). There are heavy on-the-spot fines for speeding, so visitors should take care to observe the speed restriction signs.

Mopeds
No driving licence is required for mopeds in Italy and anyone over 14 may use them.

Driving Documents and Requirements
All vehicle documents: registration, insurance and driving licence, must be carried at all times with on-the-spot penalties for offenders. Visitors should also carry a translation of their driving licence, available from the AA, RAC or Italian State Tourist Authorities. It is compulsory for front seat passengers to wear seatbelts, and children under 5 must be strapped into a child car seat. It is also compulsory to have a nationality plate and a left hand wing mirror, and to carry a red warning triangle.

Car Hire
Car hire is available at airports, main stations and in most large towns. The major international firms are represented throughout Italy, supplemented by local firms. Most British and American travel agents selling flights or package holidays to Italy will be able to offer competitive terms for car hire.

INDEX

A
Abruzzo National
    Park 84-88
Acaia 225
Acciaroli 124
Accommodation 270
Acireale 184, 186, 187
Additional Informa-
    tion 271
Adriatic Coast 242-269
Aeolian Islands 141-143
Agrigento 168-169,
    186, 187
Agropoli 121, 134
Aidone 173, 186
Alatri 45, 46, 73
Alberobello 233, 237
Albi 201
Alcamo 157
Alfedena 81, 84
Altamura 251, 266, 267
Altilia 80-81
Amalfi 117-119, 133, 134
Anacapri 116, 135
Anagni 44, 71, 73
Andria 256
Anversa d'Abruzzo 87
Appennines, Lower
    Central 76-89
Appennines, Upper
    Central 90-113
Ariacapri 135

Arsoli 105
Assergi 100
Atrani 119, 135
Augusta 183

B
Bacoli 65
Badia Morronese 94-
    96, 112
Bagheria 149, 161
Baia 65
Bari 252-254, 266, 267
Barletta 251, 254, 256,
    266, 267
Barrea 85
Belvedere 182-184, 186
Benevento 77, 77-79, 88
Bianco 193
Bisegna 86
Bitonto 252, 266, 268
Boiano 81
Bova 193
Brindisi 230, 237, 238

C
Calasibetta 172
Caltagirone 176, 186, 188
Camerota 125
Camigliatello Silano
    204, 212
Campania, Upper 49-71
Campitello Matese 81
Campo Imperatore 99

Campochiaro 81
Cantanzaro 212
Capo di Milazzo 141
Capri 116, 134, 135
Capua 49, 73, 75
Carovigno 230, 238
Carsoli 105
Casamari 46-47, 75
Caserta 50, 73, 75
Cassano allo Jonio
    206, 211
Cassino 48-49, 73, 75
Castel del Monte 99,266
Castel di Sangro 84
Casteldaccia 148
Castellabate 123
Castellamare di Stabia
    114
Castellana 233, 237, 238
Castellaneta 247, 268
Castiglione a Casauria
    96-97, 112
Castro 221, 237, 239
Castro Marina 221
Catania 183
Catanzaro 196, 199-
    200, 211
Cave 43
Cefalu 146-148, 161, 162
Cerchiara di Calabria
    206
Certara 120

Chiesa 200
Chieti 262, 265-266, 267, 268
Civitella Alfedena 85, 88, 89
Climate 272
Cocullo 86
Consulates 273
Corvara 97
Cosenza 128-129, 134, 136
Credit Cards 272
Cropalati 205
Cumae 64, 75
Currency Regulations 273
Customs Regulations 273

E
Electricity 273
Embassies 273
Emergency Services 275
Enna 167, 172-173, 186, 188
Eraclea Minoa 168, 186
Ercolano 65-68, 74, 75
Etna, Mount 184

F
Falcone 143
Fasano 233, 237, 239
Ferentino 41, 44-45, 74
Festivals 276
Fonte Cerreto 100, 112
Forca di Penne 98-99
Fossiata 204
Fragagnano 216

G
Gallipoli 218-220, 237, 239
Gatarella 260
Gerace 192, 195-196, 213
Ghibellina Nuova 158, 163
Giardini Naxos 184
Ginosa 248
Grammichele 177

H
Health Care 275
Holidays 276

I
Ionian Coast 190-213
Isernia 82-83, 88, 89

L
La Camosciara 85
Language 276
L'Aquila 97, 100-104, 112
Laterza 248
Lazio 41-49
Lecce 222, 226-229, 237, 239
Lentiscosa 125
Lesina 256, 262
Lido del Sole 262
Lipari 142, 161, 163
Locorotondo 235-236, 240
Locri 193, 195, 212, 213
Longobucco 204-205
Lungomare Giacomo Matteotti 133

M
Maiori 120
Manduria 216-217
Manfredonia 257, 267, 268
Maps 280
Maratea 126, 136   •
Marina di Leuca 220
Marinella 158-160, 162
Martina Franca 229, 236, 240
Massafra 244, 244-245, 268
Matera 244, 248-251, 251, 267, 269
Melito di Porto Salvo 192
Menfi 167
Mesagne 230, 237
Messina 133, 140, 161, 163, 182
Metaponto 208, 212
Milazzo 141, 161, 164
Minori 120
Miseno 65
Monreale 156-157, 161
Monte Sant'Angelo 258-262
Morano Calabro 120, 127-128
Murge 242-269

N
Naples 50-63, 74
  Cappella San Gennaro 60, 72
  Cappella San Severo 57, 72
  Castel Nuovo 52-53, 72
  Cathedral 60-61
  Certosa di San Martino 62-63, 72
  Galleria Nazionale di Capodimonte 63, 72
  Gesu Nuovo 55
  Museo Civico Filangieri 61, 72
  Museo Nazionale 58-59, 72
  Palazzo Reale 53-55, 72
  San Domenico Maggiore 57
  San Lorenzo Maggiore 59-60
  Santa Chiara 56
  Sant'Anna dei Lombardi 55
  Teatro San Carlo 53, 72
Naples, Bay of 63-71
Nardo 218
Nicolosi 184
Nicotera 132

O
Ortigia 179
Ortona 265
Ostuni 230-232, 237, 240, 241
Otranto 222-225, 241

P
Paestum 114, 120-121, 134, 136
Palagianello 247
Palazzolo Acreide 173, 177-189, 186, 188
Palermo 149, 149-156, 164
  Cappella Palatina 153, 162
  cathedral 152, 161
  Galleria Regionale di Sicilia 155-156, 162
  Martorana 150-152, 161
  Museo Archeologico Regionale 154-155, 162
  Palazzo dei Normanni 152-153, 161
  Piazza Olivella 162
  San Giovanni degli Eremiti 153, 162
Palestrina 41-43, 75
Palinuro 125, 136
Palo del Colle 252
Patti 144, 162, 165
Pergusa 173
Pescasseroli 86, 88, 89
Peschici 261
Pescina 86
Photography 281
Piazza Armerina 174-176, 186, 188
Pizzo 130
Policastro Bussentino 125

Police Registration 280
Policoro 207, 212
Pollino, Monte 126
Pompei 68-71, 75
Pompei Scavi 68-71, 73
Popoli 96
Porticello 148-149, 162
Porto Badisco 216, 222
Porto Cesareo 217
Positano 117
Postal Services 280
Pozzuoli 64, 73, 75
Praiano 117

R
Ravello 119, 134, 137
Reggio Calabria 192
Reggio di Calabria 133, 134
Ribera 168
Rocca Imperiale 207
Rocca Vecchia 225
Roccaforzata 216
Roccella Ionica 196
Rocella 199
Rodi Garganico 261, 269
Rome 11-40, 104
  Ara Pacis Augustae 32, 38
  Colosseum 21, 37
  Constantine's Arch 21
  Farnesina 27
  Fontana di Trevi 29
  Forum 17-18
  Forum Romano 37
  Galleria Borghese 31, 38
  Galleria Colonna 28, 38
  Galleria Doria-Pamphili 24, 37
  Galleria Nazionale d'Arte Antica 30, 38

  Galleria Nazionale d'Arte Moderna 31, 38
  Galleria Nazionale di Palazzo Corsini 27, 38
  Galleria Spada 38
  Gianicolo 27
  Keats and Shelley Memorial House 31, 38
  Mercati Traianei 24
  Musei Capitolini 16, 37
  Museo Barraco 26, 38
  Museo Canonica 31, 38
  Museo di Palazzo Venezia 37
  Museo di Roma 26, 38
  Museo Nazionale di Castel Sant'Angelo 32, 39
  Museo Nazionale di Villa Giulia 31, 38
  Museo Nazionale Romano 23, 37
  Palazzo Barberini 30, 38
  Palazzo dei Conservatori 16
  Palazzo della Cancelleria 26
  Palazzo della Consulta 29
  Palazzo Farnese 26
  Palazzo Spada 27
  Palazzo Venezia 13
  Pantheon 24, 38
  Piazza Barberini 30
  Piazza Navona 25
  Piazza Venezia 13
  San Clemente 21, 37

San Giovanni in Laterano 20
San Pietro in Vincoli 22, 37
San Stefano Rotondo 20
Santa Maria degli Angeli 23
Santa Maria in Cosmedin 28
Santa Maria Maggiore 22
Santa Trinita dei Monti 30
Santissimi Giovanni e Paolo 18
Scalinata della Trinita dei Monti 30
St Peter's Basilica 33
Teatro di Marcello 28
Terme di Caracalla 37
Trastevere 27
Vatican 33-37
Vatican Museums 34-37, 39
Villa Borghese 31
Villa Celimontana 20
Rossano 200, 205, 212, 213

S
Saepinum 77, 81
Salentine Peninsula 214-241
Salerno 120
Salina 142, 165
San Benedetto dei Marsi 86

San Calogero 142
San Cesarea Terme 221, 237, 241
San Clemente a Casauria 92, 96, 97
San Giovanni a Piro 125
San Giovanni in Fiore 203
San Marco 124
San Vito dei Normanni 230, 241
Sant-Agnello 116
Santa Maria al Bagno 218
Santa Maria Capua Vetere 49
Santa Maria di Castellabate 123
Sant'Agata Sui Due Golfi 117
Sapri 126
Sava 216
Scanno 87-88, 89
Sciacca 167-168, 187, 189
Scilla 133
Segesta 157-158, 162
Selinunte 156, 158-160, 162, 167
Serra San Bruno 198
Sibari 206, 212
Sicily, Northern 138-166
Sicily, Southern 167-189
Siracusa 177-182, 187, 189
Soluto 144, 148-149
Sorrento 116, 134, 137
Soverato 198, 213
Stilo 196-198, 212
Stromboli 142, 166
Strombollichio 142
Subiaco 105-106, 112, 113

Sulmona 84, 92, 92-94, 112, 113
Sybaris-Copia 206

T
Tagliacozzo 104
Taormina 184-185, 187, 189
Taranto 205, 208-211, 212, 213, 216
Taverna 201
Telephone Services 280
Termini Imerese 148
Termoli 262-263
Tindari 140, 143-144, 144, 162, 166
Tivoli 107-111, 112, 113
Torre dell'Orso 225
Trani 254
Travel 281
Tremiti Islands 261
Tricase 221
Tropea 130-132, 137
Tyrrhenian Coast 114-137

V
Vasto 264, 267, 269
Velia 124-125, 134
Venere 264-265
Veroli 46
Vesuvius 68
Vico Equense 114
Vicovaro 107
Vieste 260, 269
Vietri sul Mare 120, 134
Villa Adriana 109-111
Villa Romana di Patti 144-147
Villa San Giovanni 128
Villagio Mancuso 203
Villetta Barrea 89
Vizzini 177
Vulcano 141, 166